Pre-Decian Acts of Martyrs
and Commentarii

Harvard Dissertations in Religion

Editors

Margaret R. Miles
and
Bernadette J. Brooten

Number 22

*Pre-Decian Acts of Martyrs
and Commentarii*

Gary A. Bisbee

Pre-Decian Acts of Martyrs and Commentarii

Gary A. Bisbee

Fortress Press   Philadelphia

Library of Congress Cataloging-in-Publication Data

Bisbee, Gary A.
    Pre-Decian acts of martyrs and commentarii / Gary A. Bisbee.
        p.   cm. — (Harvard dissertations in religion)
    Includes bibliographical references.
    ISBN 0 – 8006 – 7074 – 4
    1. Martyrologies—History and criticism. 2. Martyrdom
(Christianity)—History. 3. Martyrdom—History. I. Title.
II. Series.
BR1609.B57 1988
272'.1—dc19

3570F88   Printed in the United States of America   1–7074

To My Dad

Contents

Abbreviations

AJT	*American Journal of Theology*
AnBoll	Analecta Bollandiana
ANRW	Aufstieg und Niedergang der römischen Welt
ArchP	*Archiv für Papyrusforschung*
BASP	Bulletin of the American Society of Papyrologists
Hermes	*Hermes: Zeitschrift für classische Philologie*
HTR	Harvard Theological Review
IDBSup	Supplementary volume to G. A. Buttrick (ed.), *Interpreter's Dictionary of the Bible*
JRomS	*Journal of Roman Studies*
JTS	*Journal of Theological Studies*
LCC	Library of Christian Classics
LCL	Loeb Classical Library
LSJ	Liddell-Scott-Jones, *Greek-English Lexicon*
NAWG	Nachrichten von der Akademie der Wissenschaften in Göttingen, Philologische-Historische Klasse
NHC	Nag Hammadi Codices
OxCD	*The Oxford Classical Dictionary*
PAAR	American Academy in Rome, Papers and Monographs
PG	J. Migne, Patrologia graeca
PW	Pauly-Wissowa, *Real-Encyclopädie der classischen Altertumswissenschaft*
REA	*Revue des études Augustiniennes*
REJ	*Revue des études juives*
RivFil	*Rivista di filologia*
SPAW	Sitzungsberichte der preussischen Akademie der Wissenschaften zu Berlin
TDNT	G. Kittel and G. Friedrich, eds., *Theological Dictionary of the New Testament*
ThLz	*Theologische Literaturzeitung*
VC	*Vigiliae christianae*
ZNW	*Zeitschrift für die neutestamentliche Wissenschaft*

Papyrological / Inscriptional Publications

(For full bibliographic data on Greek papyri, see John F. Oates, Roger S. Bagnall, and William H. Willis, "Checklist of Editions of Greek Papyri and Ostraca," *BASP* 11 (1974) 1 – 35.)

BGU	*Aegyptische Urkunden aus den Staatlichen Museen zu Berlin, Griechische Urkunden* (Berlin, 1895 –)
Bruns[7]	C. G. Bruns, *Fontes iuris Romani antiqui* (7th ed.; 1919)
Chrest.	see M.*Chr.*
CIG	*Corpus inscriptionum graecarum*
CIL	*Corpus inscriptionum latinarum*
CPL	*Corpus Papyrorum Latinarum*, ed. R. Cavenaile (Wiesbaden, 1958)
CPR	*Corpus Papyrorum Raineri*, vol. 1: *Griechische Texte, Rechtsurkunden*, ed. C. Wessely (Vienna, 1895)
FIRA	S. Riccobono, *Fontes Iuris Romani AnteIustiniani*, 1941
M.*Chr.*	L. Mitteis and U. Wilcken, *Grundzüge und Chrestomathie der Papyruskunde*, (Band I by Wilcken; Band II by Mitteis; Leipzig, 1912; reprinted Hildesheim, 1963)
P.Amh.	*The Amherst Papyri*, vol. 2, ed. Bernard P. Grenfell and Arthur S. Hunt (London, 1900)
P.Ant.	*The Antinoopolis Papyri*, ed. J. W. B. Barnes and H. Zilliacus (London, 1960)
P.Aberd.	*Catalogue of Greek and Latin Papyri and Ostraca in the Possession of the University of Aberdeen*, ed. E. G. Turner (Aberdeen, 1939)
P.Berol.	*Papyri graecae berolinenses*
P.Bour.	*Les Papyrus Bouriant*, ed. P. Collart (Paris, 1926)
P.Brem.	*Die Bremer Papyri*, ed. U. Wilcken (Berlin, 1936)
P.Brux.	*Papyri Bruxellensis Graecae*, ed. G. Nachtergael (Brussels, 1974)
P.Erl.	*Die Papyri der Universitätsbibliothek Erlangen*, ed. W. Schubart (Leipzig, 1942)
P.Fam.Teb.	*A Family Archive from Tebtunis*, ed. B. A. van Groningen (Leiden, 1950)
P.Fay.	*Fayum Towns and their Papyri*, ed. B. P. Grenfell, A. S. Hunt, and D. G. Hogarth (London, 1900)
P.Flor.	*Papiri greco-egizii, Papiri Fiorentini*, vol. 1: *Documenti pubblici e privati dell'età romana e bizantina*, ed. G. Vitelli (Milan, 1906)
P.Fouad	*Les Papyrus Fouad I*, ed. A. Bataille et al. (Cairo, 1939)
P.Goodsp.	*Greek Papyri from the Cairo Museum*, ed. Edgar J. Goodspeed (Chicago, 1902)
P.Giss.	*Griechische Papyri im Museum des oberhessischen Geschichtsvereins zu Giessen*, ed. P. Eger, E. Kornemann, and P. M. Meyer (Leipzig/Berlin, 1910 – 1912)
P.Hamb.	*Griechische Papyrusurkunden der Hamburger Staats- und Universitätsbibliothek* I (in 3 parts), ed. P. M. Meyer (Leipzig/Berlin, 1911 – 1924)

P. Harr.	*The Rendel Harris Papyri of Woodbrooke College, Birmingham*, ed. J. E. Powell (Cambridge, 1936)
P. Herm.	*Papyri from Hermopolis and Other Documents of the Byzantine Period*, ed. B. R. Rees (London, 1964)
P. Lips.	*Griechische Urkunden der Papyrussammlung zu Leipzig*, ed. L. Mitteis (Leipzig, 1906)
P. Lond.	*Greek Papyri in the British Museum*, 1893 –
P. Louvre	*Notices et textes des papyrus grecs du Musée du Louvre et de la Bibliothèque Impériale*, ed. J. A. Letronne, et al. (Paris, 1865)
P. Lug.Bat.	*Papyrologica Lugduno-Batava* (Leiden, 1941 –)
P. Mert.	*A Descriptive Catalogue of the Greek Papyri in the Collection of Wilfred Merton*, vol. 1, ed. H. I. Bell and C. H. Roberts (London, 1948)
P. Mich.	*Michigan Papyri*, 1931 –
P. Mil.Vogl.	*Papiri della R. Università di Milano*, vol. 1, ed. A. Vogliano (Milan, 1937)
P. Oslo	*Papyri Osloenses*, ed. S. Eitrem and L. Amundsen (Oslo, 1925 –)
P. Oxford	*Some Oxford Papyri*, ed. E. P. Wegener (Leiden, 1942)
P. Oxy.	*The Oxyrhynchus Papyri* (Egypt Exploration Society, 1898 –)
P. Paris	*Notices et textes des papyrus grecs du Musée du Louvre et de la Bibliothèque Impériale*, ed. J. A. Letronne, W. Brunet de Presle, and E. Egger (Paris, 1865)
P. Phil.	*Papyrus de Philadelphie*, ed. J. Scherer (Cairo, 1947)
P. Rainer	*Mitteilungen aus der Sammlung der Papyrus Erzherzog Rainer*, ed. J. Karabacek
P. Rein.	*Papyrus grecs et démotiques recueillis en Égypte*, ed. T. Reinach, W. Speigelberg, and S. de Ricci (Paris, 1905)
P. Ross. Georg.	*Papyri russischer und georgischer Sammlungen*, 1925 –
PRUM	see *P. Mil.Vogl.*
P. Ryl.	*Catalogue of the Greek Papyri in the John Rylands Library, Manchester*, vol. 2: *Documents of the Ptolemaic and Roman Periods*, ed. J. de M. Johnson, V. Martin, and A. S. Hunt (Manchester, 1915)
PSI	*Papyri greci e latini (Pubblicazione della Società Italiana per la ricerca dei papiri greci et latini in Egitto)* (Florence, 1912 –)
P. Stras.	*Griechische Papyrus der kaiserlichen Universitäts- und Landesbibliothek zu Strassburg*, ed. F. Preisigke (Leipzig, 1912 –)
P. Teb.	*The Tebtunis Papyri*, ed. B. P. Grenfell et al. (London, 1902 –)
P. Thead.	*Papyrus de Theadelphia*, ed. P. Jouguet (Paris, 1911)
P. Wisc.	*The Wisconsin Papyri*, ed. P. J. Sijpesteijn (Leiden, 1967)
P. Yale	*Yale Papyri in the Beinecke Rare Book and Manuscript Library*, vol. 1, ed. J. F. Oates, A. E. Samuel, and C. B. Welles (New Haven/Toronto, 1967)
SB	*Sammelbuch griechischer Urkunden aus Aegypten*, ed. F. Preisigke et al. (Strassburg/Heidelberg/Wiesbaden, 1915 –)
SEG	*Supplementum epigraphicum graecum*
W.Chr.	see M.Chr.

Short Titles

Information appears here for frequently used works which are cited by short title. A few short titles do not appear in this list, but in each instance full bibliography is given on the page(s) preceding such references.

Aigrain, *L'hagiographie*
> Aigrain, René, *L'hagiographie: ses sources ses méthodes, son histoire* (Poitiers: Bloud & Gay, 1953).

Barnes, "Pre-Decian *Acta Martyrum*"
> Barnes, Timothy David, "Pre-Decian *Acta Martyrum*," *JTS* 19 (1968) 509–31.

Bickermann, *Chronology*
> Bickermann, E. J. *Chronology of the Ancient World* (2d ed.; Ithaca, NY: Cornell University Press, 1980).

Von Campenhausen, "Bearbeitungen und Interpolationen"
> Von Campenhausen, Hans, "Bearbeitungen und Interpolationen des Polykarpmartyriums," *SHAW* 3 (1957) 1–48.

Coles, *Reports of Proceedings*
> Coles, Revel A., *Reports of Proceedings in Papyri* (Papyrologica Bruxellensia 4; Brussels: Fondation Egyptologique Reine Elisabeth, 1966).

Delehaye, *Les passions des martyrs*
> Delehaye, Hippolyte, *Les passions des martyrs et les genres littéraires* (1921; reprinted Brussels: Société des Bollandistes, 1966).

Finley, ed., *Studies in Ancient Society*
> Finley, M. I., ed., *Studies in Ancient Society* (London/Boston: Routledge and Kegan Paul, 1974).

Garnsey, "Criminal Jurisdiction"
> Garnsey, Peter, "The Criminal Jurisdiction of Governors," *JRS* 58 (1968) 51–59.

Grant, *Eusebius*
> Grant, Robert M., *Eusebius as Church Historian* (Oxford: Clarendon, 1980).

Hammond, *Antonine Monarchy*
> Hammond, Mason, *The Antonine Monarchy* (PAAR 19; Rome: American Academy in Rome, 1959).

Hunt and Edgar, *Select Papyri*
> Hunt, A. S., and C. C. Edgar, *Select Papyri* (2 vols.; LCL; Cambridge: Harvard University, 1963).

Jones, *Cities of the Eastern Roman Provinces*
> Jones, A. H. M. *The Cities of the Eastern Roman Provinces* (2d ed.; rev. Michael Avi-Yonah, et al.; Oxford: Clarendon, 1971).

Jones, *Criminal Courts*
> Jones, A. H. M., *The Criminal Courts of the Roman Republic and Principate* (Oxford: Blackwell, 1972).

Koester, *Introduction to the New Testament*
> Koester, Helmut, *Introduction to the New Testament* (2 vols.; Foundations and Facets; Philadelphia: Fortress, 1982; Berlin/New York: De Gruyter, 1983).

Lawlor and Oulton, *Eusebius*
> Lawlor, Hugh Jackson, and John Ernest Leonard Oulton, *Eusebius: The Ecclesiastical History and the Martyrs of Palestine* (2 vols.; London, SPCK, 1927).

Lazzati, "Atti di S. Giustino"
> Lazzati, Giuseppe, "Gli Atti di S. Giustino Martire," *Aevum* 27 (1953) 473–97.

Lazzati, *Gli sviluppi della letteratura sui martiri*
> Lazzati, Giuseppe, *Gli sviluppi della letteratura sui martiri nei primi quattro secoli* (Torino: Società editrice internazionale, 1956).

Lightfoot, *Apostolic Fathers*
> Lightfoot, J. B., *The Apostolic Fathers*, part 2: *S. Ignatius; S. Polycarp* (2 vols.; London: Macmillan, 1885).

Millar, *Emperor*
> Millar, Fergus, *The Emperor in the Roman World* (Ithaca, NY: Cornell University Press, 1977).

Musurillo, *Christian Martyrs*
> Musurillo, Herbert, *The Acts of the Christian Martyrs* (Oxford: Clarendon, 1972).

Musurillo, *Pagan Martyrs*
> Musurillo, Herbert, *The Acts of the Pagan Martyrs: Acta Alexandrinorum* (Oxford: Clarendon, 1954).

Posner, *Archives*
> Posner, Ernst, *Archives in the Ancient World* (Cambridge: Harvard University Press, 1972).

Von Premerstein, "Commentarii"
> Von Premerstein, Anton, "Commentarii," PW 4 (1901) 726–70.

Reinmuth, *Prefect of Egypt*
    Reinmuth, Oscar William, *The Prefect of Egypt from Augustus to Diocletian* (Beiträge zur alten Geschichte 21; Leipzig: Dieterich'sche Verlagsbuchhandlung, 1935).

Taubenschlag, *Law of Greco-Roman Egypt*
    Taubenschlag, Raphael, *The Law of Greco-Roman Egypt in the Light of the Papyri, 332 B.C. – 640 A.D.* (New York: Herald Square, 1944).

Wilcken, "Ὑπομνηματισμοί"
    Wilcken, Ulrich, "Ὑπομνηματισμοί," *Philologus* 53 (1894) 80 – 126.

Introduction

> The aim of history . . . is to know the elements of the present by under-
> standing what came into the present from the past. For the present is
> simply the developing past, the past the undeveloped present. . . . The
> first lesson the student of history has to learn is to discard the conception
> that there are standard ultimate histories. In the nature of the case this is
> impossible. History is all the remains that have come down to us from
> the past, studied with all the critical and interpretative power that the
> present can bring to the task.[1]

Historians are often tempted to regard their methods and their writings as
final, ultimate, and definitive. In me, one is tempted to think, Clio has
spawned a historian who has actually succeeded in accomplishing Ranke's
goal: to present history "as it actually happened." But, as Turner reminds
us, definitive histories can never be written; the advances of one generation
of scholars make possible further advances by the next generation. The
present age cannot be properly understood apart from a knowledge of the
past, and the past is properly understood only when *all the critical and interpretative powers that the present can bring to the task* are applied. To understand this is to understand that a future generation may, indeed *should*, possess even greater critical and interpretative powers than does the present.

---

[1] Frederick Jackson Turner, "The Significance of History" (1891), reprinted in Fritz Stern,
ed., *The Varieties of History* (New York: Vintage Books, 1973) 200–201.

In an analysis of the past two hundred years of historiography, Fritz Stern observed that

> modern historians have written in a variety of genres, but the multiplicity of style cannot obscure the two basic tendencies which have affected all modern historians. First, the transformation of history into an academic discipline—indeed, according to some into a science. . . . Second, society's growing demand for history. . . . These two developments are both manifestations of the cultural revolution which has shaped modern times: the secularization of thought, the growth of science and the questioning of all systems embodying eternal truths.
>
> Related in origin though they may be, the two tendencies are nevertheless at odds with one another. The scientific historian . . . has become a specialist, ill-equipped to meet the heightened demands of society. . . . In short, just as the historian was getting ready to become an academic monk, shut up in his study with his sources, the world about him sought him as a preacher.
>
> Nothing is more characteristic of the history of the last two hundred years than the demand from within the profession that history must once again become broader, more inclusive, more concerned with the deeper aspects of human experience. . . . as long as society seeks knowledge of the past, the historian must accept responsibility to society, without violating responsibility to the past.[2]

The acts of the martyrs have been read during the past eighteen hundred years or so primarily for their edificatory value. The Christian acts have been studied, more often than not, for similar reasons. The acts of the martyrs tell of the heroic deaths of heroes, of philosophers against tyrants and of Christians against pagans. Yet the historian knows both that it is the victors who write the "histories" and that scientific, that is, objective, history is a phenomenon of only the recent past. A Polycarp or a Cyprian would be quite differently remembered, if at all, had paganism defeated Christianity and not vice versa. How different history would have been had the pagans won! The historian of ancient Christianity also knows that the role played by martyrs in the eventual outcome was enormous: without its martyrs and theology of martyrdom, Christianity might have become just another ancient mystery religion.

That Christianity had martyrs and a theology of martyrdom were important ingredients in the formula for triumph, but by no means the only ingredients. George La Piana remarked:

It is amazing to see what a small part, after all, reason has played in the course of human history in comparison with such other motive forces as faith, feelings, passions, and instincts. . . . Especially in the field of religious history do we find that reason has been confined mostly to the humble task of patching together bits and fragments of beliefs and traditions, principles and experiences, all kinds of odds and ends, and combining them in a frame which to the happy believer could give at least the impression of a consistent unity.[3]

R. A. Markus asked, "Did the Christian church of the fourth, fifth and sixth centuries live with a self-awareness distorted by an image projected from its own heroic age . . .?"[4] The honest hagiographer knows that the Christian church in the second and third centuries too lived with a self-awareness that was distorted by images projected from its heroic present. "What actually happened" and what was "remembered to have happened" were often quite different. The importance today of objective inquiry into the origins, development, and uses of acts of martyrs cannot be overstated, for the knowledge so acquired may shed much light not only upon ancient Christianity but also upon the human experience in general.

When the research for the present study was begun, the goal was to establish the definitive method for studying all the genres present in all the acts of all periods. This study was to make possible the presentation of a history "as it actually happened!" Moreover, the original focus was entirely upon the acts of Christian martyrs, the topic of Chapters Four through Seven, without consideration of acts of pagan martyrs, the topic of Chapter Three. As the study progressed, it became apparent how very much remained to be learned about *commentarii*, archives, and judicial scribes—the topics of Chapters One and Two, which, along with the Appendices, are perhaps the most important contributions of this study.

The audacity of the original goal soon became apparent. Besides violating Turner's dicta, such a study could not and can not be written for several reasons. It would require covering several centuries, in which all differences of development and digression of all locations and periods would have to be taken into account. It would require isolating and defining all of the various

---

[3] La Piana, "Ancient and Modern Christian Apologetics," *HTR* 24 (1931) 2–3. In the less sympathetic words of Karl Marx, "Religion is the sigh of the oppressed creature, the heart of a heartless world, just as it is the spirit of an unspiritual situation. It is the *opium* of the people" (Karl Marx, *Toward the Critique of Hegel's Philosophy of Right*, excerpted in Lewis S. Feuer, ed., *Marx & Engels: Basic Writings on Politics & Philosophy* [Garden City, NY: Doubleday/Anchor Books, 1959] 263).

[4] Markus, "Church history and early church historians," in Derek Baker, ed., *The Materials, Sources and Methods of Ecclesiastical History* (Papers Read at the Twelfth Summer Meeting and the Thirteenth Winter Meeting of the Ecclesiastical History Society; Oxford: Blackwell, 1975) 1.

genres present in the acts of martyrs. The origin and development, including the influence of non-Christian genres, for each genre would have to be traced. Narrower perimeters were clearly required; the single large study would have to become many smaller studies. The present study perhaps raises more questions than it succeeds in answering, but it is hoped that it will provide the means and stimulus for more definitive studies in the future by scholars possessing greater scholarly resources.

Before proceeding, a few terms must be defined. Past studies have tended to use the term *acta martyrum* for the general category "acts of the Christian martyrs." Studies of the pagan acts since Herbert Musurillo's work[5] have tended to refer to "acts of the pagan martyrs" as *Acta Alexandrinorum*. The present study departs from these designations. Here the term *acta paganorum* will be used for any account of the general category "acts of pagan martyrs"; *acta Christianorum* will be used for the general category "acts of the Christian martyrs"; and *acta martyrum* will be used for acts of either pagan or Christian martyrs.

The consensus of scholarship to date is that the earliest "authentic" *acta Christianorum* that we now possess are the *Martyrdom of Polycarp* (died between 155–177), the *Martyrdom of Ptolemaeus and Lucius* (*apud* Justin *2 Apology* 2; died before 160), and the *Acts of Justin* (died between 162–167). Eusebius apparently knew of no earlier Christian acts, even though the names of a few earlier martyrs were known by him.[6] Goodspeed and Grant, having observed this fact, concluded that "with the Martyrdom of Polycarp and the Martyrdom of Justin begins a new form of Christian literature that became immensely popular, the 'acts of martyrdom.'"[7] It would seem, then, that the genre *acta Christianorum* arises about the mid-second century. That we apparently possess no, or at best very few, acts of Christian martyrs that predate the mid-second century is striking when we consider the emphasis that Christians came to place on martyrs and martyrdom. It is known, largely from pagan sources, that the Christians did undergo isolated, although occasionally violent, periods of local persecution in the pre-Antonine period. Yet the Christians themselves do not seem to have produced contemporary descriptions of these persecutions or to have had any interest in generating anything resembling acts of martyrs. All this presupposes, however, that the *Acts of Ignatius* are completely fictional. Scholarship since Lightfoot's

[5] Musurillo, *The Acts of the Pagan Martyrs: Acta Alexandrinorum* (Oxford: Clarendon, 1954).

[6] See Robert M. Grant, *Eusebius as Church Historian* (Oxford: Clarendon, 1980) 114–21. It should be noted that there presumably existed a *commentarius* of the trial for those early Christians who were tried before Roman magistrates.

[7] Edgar J. Goodspeed, *A History of Early Christian Literature* (rev. Robert M. Grant; Chicago: University of Chicago, 1966) 25.

analysis of these acts,[8] has omitted the *Acts of Ignatius* from discussions on the origins and developments of the genre *acta Christianorum*. It was not until a very late stage in the production of the present study that I decided that the *Acts of Ignatius* should not be omitted from such discussions.

This study will focus upon the earliest acts and will be limited to the *acta martyrum* whose dramatic date occurs during the first or second centuries. In addition, this study will be limited to a single genre of the acts, namely, the *commentarius*-form. Most scholars believe that many of the earliest *acta martyrum* originated as copies of ὑπομνηματισμοί, the legal term for records of trials taken down by official scribes. The Latin equivalent of ὑπομνηματισμός is *commentarius, -i* and is the term that will be used hereafter for official records of trials.

The term "*commentarius*-form," which was used above, requires definition. The title "Acts of . . ." (*acta* or *gesta*) is normally reserved for accounts that primarily consist of discourses between magistrates and martyrs in the courtroom (e.g., the *Acts of Justin Martyr* and the *Acts of the Scillitan Martyrs*). The title "Martyrdom of . . ." (*passiones* or *martyria*) is given to Christian accounts whose focus is upon descriptions (purportedly of eyewitnesses or contemporaries) of the last events and heroic sufferings of martyrs (e.g., *Martyrdom of Polycarp*). However, "Martyrdom of . . ." is also given to rather simple pieces consisting primarily of courtroom discourses, such as the *Martyrdom of Carpus, Papylus, and Agathonicê*. Moreover, the general category "acts of [pagan or Christian] martyrs," encompasses a diverse body of literature that ranges from unadorned accounts such as the *Acts of the Scillitan Martyrs* to complex pieces such as the *Martyrdom of Perpetua* and *Martyrdom of Pionius*. "*Commentarius*-form" is used to describe a writing, pagan or Christian, whose literary form resembles a *commentarius*.

A distinction has been drawn between the genre "Acts" and "*commentarius*-form" because "Acts" usually contain descriptions of the martyr's death (the focus of a Martyrdom), and "Martyrdoms" normally contain sections of direct discourse between magistrates and martyrs (the focus of "Acts"). The present study is principally concerned with those accounts or sections of accounts that purport to be, resemble, or indeed are, copies of *commentarii*. One goal of this study seeks to develop a methodology, to supplement existing methodologies, for answering such questions as:

1) Is such and such account or portion of an account an authentic *commentarius*?
2) Is such and such account an edited version of a *commentarius*?

---

[8] J. B. Lightfoot, *The Apostolic Fathers*, part 2: *S. Ignatius; S. Polycarp* (2 vols.; London: Macmillan, 1885) esp. 2. 363–584.

3) If it is an edited version, in what ways has it been edited?
4) If it has been edited, why has it been so edited?

The analysis of the *acta martyrum* with questions such as these in mind may provide fresh insights into (1) the origin and development of the general genre *acta martyrum*; (2) the origin and development of the Christian concepts and theologies of martyrdom; (3) the uses to which the pagans and Christians put these accounts; and (4) the confrontation between provinces and the Empire and between the Empire and Christianity.

Scholarship on the *acta Christianorum*, from the earliest work by the Bollandists in the seventeenth century up to the present,[9] has resulted in the formation of a "canon" of "authentic" acts. Several problems have resulted from this process of canonization. First, the existence of a canon has resulted in a "true-false" attitude in many scholars. That is, they tend to treat as authentic only those writings that have been included in the canon. Even Timothy D. Barnes, a first-rate scholar, tends to put the *acta Christianorum* into two neat piles, one "authentic" and one "inauthentic." He says:

> Of the vast mass of hagiographical literature preserved from late antiquity the greater part has no relevance to the realities of early Christian history. Comparison of the *Acta Sanctorum* and the Bollandist *Bibliotheca Hagiographica* with the successive prunings in T. Ruinart's *Acta Primorum Martyrum Sincera et Selecta* (first published in 1689) and in any modern collection will show how much has rightly been discarded. But has the process of rejection gone far enough? ... Many other *acta* may contain something of value or be based on historical fact. But no more than nine from the period before Decius have been accepted as wholly authentic by competent scholars of the present century.[10]

Acts which have been labelled "authentic" are placed in one pile and receive the attention of the community of scholars. Those labelled "inau-

---

[9] On the work of the Bollandists, see Hippolyte Delehaye, *L'oeuvre des Bollandistes à travers trois siècles* (Brussels: Société des Bollandistes, 1920).

[10] Barnes, "Pre-Decian *Acta Martyrum*," *JTS* 19 (1968) 509. The "nine authentic acts" alluded to by Barnes are: *Martyrdom of Polycarp, Acts of Carpus, Papylus, and Agathonicê, Martyrdom of Ptolemaeus and Lucius, Acts of Justin Martyr, Martyrs of Lyons, Acts of the Scillitan Martyrs, Acts of Apollonius, Martyrdom of Perpetua and Felicitas, Martyrdom of Potamiaena and Basilides.* Barnes cites the following studies: Karl Johannes Neumann, *Der römische Staat und die allgemeine Kirche bis auf Diocletian*, i (Leipzig: Veit, 1890) 274ff.; Karl Bihlmeyer, *Die "syrischen" Kaiser zu Rom (211–35) und das Christentum* (Rottenburg: Bader, 1916) 157ff.; H. Delehaye, "Les actes de saint Timothée," in W. M. Calder and Josef Keil, eds., *Anatolian Studies presented to W. H. Buckler* (Manchester: Manchester University Press, 1939) 77.

thentic" are simply discarded and given no further thought.[11] New Testament scholars do not ignore 2 Peter, even though it could not possibly have been written by the disciple Peter, nor do they ignore the deutero-Pauline epistles. But with regard to the process of pruning the list of "authentic" *acta Christianorum*, Barnes stated, with approval, that Edmond Le Blant's "attempt to reverse the process stands . . . in virtual isolation."[12] Although the present study is written with the intention that a means (a methodology) of reversing the process might be found, it is hoped that the study will prove to be of more use than did Le Blant's, which is now regarded by scholars as useless.[13]

Scholars have rejected several pre-Decian *acta Christianorum* because of the obvious lateness of the extant account, but as long ago as 1894 Conybeare demonstrated that many of the Armenian martyrdoms were derived from earlier, less-interpolated recensions—either Greek or Syrian—than the extant Greek or Latin version.[14] This brings us to a second problem. Acts which appear to be purely fictional may, in fact, derive from historical accounts. The question that must be asked of the Christian acts is not which are authentic, as though accounts are homogeneously true or false, but rather, as Ulrich Wilcken asked of the *acta paganorum*, "What is original in the transmitted text of our . . . acts and what is revised?"[15] As the discussion below will indicate, however, the search for "original" has often, if not usually, been carried out without a proper understanding of what forms an original account might have taken.

[11] The "canonization" of the "authentic" *Acta Christianorum* of martyrs has followed a path remarkably like the process by which the New Testament writings probably became canonized. On the canonization of the New Testament, see Helmut Koester, *Introduction to the New Testament* (2 vols.; Foundations and Facets; Philadelphia: Fortress, 1982; Berlin/New York: De Gruyter, 1983) 2. 5 – 12, 330 – 31; and see the secondary sources he lists at p. 6.

[12] Barnes, "Pre-Decian *Acta Martyrum*," 509, with reference to Edmond Le Blant, *Les Actes des martyrs: Supplement aux Acta sincera de Dom Ruinart* (Paris: Imprimerie Nationale, 1882). Note, however, Henri Leclercq's fifteen-volume collection, *Les Martyrs: recueil de pièces authentiques sur les martyrs depuis les origines du christianisme jusqu'au XXe siècle* (Paris: Oudin, 1903 – 24).

[13] Le Blant's *Les Actes des martyrs* is primarily a legal historical study that compares legal terms found in the *Acta Christianorum* with terms found in Roman law. His method, as Musurillo noted, "could merely isolate gross, unskilful forgeries" (*The Acts of the Christian Martyrs* [Oxford: Clarendon, 1972] li).

[14] F. C. Conybeare, *The Apology and Acts of Apollonius and Other Monuments of Early Christianity* (London: Swan Sonnenschein, 1894); see esp. the *Acts of Eugenia*, who is said to have been martyred under Commodus. See also idem, "The Armenian Acts of Cyprian," *ZNW* 21 (1922) 269 – 77. See also Grant, *Eusebius*, 120 – 21.

[15] Wilcken, "Zum alexandrinischen Antisemitismus," *Abhandlungen der königlich-sächsischen Gesellschaft der Wissenschaften* 27 (1909) 832.

Commentarii and the *Acta Martyrum*

Prior to the spectacular discoveries of papyri in Egypt beginning in the 1870s, especially the finds of Grenfell and Hunt at Oxyrhynchus and Tebtunis beginning in 1897, few *commentarii* were available to scholars.[16] Then came the exciting period in which, to use Raphael Taubenschlag's words,

> A new and fascinating science was developed at the end of the Nineteenth Century: papyrology. . . . the first scholar to study (the) juristic side of the papyri was Ludwig Mitteis. His great work on juristic papyrology, "Grundzüge und Chrestomathie der Papyruskunde, 1912," was a brilliant achievement for this epoch. . . . Since 1912 many thousands of new papyri have been discovered. . . . From these it is now possible to work out the solutions to many problems for which Mitteis could find no answers.[17]

It is not surprising that it was the Germans who initially began the process of assimilating the new data. Even earlier than Mitteis's legal study of the papyri was Wilcken's " Ὑπομνηματισμοί,"[18] a form-critical study of the *commentarii* which had been occasionally discovered among the other papyri. Relatively few *commentarii* had been published, or discovered, at the time of Wilcken's study in 1894. Papyrological discoveries of *commentarii* continued, and a period of hectic literary analysis resulted in which Richard Reitzenstein, Karl Holl, Adolf Bauer, Ulrich Wilcken, W. Weber, Anton von Premerstein, E. von Dobschütz and many other scholars wielded the pen in academic battle until the outbreak of World War I, when Europe traded pens for guns and ink for mustard gas.

Since the early decades of the twentieth century many advances have been made in the study of Roman law in general and of the *commentarii* in particular. In 1910 Johannes Geffcken complained that to provide historical or philological objections to the *acta martyrum* based upon arguments from legal procedure was completely meaningless, since in so doing one was in

---

[16] For an excellent survey of this period of discovery, see Eric G. Turner, *Greek Papyri: An Introduction* (Oxford: Clarendon, 1968) chaps. 2–4.

[17] Taubenschlag, *The Law of Greco-Roman Egypt in the Light of the Papyri, 332 B.C.–640 A.D.* (New York: Herald Square, 1944) vii-viii. The circumstances under which Taubenschlag wrote his legal study are worth noting: he began the work in 1938 in Cracow but was forced to flee Poland for Aix-en-Provence. When France collapsed, he was again forced to flee, this time to Columbia University in New York, where the book was finished in 1944. *Per angusta ad augusta.*

[18] Ulrich Wilcken, " Ὑπομνηματισμοί," *Philologus* 53 (1894) 80–126.

effect comparing acts to knowledge obtained primarily from those acts.[19]
Since 1910 the studies of Raphael Taubenschlag,[20] A. H. M. Jones,[21] A. N.
Sherwin-White,[22] Peter Garnsey,[23] and other legal historians have illum-
inated our understanding of Roman criminal procedure without reliance upon
acta martyrum as primary resources. More important for the present study
are the many *commentarii* that have been published since the early decades
of this century. Revel Coles's *Reports of Proceedings in Papyri*, which is a
literary study of extant *commentarii*, in 1966 listed eighty-seven *commentarii*
dating to the second century and fifty-eight from the Antonine period alone.[24]
To these can now be added at least twelve more *commentarii* dating before
218 CE, and there are no doubt others of which the present writer is unaware.
If scholars wish to prove (most assume without proving) that some *acta martyrum* originated as copies of *commentarii*, then those acts must be form-
critically analyzed over against *commentarii* and not over against other *acta
martyrum* that have been assumed to derive from *commentarii*. The point
seems almost too obvious to make, but the best of scholars have built cases
based upon such circular evidence.

As indicated above, the discoveries of texts belonging to the *Acta Alexandrinorum* and *commentarii* genres caused a flurry of literary activity, with the
historical school contending that the Christian and pagan accounts originated
from authentic *commentarii* and the history-of-religions school attempting to
prove a fictional origin.[25] Perhaps the most recent pronouncement on the
mutual dependencies of the genres is that of Ramsay MacMullen:

> The similarity arises from no literary borrowings but from the depen-
> dence of both types of document on official acta emphasized for the sake
> of credibility; and everyone acknowledged that both pagan and Christian

[19] Geffcken, "Die christlichen Martyrien," *Hermes* 45 (1910) 484. Barnes, too, notes that
with regard to the legal basis of the persecutions of the Christians "an important part of the evidence consists of accounts of how Christians were actually tried" ("Pre-Decian *Acta Martyrum*," 509).

[20] *Law of Greco-Roman Egypt.*

[21] See esp. *The Criminal Courts of the Roman Republic and Principate* (Oxford: Blackwell,
1972); and idem, *Studies in Roman Government and Law* (Oxford, 1960).

[22] *Roman Society and Roman Law in the New Testament* (Oxford: Clarendon, 1963).

[23] "The Criminal Jurisdiction of Governors," *JRomS* 58 (1968) 51–59; idem, "Legal
Privilege in the Roman Empire," in M. I. Finley, ed., *Studies in Ancient Society* (Lon-
don/Boston: Routledge and Kegan Paul, 1974) 141–65; Garnsey, *Social Status and Legal
Privilege in the Roman Empire* (Oxford: Clarendon, 1970); idem, "Why Penalties Became
Harsher: The Roman Case, Late Republic to Fourth-Century Empire," *Natural Law Forum* 13
(1968) 141ff.

[24] Coles, *Reports of Proceedings in Papyri* (Papyrologica Bruxellensia 4; Brussels: Fondation
Egyptologique Reine Elisabeth, 1966).

[25] For a brief summary of the principal arguments, see Musurillo, *Pagan Martyrs*, 259–66.

martyr tales really did draw, some more, some less, on court minutes. . . .
A few key words shared by Epictetus and Diogenes, and by Christian
hagiographers, once led to theories of dependence later disproved, nor
could any direct link be established joining early *Acta Christianorum* to
the *exitus* stories and the *Acta Alexandrianorum*, whatever might be said
of the possibility of a common source.[26]

But since the battles between the historical and history-of-religions schools
during the first decades of this century, when scholars had only a few *commentarii* upon which to base their arguments, few studies have actually compared the *acta paganorum* or *acta Christianorum* to *commentarii*. No study
has done so in sufficient depth as to provide us with the tools necessary for
redaction criticism.

One of the few comparative studies was made by Hans Niedermeyer, one
of Reitzenstein's students. Niedermeyer was convinced that "ancient *commentarii* (*Aktenabschriften*) had contained and preserved the date as an
essential element of form,"[27] but his form criticism of the *acta Christianorum* consisted of little more than a categorization according to the position of the date formula. He noted that "it was necessary for the authors of
martyr accounts also to give the date of the death day."[28] Niedermeyer's
study of the *acta Christianorum* was directed to the *Acts of Cyprian*, and certainly his statement was true by the time of Cyprian, for Cyprian directs his
presbyters and deacons thus: "Denique et dies eorum, quibus excedunt,
adnotate, ut commemorationes eorum inter memorias martyrum celebrare
possimus."[29] But many of the pre-Decian *acta Christianorum* bear no date,
as is the case of the Greek recension of the *Acts of Carpus* (the Latin version
gives April 13) and of the three recensions of the *Acts of Justin*.[30] Even the
date 23 February for the martyrdom of Polycarp may be a later addition,
since, as New Testament scholarship has shown, dates are often interpolated

[26] MacMullen, *Enemies of the Roman Order: Treason, Unrest, and Alienation in the Empire*
(Cambridge: Harvard University, 1966) 89. Not everyone has acknowledged that Christian acts
drew upon *commentarii*, but the vast majority indeed have.

[27] Niedermeyer, *Über antike Protokoll-Literatur* (Göttingen: Dieterich'schen University,
1918) 29.

[28] Ibid.

[29] Cyprian *Ep* 12.2. See Victor Saxer, *Morts, Martyrs, Reliques en Afrique Chrétienne aux
premiers siècles: les témoignages de Tertullien, Cyprien, et Augustin à lumière de l'archéologie
africaine* (Paris: Éditions Beauchesne, 1980).

[30] The traditional dates of Justin's martyrdom are: Greek and Maronite: 1 June; Roman: 13
April; Coptic: 31 March and 11 August.

to fill out detail, and *Martyrdom of Polycarp* has been thoroughly interpolated.[31]

The best literary study of the *acta Christianorum* is still that of the Bollandist Hippolyte Delehaye, *Les passions des martyrs et les genres littéraires*.[32] The questions Delehaye would initially ask concerning our acts are sound: "Did the hagiographer have at his disposition an official document? To what degree was it respected? Were some things omitted? What has been interpolated to it?"[33] His approach to answering these questions, however, is not sound. He uses as "les meilleurs modèles du style strictement protocolaire" two Christian documents, *Gesta apud Zenophilum* (13 December 320) and *Acta purgationis Felicis* (314), which derive from the Donatist controversy.[34] From these accounts Delehaye proceeded to discuss the form of the *procès-verbal* (*commentarius*), at times providing corroboration for his conclusions from two papyri—P. Theadelphia 15 (280/81 CE) and P. Rainer 18 (124 CE).[35] The principal difficulty with this approach is that one can do little more than generalize the form of a *commentarius* from these few examples covering several centuries. The form of fourth-century *commentarii* differs in several significant respects from the form of second-century *commentarii*. Delehaye's conclusions, therefore, only hold true in a general sense for the *acta martyrum* of the Antonine period, or are inaccurate, and are not sufficiently detailed for redaction criticism.[36]

---

[31] See esp. Hans von Campenhausen, "Bearbeitungen und Interpolationen des Polykarpmartyriums," *SHAW* 3 (1957) 1–48; and Hans Conzelmann, *Bemerkungen zum Martyrium Polykarps* (NAWG; Göttingen: Vandenhoeck & Ruprecht, 1978) 40–58.

[32] Delehaye, *Les passions des martyrs et les genres littéraires* (1921; reprinted Brussels: Société des Bollandistes, 1966).

[33] Ibid., 125–26.

[34] These documents are investigations into the charges that Silvanus (in *Gesta apud Zenophilum*) and Felix of Aptungi (in *Acta purgationis Felicis*) had been *traditores*, ones who had "handed over" scriptures during persecution.

[35] See Delehaye, *Les passions des martyrs*, 125–31 for his form criticism of the *commentarii*.

[36] The two most recent book-length treatments of the Christian acts are Musurillo, *Christian Martyrs*, and Giuliana Lanata, *Processi contro Cristiani negli atti dei martiri* (Torino: Giappichelli, 1975). Both works are collections of texts and translations with general introductions and discussions. By comparison with his superlative *The Acts of the Pagan Martyrs: Acta Alexandrinorum* (Oxford: Clarendon, 1972), Musurillo's study of the *acta Christianorum* is disappointing, and it has received a scathing review by Fergus Millar (*JTS* n.s. 24 [1973] 239–43) who is typically a tough reviewer. Musurillo's translations have received criticism in a recent article by Jan den Boeft and Jan Bremmer ("Notiunculae Martyrologicae," *VC* 35 [1981] 43–56).

Trends of Scholarship on the *Acta Christianorum*

Previous generations of scholars have not always approached the *acta Christianorum* with the attitude that the acts should be understood by means of all critical and interpretative powers. Guiseppe Lazzati observed that "the literature about the martyrs is examined more . . . with hagiographical interest than literary and this has perhaps done harm to the literary evaluation of these documents."[37] There can be no doubt that it has. Hippolyte Delehaye, the most formidable scholar of the *acta Christianorum*, complained that

> religious-minded people who regard with equal veneration not only the
> saints themselves but everything associated with them, have been greatly
> agitated by certain conclusions assumed by them to have been inspired
> by the revolutionary spirit that has penetrated even into the Church, and
> to be highly derogatory to the honour of the heroes of our faith. This
> conviction frequently finds utterance in somewhat violent terms.[38]

Indeed it has!

Moreover, many scholars would place the goal of "protecting the honor of the saints" above the goal of thoroughly understanding the past. The scholarship of Adolf von Harnack, whose *Geschichte der altchristlichen Literatur* probably marks the beginning of critical study of the *acta Christianorum* as it is understood today, typifies the "protect-and-don't-look-too-closely" approach.[39] Like most scholars of the eighteenth and nineteenth centuries, Harnack was inclined to accept much on faith. He argued from such texts as Matt 10:19–20 that "the martyr accounts are the true continuation of the New Testament accounts and miracles, because Christ speaks and acts in the martyrs."[40] As supplements to the New Testament, the authenticity of the *acta Christianorum* must have been jealously preserved by the early church:

> Whoever would falsify here [the acts of the martyrs], set themselves up
> to the most serious reproach, because such a one would falsify the words
> of the Holy Spirit, i.e., of Christ. It was most certain, therefore, that per-
> sons themselves obtained records from the confessors in the prisons
> whenever possible; if that was not possible, one sent trustworthy

---

[37] Lazzati, "Gli Atti di S. Giustino Martire," *Aevum* 27 (1953) 473.

[38] Delehaye, *The Legends of the Saints: An Introduction to Hagiography* (Notre Dame: University of Notre Dame Press, 1961) ix.

[39] Harnack, *Geschichte der altchristlichen Literatur bis Eusebius* (3 vols.; 1904; reprinted Leipzig: Hinrichs, 1958).

[40] Harnack, "Das ursprüngliche Motiv der Abfassung von Märtyrer- und Heilungsakten in der Kirche," *SPAW* 7 (1910) 115.

brethren to them to hear their testimony. One sought to examine the trial records, but since these were not completely adequate—because they did not completely contain the speeches of the defendants—one sent brethren to the trial, who must have faithfully recorded the words of the confessors.[41]

Delehaye found Harnack's theory regarding the early church's concern to gather the last words of the martyrs "seductive and not inspired by an exaggerated distrust with regard to the hagiographical literature. But it is conceived apart from the facts, and nothing in our documents justifies it."[42] But he had scarcely more sympathy with Harnack's nemeses in the history-of-religions school. According to Delehaye, the heroic γένος prevalent in the Roman world, such as found in Diogenes Laertius's *Lives of Philosophers* and Philostratus's *Apollonius of Tyana*, exhibited to the *acta Christianorum* "simple parallels, resemblances entirely exterior from form, thought, and expression."[43] These slight resemblances were merely the result of both types being derived from *commentarii*.

One can quickly see from the quotations of Harnack above that he was not adverse to a priori reasoning. His method and conclusions provoked a strong response from proponents of the philological-historical method, especially from Reitzenstein, Geffcken, and other members of the history-of-religions school in Germany at the turn of the century. Richard Reitzenstein's work largely focused upon the Hellenistic models, with the conclusion that "the Christian literature offers to the philologist various instructive mirror-images of the various forms of the pagan *exitus*-literature."[44] Harnack's unequivocal reply to the history-of-religions school's philological hypercriticism was that

> it gives a disorder of comparisons, reductions and neutralizations, which deceives the eye and threatens to suffocate everything unique and individual. Against it one is well inclined to give the warning cry of the English: "Make no comparison!"[45]

Yet the "make-no-comparison" approach itself threatens to suffocate the search for truth, for it implies that certain things must be accepted as "givens." The historian cannot assume with Harnack that the genre *acta Christianorum* was not influenced by pagan genres, but neither should one

---

[41] Ibid., 116.

[42] Ibid., 112.

[43] Ibid., 114.

[44] Reitzenstein, *Ein Stück hellenistischer Kleinliteratur* (*NAWG*; Göttingen: Vandenhoeck & Ruprecht, 1904) 331–32.

[45] Harnack, "Das ursprüngliche Motiv," 125.

assume with Reitzenstein that it was. More dangerous than the "make-no-comparison" approach, however, is the "protect-the-honor-of-the-saints" approach, for it implies that certain topics and conclusions are to be avoided, that truth is not paramount to all else. The historian's ideal, to present "history as it actually happened," must be pursued without hindrances from religious or political convictions, but also without allowing neutrality or the knowledge that the ideal is unobtainable to enfeeble the presentation.

The concern to distinguish authentic from inauthentic and to understand the origin and development of writings and events are proper concerns of any historian. The *acta martyrum* have been assaulted by so many historical and text-critical studies that it is doubtful whether these methods will bring many fresh insights to our understanding of the acts. The present study makes no claim to overturn the results of centuries of scholarship but rather to build upon and go beyond those results. The historical approaches have naturally recognized that the acts were interpolated and went through successive editions, and this approach has enabled scholars partially to reconstruct the "authentic text" by recognizing the anachronisms or other "mistakes" of a historical nature which probably would not have been present in the original. When two or more recensions are extant, the historical method can usually succeed in correctly labelling a text as a whole "earlier" or "later," as Lazzati has also done by the text-critical method for the *Acts of Justin.* However, if we assume that some *acta martyrum* did actually derive from *commentarii,* it is difficult to see how any attempt to establish the authentic text, or at least to recognize redactional elements, can hope to succeed before it is known what an original text looked like.

A necessary preliminary, then, to establishing methodological controls is some understanding of what form the acts originally took. If it is established that several of the acts did in fact originate as copies of *commentarii,* we are well on our way toward knowing much about this form, since, as will be seen in Chapter Two, the form of second-century *commentarii* was quite uniform. The earliest recensions of our acts may or may not have been so uniform, however, depending upon the degree to which the authors faithfully followed the *commentarius*-form when producing copies.[46]

The question becomes how to arrive at the earliest state of an account, even when we are in possession of only a single manuscript that is manifestly late. Form critism—in conjunction with historical, source-, and text-critical

---

[46] Here a study of the *Martyrdom of Ptolemaeus and Lucius* found in Justin's *2 Apology,* the accounts found in Eusebius, and *P. Bodmer* 20 (which dates to the fourth century, possibly only two decades after the event described) with the extant MSS from the ninth and later centuries could provide additional data useful for a comparison of the acts with the *commentarii* and *Exitus inlustrium virorum.*

methods—is a, if not the *proper*, means of "getting behind" a late recension to an earlier, no longer extant, stage. Scholars have unanimously rejected the *Acts of Ignatius* because of the obvious lateness of the extant text, yet few scholars today, if any, doubt the authenticity of Ignatius's *Epistle to the Romans*, the text of which has been extracted from the *Acts of Ignatius*. Scholarship has saved the epistle and thrown away the acts. If New Testament scholars treated the Gospels in the same fashion, perhaps they would also save only the epistles (i.e., there would be nothing left of the Gospels). The wholesale disposal of accounts is not an acceptable solution. A thorough acquaintance with the *commentarius*-form and the application of form and redaction criticism provide the means to rehabilitate many of the discarded *acta Christianorum*.

The term "form criticism" as applied to the aimed-for methodology of this study requires explanation. Perrin defined redaction criticism as the discipline "concerned with studying the theological motivation of an author as this is revealed in the collection, arrangement, editing, and modification of traditional material, and in the composition of new material or the creation of new forms within the traditions of early Christianity."[47] Redaction is simply the reworking (editing) of older materials to meet new ends. Form criticism is sometimes described as a stage prior to redaction criticism, although this is not strictly or necessarily true. Form criticism attempts to move from an existing text to a prior stage by recognizing, delimiting, and categorizing smaller units within the text which already had a "form" of their own. In criticism of the Old and New Testament writings, this "prior stage" is normally assumed to be oral tradition. The smaller units of the literature, such as apothegm and paradigm, are assumed to each have a definite form which functioned in a precise *Sitz im Leben* ("life situation"; the historical, social, theological context).[48] The *mutatis mutandis* for this study's application of the term "form criticism" to the *acta martyrum* may be easily seen from the chart below:

Gospel Schema:

Jesus' words	social context 1
period of oral tradition	social contexts 2-
oral becomes written	social contexts 3-
written is edited/copied	social contexts 4-

---

[47] Norman Perrin, *What Is Redaction Criticism?* (Philadelphia: Fortress, 1969) 1. As Perrin also notes, redaction criticism is sometimes called "composition criticism" because "it is concerned with the composition of new material and the arrangements of redacted or freshly created material into new units and patterns, as well as with the redaction of existing material" (ibid.).

[48] In this study the term "social context" bears the connotations of Sitz im Leben and, in this writer's estimation, is preferrable to "life situation," "world-view," and other such terms.

Acts Schema:

trial	social context 1
commentarius	social context 1
acta	social context 2
edited/copied *acta*	social contexts 3-

Alternate Schema:

trial with *commentarius*	social context 1
period of oral tradition	social contexts 1-
oral becomes written *acta*	social contexts 2-
written *acta* edited/copied	social contexts 3-

In this study, "form criticism" is used to recognize form that was at the outset written. If we assume that an account was ultimately derived from a *commentarius*, the earliest stage would have been written, even though it may have passed through an intermediate stage that was oral. The methodology for determining whether an account did in fact derive from a *commentarius* is an object of this study.

The reader may have already noticed that there is no chapter entitled "Conclusion." This study is focused upon the trial sections of *acta martyrum*, which purport to record the ipsissima verba of martyrs' trials. The early objective of the study was to establish a method for discovering whether the extant account of a particular *acta* originated from a *commentarius* and therefore might be discovered to contain, in part or entirely, the historical account. After much study, I concluded with Theodor Mommsen that historians are "not trained but born, not educated but self-educated,"[49] and that there are no substitutes for a thorough acquaintance with the primary literature. Thus the basic conclusions of this study are few:

1) Records of trials, *commentarii*, from the same period are of a consistent form.
2) The overall form of the *commentarius* may be divided into four sections: *caput*, body, κρίσις, and concluding matters.
3) Within these four sections there are smaller units that also assume definite forms.
4) Form criticism that analyzes *acta martyrum* according to *commentarius*-form is often able to reveal whether the *acta* were derived from a *commentarius* and provides the foundation for redaction criticism.

As such, Chapters One and Two and the Appendices are meant to facilitate the scholar's own reading of the *commentarii*. The studies of the *acta paganorum* and *acta Christianorum* found in Chapters Three through Seven

---

[49] Mommsen, "Rectorial Address" delivered to the University of Berlin, 1874, reprinted in Fritz Stern, ed., *The Varieties of History* (New York: Vintage Books, 1973) 193.

are not intended as "definitive studies." Rather, they briefly illustrate and advocate form criticism according to *commentarius*-form. This in turn advocates future form-critical studies of the *acta martyrum* in the hope and expectation that yet other forms will be isolated.

1

Judicial Procedure,
Scribes, and Archives

A study of Roman law, trial records, and administrative system should be a prerequisite to any study of Christian persecutions and martyrdom literature. However, the vexed questions of why the Christians were persecuted and the charge(s) upon which they were brought to trial will in this study be treated only in passing.[1] Nor will the social and political background to the *acta paganorum* be treated at much length here. The present chapter is intended to provide the reader with a general, and at times specific, understanding of the background of the documents analyzed in Chapter Two. Chapters Three through Seven, in turn, rely upon the analysis there.

What we have just called "trial records" were called ὑπομνηματισμοί or *commentarii* during the Empire. In English these words have been variously translated as "minutes," "memoranda," "trial records," "records of pro-

---

[1] The secondary literature on these topics is enormous. The early study by Leon Hardy Canfield (*The Early Persecutions of the Christians* [Studies in History, Economics and Public Law 55/2; New York: Columbia University, 1913]) is somewhat dated but contains much useful source material and a summary of previous scholarship on the topic. Still astounding and useful is J. B. Lightfoot's mammoth study, which contains a surprising amount of source material: *The Apostolic Fathers*, part 2: *S. Ignatius; S. Polycarp* (2 vols.; London: Macmillan, 1885). These volumes cover, in great detail, much more than just Ignatius and Polycarp. Any reader who has not become acquainted with the unabridged edition of Lightfoot's *Apostolic Fathers* should do so—for most of us it is a humbling experience.

The best study on the legal bases of the persecutions, the view that the present writer is inclined to accept, is Ste Croix's "Why Were the Early Christians Persecuted?" *Past and Present* 26 (1963) 7–38; reprinted in Finley, ed., *Studies in Ancient Society*, 210–49.

ceedings," or "protocols." The French and German translations are normally *procès-verbaux* and *Protokolle* respectively. Hereafter the Latin *commentarius/commentarii* will be used to refer to such documents, whether in Greek or Latin.

The Trial Procedure:
Summons and Arrest to Arraignment

The overriding concern of the Roman government was to preserve the *pax et tranquillitas* of the Empire, and it was only when these were threated that criminals were arrested, prosecuted, and punished.[2] In most cases it was necessary for the plaintiffs themselves to bring defendants to trial, or, in the case of murder, the deceased person's family acting as plaintiffs.[3]

> If an accused ... failed to appear to defend himself, he was not condemned in absence. The governor posted him as wanted, announcing this by edict and informing the magistrates of his town by letter, and his property was sequestrated. If he appeared within a year and stood his trial, and was acquitted, he recovered his property; if he did not appear the property was confiscated, and that was all the penalty he suffered.[4]

Although more will be said about the process of accusation in the discussion of *delatores* below, it may be appropriate to give here an example of the

---

[2] J. L. Strachan-Davidson, *Problems of the Roman Criminal Law* (2 vols.; Oxford: Clarendon, 1912) 2. 165; cf. Jones, *Criminal Courts*, 116: "The imperial mandates to provincial governors contained the clause: 'the man in charge of a province must see to it that he clears the province of criminals.' Ulpian expands this: 'it is the duty of a good and conscientious governor to see that the province he rules is peaceful and tranquil, and this result he will achieve without difficulty if he takes careful measures to ensure that the province is free from criminals and searches them out. He should search out persons guilty of sacrilege, brigands, kidnappers and thieves and punish them according to their offences. . . .' Apart from the above cases the detection of crime and the bringing of its perpetrators to justice was still left to private citizens, either injured parties or personal enemies of the accused or else *delatores* for the sake of the financial reward."

It should be noted here that the Roman criminal "system" never "passed through a stage of strict law" (H. F. Jolowicz, *Historical Introduction to the Study of Roman Law* [2d ed.; Cambridge: Cambridge University, 1965] 413) and that "justice" depended very much upon the social status of the persons involved. Upon this latter point see Jones, *Criminal Courts*, 109–10; Strachan-Davidson, *Criminal Law*, 2. 172–74; Ramsay MacMullen, *Roman Social Relations 50 B.C. to A.D. 284* (New Haven/London: Yale University, 1974) 8, 11, 39; and Peter Garnsey, "Legal Privilege in the Roman Empire," in Finley, ed., *Studies in Ancient Society*, 141–65.

[3] See, e.g., *SB* 7558 (148 CE); see also Taubenschlag, *Law of Greco-Roman Egypt*, 327–28; Jones, *Criminal Courts*, 116–17; cf. Jolowicz: "In *cognitio* . . . the state official began to take a part, not only in the trial, but in the summons" (*Roman Law*, 408).

[4] Jones, *Criminal Courts*, 118; see also Taubenschlag, *Law of Greco-Roman Egypt*, 411–19.

process of accusation, and an indication of the time factor involved, from what purports to be the defense speech of Apuleius before the Proconsul Claudius Maximus:

> It is only four or five days since his [Sicinius Aemilianus's] advocates of malice prepense attacked me with slanderous accusations, and began to charge me with practice of the black art and with the murder of my stepson Pontianus. . . . a day later he presented the indictment in the name of my step-son, Sicinius Pudens, a mere boy, adding that he appeared as his representative. This is a new method. . . . You, Maximus, with great acuteness saw through his designs and ordered him to renew his original accusation in person.[5]

Trials could drag on for years, however, with one magistrate passing a case on to his successor.[6]

Civil lawsuits, *actio* and *iudicium*, were normally initiated by the issuance of an *in ius vocatio* by the plaintiff, which requested that the defendant be summoned.[7] In both criminal and civil procedures, the principle of *nisi accusatus condemnari non potest*[8] seems to have applied.

In addition to these trials which involved some form of *crimen, delictum*, or *maleficium*, the *commentarii* also record appearances before magistrates dealing with civil matters, such as delegations appealing for tax relief and requests for circumcision and admission to the priesthood.[9]

---

[5] Apuleius *Apologia* 1–2; the translation used here is that of H. E. Butler, *The Apologia and Florida of Apuleius of Madaura* (Oxford: Clarendon, 1909). The crux of the dispute revolved around a potential inheritance from a wealthy widow named Pudentilla. Rufinus, the father-in-law of this woman, had hoped to gain a portion of her fortune by having her marry another of his sons. His plans were dashed when Apuleius married her. Pudentilla had had two sons, Pontianus and Pudens, by her first husband, and when Pontianus fell ill and died, Rufinus accused Apuleius in the name of the surviving son of having won the woman's heart by means of magic and of murdering the boy. The governor required that the accusation be resubmitted on the grounds that the real accuser was sheltering behind someone else's name.

[6] See, e.g., *P. Oxy.* 237 (186 CE); see also Oscar William Reinmuth, *The Prefect of Egypt from Augustus to Diocletian* (Beiträge zur alten Geschichte 21; Leipzig: Dieterich'sche Verlagsbuchhandlung, 1935) 102; and see also the examples cited there.

[7] See Taubenschlag, *Law of Greco-Roman Egypt*, 481–84.

[8] Cicero *Oratio pro Sexto Roscio Comoedo* 20.56; see also the references given by E. J. Bickermann, "Trajan, Hadrian and the Christians," *RivFil* 97 (1968) 310 n. 1.

[9] Circumcision was a long-established custom in Egypt; Egyptian priests were required to be circumcised. See H. D. Schmitz, "τὸ ἔθος und verwandte Begriffe in den Papyri" (Diss., University of Köln, 1970) 27, 81, cited by the editors of *BGU* 2216 (156 CE). Hadrian outlawed circumcision, making it punishable by death; Hadrian's edict was suspended by Antoninus Pius in 138. See Rudolf Meyer, "περιτέμνω," *TDNT* 6 (1968) 80; and see also the sources cited there.

Not much is known of the events which transpired between the *accusatio* and the *cognitio* (trial) itself. It appears that in the first place the plaintiff directed the case by petition or application (ὑπόμνημα)[10] to a particular magistrate.[11] However, in the provinces only the governors, and in Egypt the prefect, had *imperium* and hence *iurisdictio*,[12] and normally petitions would be directed to the governor or *Prefectus Aegypti*. But no governor could hear all the cases directed to him, and as a result he would delegate (ἐξ ἀναπομπῆς) cases to subordinate magistrates, *iudices pedanei* (or *dati*) or simply κριταί.[13]

In Egypt, as in the other provinces, magistrates made an annual judicial tour based upon a fixed calendar and to fixed *conventus* (sitting of the magistrate) sites.[14] In Egypt the *conventus* was held "at Pelusium in January for the eastern Delta, at Memphis or Arsinoe anywhere from late January to mid-April for middle and upper Egypt, and at or near Alexandria thereafter."[15] When a magistrate opened a *conventus* he was immediately deluged with petitions, accusations, and other matters of a judicial or administrative nature. *P. Yale* 61 (209 CE) records that 1,804 petitions were submitted to the *conventus* at Arsinoe in a period of little over two days! Lewis, noting this statistic, remarked upon "how passionately the local population looked to the annual *conventus* for redress of grievances."[16]

---

[10] See, e.g., *PSI* 1102 (3d cent.).

[11] An accusation could be addressed to the police (*centurion, praefectus alae, eirenarchus pagi, riparii, praepositus pagi, hypostrategos*, etc.—note that not all of these posts are contemporary), to the *conventus*, or directly to the prefect. Appeal could be made from a lower magistrate to a higher, including *appellatio ad Caesarem*. On *accusatio, provocatio,* and *appellatio,* see Jones, *Criminal Courts,* 100–103; Taubenschlag, *Law of Greco-Roman Egypt,* 341, 413–14; and Fergus Millar, *The Emperor in the Roman World (31 BC–AD 337)* (Ithaca, NY: Cornell University Press, 1977) 512–15.

[12] See Garnsey, "Criminal Jurisdiction," 51–55; Jolowicz, *Roman Law,* 416; Jones, *Criminal Courts,* 104.

[13] See Naphtali Lewis, "The Prefect's Conventus: Proceedings and Procedures," *BASP* 18 (1981) 125; and see the secondary sources cited in n. 24 there.

[14] On the *conventus*, see ibid., 119–29; and G. F. Talamanca, *Richerche sul processo nell'Egitto greco-romano, I: L'organizzazione del 'Conventus' del 'Praefectus Aegypti'* (Milan: Univ. of Rome, 1974); see also *P. Oxy.* 3464 (quoted on pp. 24–25 below); *P. Oxy.* 2754 (111 CE); *P. Oxy.* 3017 (176 CE); *P. Yale* 61 (209 CE); Wilcken, "Der ägyptische Konvent," *ArchP* 4 (1908) 366–433; Jolowicz, *Roman Law,* 416–17; Wolfgang Kunkel, *An Introduction to Roman Legal and Constitutional History* (2d ed., based on 6th German ed.; Oxford: Clarendon, 1973) 41; Taubenschlag, *Law of Greco-Roman Egypt,* 20.

[15] Lewis, "Prefect's Conventus," 120, who relies up Talamanca and Wilcken at this point (see preceding note).

[16] Ibid., 121.

Once the *conventus* was opened, it was largely up to private citizens to prefer charges in criminal matters. There were, however, other means whereby criminal cases might be brought before the courts:

> The principles of procedure for the standing criminal courts, as codified by Augustus in the *lex Iulia iudiciorum publicorum*, were "accusatorial"; there had to be a named accuser and a proper statement of charge. The authorities had no power, of themselves, to charge and try people. Any citizen—with a few exceptions—could bring a criminal charge, and there were rewards for the accuser if the trial resulted in a conviction—which was liable to conjure into being the professional *delator*; but on the other hand the accuser was responsible for his charge and liable to penalties for calumnious accusation. To judge from the fact that Paulus is found in the *Digest* quoting the proper statutory form of "charge-sheet" in connection with the crime of adultery, we may assume that the "accusatorial" procedure continued to be proper for the statutory offences even when they came to be judged by tribunals other than the standing courts. (The *Digest* also contains a list of people debarred from preferring charges: women and wards, soldiers, magistrates in office, "infamous" persons, and freedmen as against their patrons; but to this rule in turn there were exceptions—thus, anyone at all could bring a charge of treason—which headed the law in a new direction, towards a principle that anyone should be entitled to bring an accusation on behalf of his own interest or family—a sort of private prosecution for crime.) The magistrate judging *extra ordinem*, on the other hand, at any rate for non-statutory offences, could proceed "inquisitorially"; there need be no formal named accuser and charge, and he could simply investigate on "information received", hale into court on his own responsibility, and judge whomsoever he chose (subject to the rules of appeal). Pliny proceeded, in dealing with Christians, on the basis of an *index* or informer as well as on formal accusations, and Trajan's objection to the use of anonymous informations, "they are a bad example and not in tune with the age we live in", implies that there was nothing *ultra vires* about Pliny's use of them.[17]

If the magistrate decided to judge the case, the defendant was officially summoned by *evocatio litteris*, which will be discussed below.

At this point the case was slated for trial, presumably by the *a cognitionibus*,[18] the official whose duties included "calling in cases," or by the ὑπομνηματογράφος (the *a commentariis*). An example of the *a cog-*

---

[17] John A. Crook, *Law and Life of Rome, 90 B.C.–A.D. 212* (Aspects of Greek and Roman Life; Ithaca, NY: Cornell University, 1967) 276–77.

[18] On the *a cognitionibus*, see Millar, *Emperor*, 232, 235; von Premerstein, "Commentarii," PW 4 (1901) 761; Reinmuth, *Prefect of Egypt*, 12.

nitionibus in action, although not from a strictly historical account, is given by Philostratus:

> When his colleague was ill, and it was reported that the Emperor [Caracalla] was cancelling many of the suits, Heliodorus hastened to the military headquarters in anxiety about his own suit. On being summoned into court sooner than he expected, he tried to postpone the case till the sick man could be present; but the official who gave the notifications of the suits was an overbearing fellow and would not allow this, but haled him into court against his will, and even dragged him by the beard.[19]

A recently published papyrus from Oxyrhynchus gives an indication of both the process of summoning and the fact that a private party could, in the first century any way, request the summons:

> To C. Iulius Asinianus, strategus of the Arsinoite nome, from Mnesitheus son of Theon. After making a complaint and having a summons delivered in the fourteenth year of Divus Claudius against Heration son of Maron and other men, on the grounds that they had wrongfully taken possession of the property of my wife Maronis . . . I received from the former prefect L. Lusius Geta as judge concerning all C. Iulius Iollas(?), priest and gymnasiarch of Alexandria, who having heard both myself and the other laid down that the ownership should remain with my wife according to the record of proceedings (ἔχωι ὑπομνημα-τισμοῖς) which I have in my possession.
>
> Since Heration disappeared and did not present himself at the hearing, he was summoned by Geta through a public notice; and since even so he did not appear, I have remained away from home up until now—intentionally, since the time for the judgement had not arrived. But now, having returned and received information of the fact that M . . . son of . . . (?) is laying claim to three aruras from the six aruras of vine-land(?), and Heration himself to the other three aruras, I myself, not keeping quiet but adhering much more to the charge against the accused persons, am submitting this memorandum and I ask that it be registered with you and a copy be transmitted to the accused persons through an assistant, so that they may know to present themselves wherever the lord prefect Ti. Claudius Balbillus holds the next *conventus*, that through his intercession I may obtain justice and they may get their deserts. Farewell. (*P. Oxy.* 3464; ca. 54–60 CE)[20]

---

[19] Philostratus *Lives of Philosophers* 2.32.

[20] Translation from A. Bülow-Jacobsen and J. E. G. Whitehorne, eds., *The Oxyrhynchus Papyri nos. 3431–3521* (London: Egyptian Exploration Society, 1980).

Another example of the petitioning and summoning process may be seen in the *commentarius* of a case brought before an *epistrategus* named Achilleus:

> Gaius Julius Ptolemaeus appeared [before the court], and Julianus, advocate, said, "This man is an Antinoite. When he became the victim of an act of violence (βία) and grievous assault (ὕβρις) and false contract (ἐργολαβία), he petitioned to you against Chairemon, son of Maron. Therefore, since the latter is not present, (even though) summoned through your assistant (ὑπηρέτης) Ptolemaeus, we ask in accordance with the rights [as Antinoites?], which you have confirmed, that he be sent for trial to Antinoöpolis." Achilleus said, "From where is the defendant (ἀντίδικος)?" He answered, "From the village of Karanis of this nome." Achilleus said, "Let the strategus order that your defendant be sent to Antinoöpolis." (*P. Mich.* 6.365; 194 CE)

Antinoöpolis was founded in 130 by Hadrian, in memory of his beloved Antinous, who had drowned in the Nile that year. This city was founded with special privileges not enjoyed by other Egyptian cities until at least the reign of Septimius Severus.[21] But even Antinoöpolis was subject to the *imperium* and *iurisdictio* of the prefect. Here the prefect's deputy, an *epistrategus* of one of the three districts (nomes) of Egypt, seems to have been empowered to delegate cases to the lower court of the city. Had the prefect decided to hear the case, an *evocatio litteris* would have been issued for the parties to appear at a particular where the prefect would appear during his regular tour of inspection, and where he would hold *conventus*.[22]

A variation of the summons is found in the *commentarius P. Fouad* 23 (144 CE):

> Dius, son of Zeuxis, having appeared, said, "Having declared on oath (χειρογραφήσας) to the strategus of the Arsinoite Nome that I would present myself here on the 24th of this month to stand trial against my brothers, I came to you [. . .] on the 24th. But because it was the holiday, it was not entered in the minutes (μὴ ὑπομνηματίσω). Therefore I now ask that it be entered in the minutes that I made my appeal by the appointed date; since my defendants, although they also declared on oath, did not attend at all, I beg that, if it is pleasing to you . . . [text breaks off here][23]

---

[21] See A. H. M. Jones, *The Cities of the Eastern Roman Provinces* (2d ed.; rev. Michael Avi-Yonah, et al.; Oxford: Clarendon, 1971) 323, 327–28.

[22] On the *conventus*, see above.

[23] Translation by the editors of *P. Fouad*: A. Bataille, O. Guéraud, P. Jouguet, N. Lewis, H. Marrou, J. Scherer, and W. G. Waddell.

The strategus had in this instance seen both parties and had sworn them to appear before the court by an appointed date. In most cases, however, both parties would appear πρὸ βῆμα. The *dramatis personae* thus assembled would normally include the magistrate, his *consilium*, defendants and plaintiffs, their advocates, guards, and scribes;[24] in place of defendants and plaintiffs might appear a delegation.

Scribes

The activity of the scribes is of particular interest to the form critic. In the *commentarii* the recording scribe is variously called *notarius*, *exceptor*,[25] *commentariensis*, γραμματεύς, νομογράφος, and ὑπομνηματογράφος.[26] According to Plutarch, Latin shorthand was introduced by Cicero:

> This [a speech before the senate against Caesar] is the only speech of Cato which has been preserved, we are told, and its preservation was due to Cicero the consul, who had previously given to those clerks who excelled in rapid writing instruction in the use of signs, which, in small and short figures, comprised the force of many letters; these clerks he had then distributed in various parts of the senate-house. For up to that time the Romans did not employ or even possess what are called short-hand writers (σημειογράφους), but then for the first time, we are told, the first steps toward the practice were taken.[27]

The date for the development of Greek shorthand is difficult to ascertain.[28] It is believed that *P. Brem.* 82, from the reign of Trajan or Hadrian, contains the earliest surviving Greek shorthand text.

---

[24] The term "scribe" is used here as a translation of the various titles used for those who penned the *commentarius* in the first instance or who produced extracts of *commentarii*. Σκρείβας is, in fact, anachronistic for the second century; see Alan K. Bowman, *The Town Councils of Roman Egypt* (American Studies in Papyrology 11; Toronto: Hakkert, 1971) 39–41.

[25] On *notarii* and *exceptores*, see von Premerstein, "Commentarii," 743.

[26] On *commentariensis*, see *ibid.*, 763–66; on γραμματεύς, see Bowman, *Town Councils*, 39–41; on νομογράφοι, see the discussion of S. Eitrem and L. Amundsen, *Papyri Osloenses* (Oslo: Dybwald, 1931) vol. 2, no. 17. For a study of a particular scribe, see P. J. Sijpesteijn, "A Scribe at Work," *BASP* 16 (1979) 277–80.

[27] Plutarch *Cato Minor* 23. Trans. Bernadotte Perrin, *Plutarch's Lives* (LCL; London: Heinemann; Cambridge: Harvard University Press, 1969). The next evidence that scribes had developed a shorthand for Latin comes from Seneca *Apocolocyntosis* 9, written during the reign of Nero.

[28] On shorthand, see H. J. M. Milne, *Greek Shorthand Manuals* (London: Egypt Exploration Society, 1934); F. G. Kenyon, "Tachygraphy," *OxCD*, 1033 col. 2; Coles, *Reports of Proceedings*, 10–15, 20, 25; and Lawrence Feinberg, "A Fragment of a Shorthand Commentary," *BASP* 9 (1972) 53–58.

On the use of shorthand in recording of *commentarii*, Coles concluded that

the immediate impression is that these reports are most unlikely to be verbatim, although set out in Oratio Recta: the recorded utterances of the parties therein are usually very brief, as are the reports as a whole, and most of the cases as we have them would not have taken more than a few minutes to transact. . . . We are perhaps given the extent and form of an original report of proceedings through *P. Fam.Teb.* 24 (124 A.D.),[29] a papyrus in the British Museum recording a case also preserved in a virtually duplicate text in Berlin. There is a subscription at the end (1.110) of the British Museum version: Ἀπολώνιος ἀνέγνων τὸν προκείμενον ὑπομνηματισμὸν ἐν σελίσι τρισὶ ἡμίσει. Both the BM papyrus and the Berlin text are private copies from the official original and this phrase . . . will be a copy of the presiding official's certification of the authenticity of the official record, appended to it originally in his own hand. ἐν σελίσι τρισὶ ἡμίσει (omitted in the Berlin copy) is the mean between the length of the two copies (BM has four cols., B has three). Provided that the columns in the original were of equivalent size, then *P. Fam.Teb.* 24 must almost certainly preserve the original text, a conclusion supported by the fact that the two copies are effectively identical. In this report the majority of the speeches are given in Oratio Obliqua after an introduction with the name of the speaker and a participle in a Genitive Absolute construction, and these speeches read like a précis of what was said: they must then have been given in this summary form in the official document. We might conclude, then, that as late as A.D. 124 reports of proceedings were taken down in longhand, so that the speeches of the parties were given more or less in note-form; thus, except insofar as private copies may have omitted passages not of interest to the persons having them made, there might in general have been little difference in length between the official originals and the private copies that we possess. The Oratio Recta format, which is virtually universal in the protocols of the first century A.D., would then be artificial and only quasi-verbatim. . . .

There is, however, a possible alternative explanation for the phenomena revealed in *P. Fam.Teb.* 24: namely that shorthand was used for the recording of proceedings but that the resulting verbatim record in shorthand was used only as a preliminary draft of which the resolved version, the effectively "original" record which would be kept in the official files, would be a précis. This conjecture however must remain virtually impossible to verify directly through original material.[30]

---

[29] *P. Fam.Teb.* 24 is discussed in Chapter Two. The text is provided in the "Texts" section at the back of this study.

[30] Coles, *Reports of Proceedings*, 15–19.

As can be gathered from what Coles has said, virtually all of the extant *commentarii* appear to have been private copies and not archival originals.

Archives and Copies of *Commentarii*

If it is to be concluded that some *acta martyrum* contain the ipsissima verba of the martyr's trial, it must be proved or assumed (1) that either persons were present at the trial who could have recorded the verbal exchanges themselves, or (2) that such persons could obtain copies of the *commentarius* itself. At this point, we will concern ourselves only with the second alternative.

In the opinion of Johannes Geffcken, no writer of any account of a martyrdom, be he Christian or pagan, ever referred to a *commentarius* when composing the account,[31] but his is a minority opinion. By far the most common explanation of how Christians obtained *commentarii* is that they bribed scribes. The common "proof" of this theory is derived from the *Acts of Saints Tarachus, Probus, and Andronicus* (304 CE),[32] in which the anonymous author states at the outset that he had obtained a copy of the record from a scribe with a bribe of two hundred denarii. This is possible, since it is not difficult to imagine the susceptibility of scribes to bribes,[33] but the *Acts of Tarachus*, in their extant form at least, are so filled with fictional elements that the evidence provided therein is nearly useless to the historian. As shall be seen below, private parties could obtain copies of *commentarii* through normal channels without resorting to bribes. For the Christians, it is more likely that a bribe would be required, if ever, not for acquisition of the document but rather as a bribe *tenere silentium* to keep the scribe from becoming a *delator* and accusing them before a magistrate.

Strong evidence that private parties could obtain copies of *commentarii* is that "the vast majority of reports of proceedings in the papyri are private

---

[31] Geffcken, "Die Stenographie in den Akten der Märtyrer," *Archiv für Stenographie* 57 (1906) 81.

[32] A sample of those who have appealed to the *Acts of Tarachus* as proof are: Herbert B. Workman, *Persecution in the Early Church* (1906; reprinted Oxford/New York: Oxford University Press, 1980); Donald W. Riddle, *The Martyrs: A Study in Social Control* (Chicago: University of Chicago Press, 1931); Delehaye, *Les passions des martyrs*; and Ernst Posner, *Archives in the Ancient World* (Cambridge: Harvard University, 1972).

[33] However, cf. Trajan's edict of 111 (*P. Oxy.* 2754) prohibiting the taking of bribes by village scribes. The issue here is probably bribery to avoid holding costly magistracies. Local scribes were required to provide lists of those eligible (based primarily upon wealth) to stand for certain offices. The costs incurred by such offices usually came out of the magistrate's personal wealth, and, hence, many wished to keep their names off such lists.

copies made from the official records.''[34] This in itself indicates a relatively easy access to the records. The reader may recall the words of *P. Oxy.* 3464 (quoted above) which contains a request for a summons in which the writer, a certain Mnesitheus, writes to the prefect that he has in his possession the *commentarius* of an earlier trial of his. The majority of extant *commentarii*, then, appear to be extracts purchased through normal channels and housed in private archives for future proof of a case's outcome.[35]

Additional proof is found where extracts are quoted in petitions or are introduced and quoted during the course of a trial as legal precedent for the case at hand. One such example is found in *P. Oxy.* 237 in which a father, Chaeremon, has charged his daughter Dionysia with "transgression of law" (παρανομία) and "ungodliness" (ἀσέβεια), although the case ultimately revolves around the father's desire to remove the daughter from her husband. During the course of the trial, Dionysia was able to produce three *commentarii*—dated 87, 128, and 135 CE—as precedents for her defense. Another example is found in *SB* 7558 (148 CE), which is a petition from a certain Antinoite named C. Apollinarius Niger to an epistrategus requesting relief from guardianship. In his petition, Gaius subjoins, as a precedent for the epistrategus, a lengthy copy of a *commentarius* from the reign of Hadrian.[36]

In order to understand how a private party, such as Dionysia or Gaius, might go about obtaining copies of *commentarii*, it is necessary to understand the administrative and archival system of the Empire.[37] Enough is known about the system in Egypt to reconstruct a fairly accurate picture for this province. In the chart on the following page, I have attempted to give a graphic presentation of the administrative and archival system of second-century Egypt:[38]

---

[34] Coles, *Reports of Proceedings*, 16; see also 19 and 24.

[35] On private archives, see Posner, *Archives*, 203, 218–19.

[36] See also *P. Harr.* 67 (ca. 150?); *P. Oxford* 1 (150/51).

[37] Posner's recent study (*Archives*) presents a coherent discussion of the archival system of the Empire; however, the study appears largely to rely on secondary sources for its data. Of these secondary sources, the most thorough is Arthur Stein, *Untersuchungen zur Geschichte und Verwaltung Ägyptens unter römischer Herrschaft* (Stuttgart: Metzlersche Buchhandlung, 1915) 187–92. Stein's conclusions, however, must be modified in the light of *P. Oxy.* 1654, as was done by Reinmuth, *Prefect of Egypt*, 41.

[38] In addition to the sources cited in the preceding note, the following secondary sources were useful in preparing this chart: Elinor Husselman, "Procedures of the Record Office of Tebtunis in the First Century A.D.," in *Proceedings of the Twelfth International Congress of Papyrology* (ASP 7; Toronto: Hakkert, 1970) 221–38; Jones, *Cities of the Eastern Roman Provinces*, chap. 11; G. H. Stevenson, *Roman Provincial Administration* (2d ed.; Oxford: Blackwell, 1949); Mason Hammond, *The Antonine Monarchy* (PAAR 19; Rome: American Academy in Rome, 1959) passim; Frank Frost Abbot and Allan Chester Johnson, *Municipal Administration in the Roman Empire* (Princeton: Princeton University, 1926) 244–45 and nos. 22, 24, 26, 29, 36, and 65.

Scheme of Administration
Second-Century Egypt

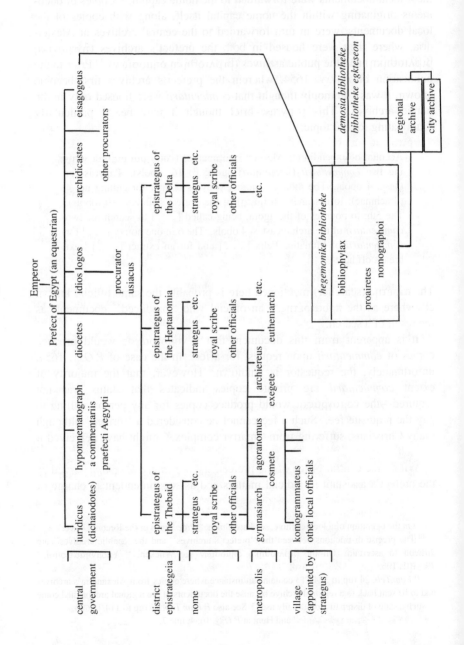

At the lowest level—villages and municipalities—records were kept by the *komogrammateus* and municipal scribes in local archives. Copies of these local documents were forwarded to the nome capital.[39] Copies of documents originating within the nome capital itself, along with copies of the local documents, were in turn forwarded to the central archives at Alexandria, where they were housed in both the prefect's archives (ἡγεμονικὴ βιβλιοθήκη) and the public archives (βιβλιοθήκη δημοσίων).[40] Prior to the publication of *P. Oxy.* 1654, wherein the prefect's archives first become known, it was commonly thought that *commentarii* were housed only in the public archives. This papyrus, brief though it may be, is particularly illuminating for our topic:

> Account of expenditure. Mesore 3: to notaries (νομογράφοις) for writing two *commentarii* (ὑπομνηματισμοὺς β) 16 (obols). Papyrus for these, 4 obols. The 4th: for another papyrus bought for cutting up, 4 (drachmae); to a searcher (αἱρέτη) of the prefect's library, 10 (obols). The 5th: to notaries of the agora, being called [. . .] to search for two *commentarii* of the archidicastes, 4 obols. The 6th: one notary [. . .] for *commentarii* of Munatius Felix [. . .] and for an extract [. . .] [text breaks off here]

The αἱρέτης (searcher) mentioned here is probably the same official known elsewhere as the προαιρέτης,[41] an official who "produced" documents as the result of a search.

It is apparent from this document that a νομογράφος would produce copies of *commentarii* upon request for a fee. In the case of *P. Oxy.* 1654, unfortunately, the requestor is unknown. However, that the majority of extant *commentarii* are private copies indicates that status was not required—the νομογράφοι would produce copies for any person willing to pay the requisite fee. Such a fee cannot be considered a "bribe," although many Christians, suffering from "martyr complex," might have perceived it as such.

Within the central office of the prefect, the *hypomnematograph* served as the prefect's assistant in judicial matters and as superintendent in charge of

---

[39] On the operation of a local archive, see Husselman, "Procedures of the Record Office."

[40] The precise distinctions between the "prefect's archives" and the "public archives" are difficult to ascertain. On the βιβλιοθήκη δημοσίων see Wilcken, " Ὑπομνηματισμοί," 99–101, 106.

P. Fam.Teb. 24 (up to 124 CE) contains an instance where copies from Alexandria's archives had to be sent back to a regional archive because the documents of the regional archive had come to such a state of disrepair from "daily use." See also *P. Fam.Teb.* 15 (up to 114/15 CE).

[41] See the discussion of Grenfell and Hunt at *P. Oxy.* 1654, line 7.

commentarii.[42] The office corresponded to the *a cognitionibus* within the emperor's central office.

In Egypt, then, a person could obtain access to and even copies of *commentarii* at the local, regional, and central governmental levels. For the system of the other provinces and for the Empire as a whole, however, it is more difficult to construct a precise picture. As Abbott and Johnson remarked, "There is little definite information to be had about the archives, or *commentarii*, of the western municipalities except that which is to be found in two or three inscriptions (e.g., *CIL* VIII, S. 15497; XI, 3614)."[43]

The provincial archival systems, from what little is known, seem not to have been very different from that of Egypt.[44] Documents from the provincial capitals appear to have been forwarded to the imperial archives in Rome. Documents originating within Rome itself were copied before being sent to their respective destinations, as is known from a well-known letter of Pliny to Trajan in which Pliny writes:

> I have not sent copies of them [an edict of Augustus and letters of Vespasian et al.] to you as they seemed to be inaccurate, and some of them of doubtful authenticity; and I felt sure that you had accurate and genuine versions among your official files.[45]

In addition to obtaining copies of *commentarii* by means of paying a scribe's fee, interested parties probably could copy documents themselves, since *commentarii* seem to have been posted publicly before being transferred to permanent archival storage.[46]

For the purposes of this study, the above discussion indicates, at the very least, that it was *possible* for Christians to obtain copies of *commentarii* through normal (i.e., legal) channels. Whether the Christians were concerned enough with the martyr's *ipsissima et ultima verba* to consult these records—a question which would be asked by a structuralist—remains to be answered later in this study.

[42] On the *hypomnematograph*, see esp. Reinmuth, *Prefect of Egypt*, 12; and see the primary sources listed in n. 4 there.

[43] Abbott and Johnson, *Municipal Administration*, 244 n. 8.

[44] For an indication of the degree to which the archives, law, and administration of Egypt were similar to other provinces of the Empire, see Posner, *Archives*, chaps. 5 and 7; Taubenschlag, *Law of Greco-Roman Egypt*, chap. 1; and Jones, *Cities of the Eastern Roman Provinces*, 314–19.

[45] Pliny *Ep.* 10.65. Trans. Betty Radice, *Pliny: Letters and Panegyricus* (2 vols.; LCL; London: Heinemann; Cambridge: Harvard University Press, 1969).

[46] See Stein, *Untersuchungen*, 187–92.

2

The Form of the Commentarius

It is commonly assumed by students of martyr literature that some accounts, or portions of those accounts, are the *ipsissima verba* of the martyr's trial record. The present chapter is a form-critical analysis of authentic trial records, that is, of trial records other than *acta Christianorum* and *acta paganorum*. The discussion below is largely based upon the data given in Appendices 1–3 to this study.

Originally the *commentarii* or ὑπομνήματα were private memoranda, but under the Empire the term came to mean "court journals," roughly equivalent to the Hellenistic ἐφημερίδες ("journals").[1] In a further restricted sense, *commentarii* referred to a subgroup of journals that were specifically the records of trials. It is in this restricted sense that *commentarii* will be used throughout this study.

During the late imperial period, the terms *acta* and *gesta* came to be used. Both nouns were general legal terms. As applied to religious literature, *acta* more properly denotes the genre *acta martyrum* in distinction to the genre

---

[1] On the term *commentarius*, see Bickermann, "Testificatio Actorum," *Aegyptus* 13 (1933) 333, 342, 354; and von Premerstein, "Commentarii," passim. On the term ὑπομνήματα, see Wilcken, "Ὑπομνηματισμοί," 113–16; Bickermann, "Testificatio Actorum," 334–36, 341, 345; and von Premerstein, "Commentarii," 726. On the term ἐφημερίδες, see Wilcken, "Ὑπομνηματισμοί," 112–20; Bickermann, "Testificatio Actorum," 349–55; and von Premerstein, "Commentarii," 736–37. On the term ὑπομνηματισμοί, see Wilcken, "Ὑπομνηματισμοί," 87, 102–3, 110; and Bickermann, "Testificatio Actorum," 334–36, 343, 349–55. On the terms *acta* and *gesta*, see Bickermann, "Testificatio Actorum," 341–48.

acta apostolorum.[2] The word "acts" in English is thus used for two somewhat different genres. The term as applied to accounts of martyrdoms is ultimately derived from ὑπομνηματισμοί by way of the later Latin legal term *acta*. As applied to *acta apostolorum*, the term is derived from the Greek noun πράξεις, which Jerome translated as the fourth declension noun *actus*.

Delehaye's and Coles's Analyses of *Commentarii*

As indicated in the Introduction, one of the few scholars who actually attempted to compare *acta Christianorum* to *commentarii* was Hippolyte Delehaye. Delehaye's form-critical analysis is worth quoting at some length, since he has become the authoritative voice on Christian martyrological literature:[3]

> At the head it [the *commentarius*] bears the date of the day and of the year: *diem habet et consulem*, St. Augustine said with regard to the discussion with the Manichean Fortunatus, written under the form of a legal debate: *excepta est a notariis veluti gesta conficerentur*, and this piece opened with the words: *Quinto kal. septembris Arcadio augusto bis et Rufino vv. cc. conss* [*Retract.* 15]. Other examples are sufficiently known, and it suffices to return to the accounts such as the *Gesta apud Zenophilum* and *Acta purgationis Felicis ep. Autumnitani*, which count among the better models of strict protocol style.
>
> The place where the session passes is sometimes indicated. It is often omitted, and the date is followed immediately by the names of the persons appearing in court:
>
> Εἰσαχθέντων Διονυσίου καὶ Φαύστου καὶ Μαξίμου καὶ Μαρκέλλου καὶ Χαιρήμονος. [Eusebius *Hist. eccl.* 7.11.6]
>
> *Inductis Frimino et Apollinario, et ceteris principalibus Antiochensium adstantibus.* [Justinian *Codex* 10.48.2]
>
> Immediately begins the series of questions posed by the judge and the answers of the accused, each being preceded by the name of the one who makes the speech. The name of the magistrate is followed by his title which is repeated each time in its entirety:
>
> Αἰμιλιανὸς διέπων τὴν ἡγεμονίαν εἶπεν. [Eusebius *Hist. eccl.* 7.11.6]
>
> *Zenophilus vir clarissimus consularis dixit.* [*Gesta apud Zenophilum* 1]

---

[2] On the genre "acts of the apostles," see Edgar Hennecke and Wilhelm Schneemelcher, *New Testament Apocrypha* (2 vols.; Philadelphia: Westminster, 1964) 2. 167–88; and Koester, *Introduction to the New Testament*, 2. 49–53.

[3] Delehaye, *Les passions des martyrs*, 126–29.

[Delehaye follows here with another example from *Gesta apud Zenophilum* and one from *P. Rainer* 18.]

The names of the accused are not accompanied by any qualification. The bishop of Alexandria, Denis, speaks under the simple rubric Διονύσιος, Victor the grammarian in the *Gesta apud Zenophilum* under that of Victor, and so forth.

In general, the response includes to whom the discourse is addressed. But it is not rare that the text says it explicitly. [Delehaye follows here with examples from Eusebius *Hist. eccl.* 7.11.9 – 10; *Gesta apud Zenophilum* 2.3 – 4; 2.8 – 10; 11.29, 31, 33.]

One is able to verify . . . that the *procès-verbal* does not record all the words which are said to the magistrate, as by the judge. [Examples from *Gesta apud Zenophilum* follow.]

The questioning begins by the accused or the witness with the procedure of identity. The habitual order of the questions is indicated in the Letter of the Churches of Vienne and Lyon. The judge asks the name, the (native) city, the condition of appearing. Is he freedman or slave?

To be less formalistic, the judge does not always follow that program to the letter. [More examples from *Gesta apud Zenophilum* are given here.]

The preliminary obligations having ended, the inquiry proper begins. The speeches which are exchanged then vary according to the persons, the cause, circumstances, and one does not know more there to guide himself according to the general rules.

The action is terminated by the judgment. . . . The sentence indicates the offence committed, the punishment encurred, and sometimes also the motives of the decision.

Musurillo, whose *Acts of the Pagan Martyrs* established him as the authority on that genre, analyzed *commentarii* in a fashion similar to Delehaye.

Delehaye's form criticism of the *procès-verbal* actually begs the question, since he principally uses Christian documents, *Gesta apud Zenophilum* (13 Dec 320 CE) and *Acta purgationis Felicis* (314), as his models of the *commentarius*. The only non-Christian corroboration he provides is from *P. Thead.* 15 (280/81) and CPR 1.18 (=*P. Rainer* 18; 124). A difficulty with this approach, besides that of using *acta Christianorum* as models, is that these accounts span a period of two hundred years. As will be seen below, the form of fourth-century *commentarii* differs in several important ways from that of second-century *commentarii*. Delehaye noted no formal distinctions, and, as will be seen below, several of his generalizations are incorrect. In his defense, however, it must be said that without Coles's work, the present study would not have been possible. The scholar who wishes to analyze *acta martyrum* form-critically will find Coles's study well worth reading. But for the form critic, there are no substitutes to a thorough acquaintance with the *commentarii* themselves.

The Form of *Commentarii*

Coles's form-critical analysis correctly divides the *commentarius* into four main sections: introductory formulae (*caput*); the body of the trial; the κρίσις; and any concluding matters. Within these sections are found several distinctive elements, which have been numbered 1 – 15 in Appendices 1 – 3. The outline of this presentation, therefore, will be as follows: introductory elements 1 – 8; trial elements 9 – 12; judgment elements 13 – 14; and concluding element 15. An overview of these elements may be found in the summary presentation of the sigla in Appendices 1 – 3.

Caput: Introductory Elements or Formulae

The introductory formulae include all the elements which precede the introductory phrase to the first *oratio recta* (direct discourse), where the body of the trial begins. One or several of the following elements may be present among the introductory formulae: (1) extract-phrase; (2) name and (usually) title(s) of the presiding magistrate; (3) date-formula; (4) location of the trial; (5) a presence-phrase; (6) a participants-formula; (7) a delegation-phrase; and (8) an "ellipsis-phrase." Very often a sentence or two of *oratio obliqua* ("indirect discourse"), summarized discourse, and/or narrative abstract (element 9) form a transition from the introductory formulae to the body of the trial. These elements are defined and illustrated in the discussion that follows.

Element 1: Extract-Phrase

The *commentarius* normally begins with some sort of extract-phrase. The forms that occur are:

> ἐξ ὑπομνηματισμῶν (normally followed genitive of magistrate's name);
> ἀντίγραφον (normally followed by a pause);
> ἀντίγραφον ὑπομνηματισμοῦ (with or without genitive);
> ὑπομνηματισμοί (followed by genitive);
> ἐκ τῶν ῥηθέντων (occurs rarely);
> *ex commentario*;
> *ex codice*.

The presence of one of these phrases seems to indicate that the record is a copy or extract from an archival original.

There seems to be no significant difference in the meanings of the various phrases listed above. Nor does there appear to be any significant chronological distinction, with the following exceptions: (1) during the third century the date more often begins the *commentarius* than it did in the second century and is there followed by an extract-phrase or the extract-phrase is omitted altogether; (2) by the late third century the extract-phrase disappears from use.

In addition to the extract-phrases listed above, there are other phrases which occasionally function in their place. For example, when more than one *commentarius* is quoted, the first may be introduced with an extract-phrase proper and those which follow introduced merely by ἄλλου or ἄλλου ὁμοίως. In the few surviving Latin *commentarii*, *infra scriptum est* and *in verba infra scripta* may serve as extract phrases. The phrases *descriptam et recognitum* and *descriptam et propositam*, which were included in Appendix 2 as extract-phrases, are, properly speaking, phrases certifying authenticity or accuracy. Authenticating phrases were included with extract-phrases in the Latin because these phrases are coupled with *ex commentario* in Bruns[7] 71a (69 CE) and in *CIL* 11.1.3614 (113/14 CE) and appear at the opening of the *commentarius*. The Greek authenticating phrases (e.g., ἀνέγνων and ὑπογραφή) appear in "concluding matters" (Appendix 1).

Another form of "extract-phrase," which serves double duty, is the magistrate's name given alone in the genitive, that is, "of/from (the proceedings of) magistrate x."

Of the twenty *commentarii* dating to the Antonine period in which an extract-phrase is extant, the most frequently occurring are ἐξ ὑπομνηματισμῶν (9 occurrences) and ἀντίγραφον ὑπομνηματισμοῦ (6 occurrences). Representative examples of such extract-phrases, in the immediate context of the introductory formulae, read as follows:

Ἐξ ὑπομνηματισμῶν Σεμπρωνίου Λιβεράλις ἡγεμόνος, (ἔτους) ι
Ἀντωνίνου Καίσαρος τοῦ κυρίου, Φαρμοῦθι β, δικαιοδοσία ἐν τῷ ἱερῷ. Μεθ᾿ ἕτερα . . .

From the *commentarii* of the Prefect Sempronius Liberalis, in the 10th year of the lord Antoninus Caesar, Pharmuthi 2, trial in the temple. After some text . . . (*SB* 8261; 154–58 CE)

Ἀντίγραφον ὑπομνηματισμοῦ. (Ἔτους) η Ἀντωνείνου Καίσαρος τοῦ κυρίου, Φαμενὼθ κϛ.

Transcript of a *commentarius*. In the 8th year of our lord Antoninus Caesar, Phamenoth 26. (*P. Fouad* 23; 144 CE)

In five *commentarii* from the Antonine period, the element which appears first in the formulae is the date:[4] *BGU* 587 (141); *P. Wisc.* 23 (143); *P. Ryl.* 678 (ca. 150); *P. Oxy.* 899r (154); and *P. Oxy.* 2340 (192), and in all five the extract-formula is absent.[5] For the form of the Latin *commentarius,* our conclusions must remain very tentative, since only a handful of these records are preserved to us. For this reason the discussion of the Latin forms will often be nothing more than passing observations. Here it can only be conjectured that the phrase *ex commentario* served an analogous function in Latin extracts to ἐξ ὑπομνηματισμῶν in the Greek.

Element 2: The Presiding Magistrate

By far the most common position of the presiding magistrate's name and, normally, title is immediately following the extract phrase:

Ἐξ ὑπομνηματισμῶν Οὐηδίου Φαύστου τοῦ κρατίστου ἐπιστρατήγου. Μεθ' ἕτερα . . .

From the *commentarii* of the most excellent epistrategus Vedius Faustus. After some text . . . (*PSI* 1100; 161 CE)

Occasionally, however, the extract gives only the magistrate's name, without title, as in the following:

(Ἔτους) ι̅ς̅ Φαρμοῦθι ι̅ς̅. Ἐξ ὑπομνηματισμῶν Σουβατιανοῦ Ἀκύλα ἐν Ὀξυρυγχείτῃ· μετ' ἄλλα . . .

(Year) 16, Pharmouthi 16. From the *commentarii* of Subatianus Aquila, in (the) Oxyrhynchite (nome). After other things . . .[6] (*P. Oxy.* 2341; 208 CE)

The distinction between the two forms is perhaps significant for the purposes of dating. Since these documents are extracts, which could have been obtained from the archives any time after the event, the absence of the magistrate's title probably indicates a date close to the event—a date when the magistrate was still remembered and, hence, the title was regarded as

---

[4] From this point forward, the number given in parentheses following a papyrus number will be the date of the *commentarius* given in the papyrus, inscription, etc.

[5] When the date appears first, it is very rare that it is followed by an extract-phrase, although this sequence does occur, as, e.g., in *P. Oxy.* 2341 (208).

[6] The editors of *P. Oxy.* 2341 translated μετ' ἄλλα here as *inter alia* ("among other things"). I have preferred the accusative of sequence, "after," to the local accusative "among" for the reasons given in my discussion of the "ellipsis phrase" (Element 8 below).

superfluous.[7] This is more than conjecture, since an inverse tendency is also seen in the *commentarii*. For example:

Ἐξ ὑπομνηματισμῶν Θέωνος γενομένου στρατηγοῦ Προσωπίτου (ἔτους) κ̄ θεοῦ Ἀδρανοῦ Ἐπεὶφ κ̄δ.[8]

From *commentarii* of Theonos, former strategus of Prosopitus, (year) 20 of the god Hadrian, Epeiph 24. (*P. Oslo* 17; 136 CE)

Significant here is the addition of γενομένου (former). Theonos was not "former strategus" but strategus at the time, and the *orationes rectae* of Theonos in the *commentarius* are introduced by ὁ στρατηγός. P. J. Sijpesteijn observed the same tendency in the copy of Valerius Clemens' ἐπίκρισις (judgment) produced by a scribe and later corrected by the βιβλιοφύλαξ Gavius Callimachus (*P. Mich. Inv.* 2930; 188 CE).[9] Lines 1–2 of this document read:

ἐκ τόμου ἐπικρίσεων, οὗ παρεπιγραφή· ἐπικρίσεις Λογγαίου Ῥούφου γενομένου ἡγεμόνος.

From a volume of judgments, corrected: a judgment of Longaeus Rufus, former prefect.

At the dramatic date, 185, T. Longaeus Rufus was acting Prefect of Egypt. In the original document, he would have been referred to as ἡγεμών without the addition of γενομένου. Sijpesteijn concluded that

either the scribe who wrote this document or possibly another scribe must have added γενομένου. We must assume that whoever did so knew and wished to show that T. Longaeus Rufus was now former prefect as the scribe was copying under the new prefect M. Aurelius Verianus. This indicates a concern for chronological accuracy, but at the expense of a historical conception of a faithful copy of a document.[10]

Callimachus "corrected" γενομένου merely by drawing lines through the letters ενου, that is, by abbreviating it.

On the other hand, γενομένου was not always added by later scribes to indicate that the magistrate was no longer in office. An example of this is found in *SB* 9050 (after 114), which contains three extracts from an

---

[7] See Gary A. Bisbee, "The Acts of Justin Martyr: A Form-Critical Study," *Second Century* 3 (1983) 136.

[8] See also, e.g., *P. Wisc.* 23 (143).

[9] Sijpesteijn, "A Scribe at Work," *BASP* 16 (1979) 277–80.

[10] Ibid., 278.

Amtstagebuch ("journal of court-days") dated 100, 114, and 105 (produced in that sequence). The extract from the year 105 is introduced thus:

Οὐβίου Μαξίμου. (Ἔτους) η̄ Θεοῦ Τραιανοῦ Φαρμοῦθι κ̄δ̄ ἐν Μέμφει.
(From the *commentarii*) of Vibius Maximus. The 8th year of the god Trajan, Pharmuthi 24, in Memphis.

Vibius Maximus was *Praefectus Egypti* from 103 to 107, and the extracts were obviously copied some years after he had left office, since the extract from the year 105 is preceded by a *commentarius* of Sulpicius Similis, who succeeded Vibius Maximus as *Praefectus Egypti.*[11]

However, we can also find instances where γενάμενος is used to indicate former titles held by persons. For example:

Ἀπολλώνιος γενάμενος στρατηγὸς Θεμείστου μερίδος ὁ κριτής·...
Apollonios, former strategus of the Themistes district, the arbiter, (said):
... (*P. Fam.Teb.* 24; up to 124)

Thus we have instances where a participial form of γίγνομαι is added to the magistrate's title when he had been out of office only a few years; and we have instances where the magistrate's name is given without title, even when the magistrate had been out of office for several years or more. We may conclude, then, that normally the *commentarii* give both the name and title of the presiding magistrate in the introductory formulae,[12] but a form of γίγνομαι may be added or the title omitted at a later date, depending upon the inclinations of the scribes and the reputation of the magistrate involved in the case.

Element 3: Date Formula

The occurrence and position of the date in the *commentarius* is generally regarded by martyrologists as of crucial importance. This is so because it is recognized that, for practical purposes, the *commentarius* required a date and, for liturgical purposes, the Christian community needed to know (or made up) the date of the martyr's death. Especial emphasis was placed on this point by Niedermeyer:

> One asks himself how it was possible that the transcript of a given individual case could be traced back to the original resting in an archive.

[11] A similar example is *PSI* 281 (2d cent.).
[12] However, the magistrate's name and title are not both used consistently throughout a *commentarius.*

Thus it is noticeable that the most constant, i.e., the most rarely missing, recurring element of the formal elements in the transcripts is the date. [Niedermeyer cites *Codex* Theodotus 1.1.1, *Codex* Justinian 1.23.4, and Justinian *Institutes* 7.45.13, and then proceeds:] Therewith we brought to light the most convincing and most important element of the acts, the date. . . . The original purpose of the addition of the dating of the transcripts must have been this, the transcripts led back by this means [the date] to the original in the archive.[13]

Niedermeyer's arguments are compelling until we learn that *commentarii* were not necessarily filed according to date. On the storage and filing of such official records, Posner found that

record documents were pasted together to form a roll (*rotulus*). This was done by covering with paste the left margin of the item to be added and placing it under the right margin of the last document on the roll. A *titulus*, attached to one end of the roll, helped to identify the record unit. . . . To facilitate searches, there were probably inventories or lists of the type of the *diastromata* found in Roman Egypt. Servicing and searching the records was the job of an official called *regendarius*.[14]

If Posner is correct, what was written on the *titulus* was the all important "call number" to those searching for a particular document. Unfortunately Posner does not cite examples of *tituli*, nor does this writer know of any. We may theorize, nevertheless, that the *titulus* was likely to bear something other than, or in addition to, the date, such as "*commentarii* of magistrate X" or perhaps merely an inventory list number.

Niedermeyer's contention that the date is "the most compelling and most important formal element" of the *commentarius* is true only to the extent that the date does seem to be present in all such documents. But an analysis of the *commentarii* reveals that to categorize *acta martyrum* according to the position of the date, as Niedermeyer did, is a pointless exercise.[15] This will become apparent in what follows.

[13] Niedermeyer, *Über antike Protokoll-Literatur* (Göttingen: Dieterich'sen University, 1918) 43–44.

[14] Posner, *Archives*, 197; see also Reinmuth, *Prefect of Egypt*, 42. On the "searcher of records," see the discussion of αἱρέτης on p. 31 above.

[15] Niedermeyer, having concluded that the date is the most important element, divides the acts into "eine Dreiteilung von Zeitbestimmungsarten": those acts of "allgemeine Zeitangabe," those with the date "an der Spitze," and those with the date "am Schlusse der Erzählung" (*Protokoll-Literatur*, 62–74). On the date, see also Wilcken, "'Υπομνηματισμοί," 87–88, 90, 92, 97–98.

In the *commentarii* of the Antonine period in which the date is extant, we find the following patterns:[16]

a) date in first position, that is, preceding all other elements (5 occurrences);
b) date in second position, following an extract phrase (5 occurrences);
c) date in third position, following an extract phrase and the magistrate's name and title (10 occurrences);
d) date in final position, following all other elements (3 occurrences)
   (*PSI* 1100 [161]; *P. Oslo* 18 [162]; *SB* 9329 [171]).

Thus for the Antonine period we can conclude only that the date rarely appears at the end, and that it appears more often in third position. About the mid-third century, however, the date is found predominately in first position. But since the date is also found in first position in *commentarii* from the Antonine period, no convincing rule may be formulated for the position of the date in Antonine *commentarii*.

Latin and bilingual *commentarii* exhibit the same variety of positions. In two Latin *commentarii*, however, yet another position is found. In *CIL* 11.1.3614 (113/14) and Bruns[7] 188 (244)[17] the date is given as the next-to-last element. In the former, it is followed by the magistrate's name and title, and in the latter by the names of the consuls for the year. Appending the consuls' names, however, may be considered an additional form of date in Latin documents, since the consuls' year could be used as a chronographic unit. Thus, for example, does Horace date the birth of his "companion": "O faithful jar of wine, born with me in the consulship of Manlius."[18]

In Latin *commentarii* the date-formula, as we would expect, is more elaborate than in Greek *commentarii*. In the Latin date-formulae, the imperial formula is often given at length, as in *SEG* 17.759 (216), a trial before Caracalla:

Sabino et Anulino cos. [VI] Kal. Iunias Antiochiae Imp. Caesar M̃.
Aurelius Antoninus Pius Fel. Aug. Par. Max. Brit. Germ. Max.

Here we find both elements of the imperial formula—Imperator Caesar ... Augustus and the personal names included therein[19]—although this formula is nowhere near as elaborate as that given for Caracalla in *CIL* 16.137, which

---

[16] General-date examples from Appendix 1 are not included in the counts below; they exhibit the same variety.
[17] *CIL* 11.1.3614 = *FIRA* III no. 113; Bruns[7] 188 = *CIL* VI 266 = *FIRA* III no. 165.
[18] Horace *Odes* 3.21, quoted in E. J. Bickermann, *Chronology of the Ancient World* (2d ed.; Ithaca, NY: Cornell University, 1980) 65.
[19] On these elements in the imperial formulae, see Hammond, *Antonine Monarchy*, 58–91.

contains both republican and imperial elements.[20] In Greek *commentarii*, on the other hand, the date is given a simplistic formulation. By far the most common form is thus: "Year x of (cognomen; nomen) τοῦ κυρίου month day." For example:

Ἔτους δ΄ Ἀντωνείνου Καίσαρος τοῦ κυρίου, Φαρμοῦθι κ̄. (*BGU* 587; 141 CE)

Hammond observed that "*Caesar* alone after the personal name became the regular style for a subordinate heir."[21] The consistent use of the emperor's cognomen followed by Καίσαρος in Greek *commentarii*, even when the person named was fully emperor, merely exhibits the use of *Caesar* as the gentile nomen.

The imperial formula is also occasionally found in a longer form that included the praenomen, additional cognomina and filiation. For example, the same emperor whose formula was quoted above, Antoninus Pius, is also given as follows:

(Ἔτους) ῑᾱ Αὐτοκράτορος Καίσαρος Τίτου Αἰλίου Ἀδριανοῦ Ἀντωνίνου Σεβαστοῦ Εὐσεβοῦς, Μεσορὴ ς̄. (*SB* 7558; 148 CE)

For the date-formula, then, we may conclude that it might appear either at the head of the *commentarius*, in first, second, or third position, or at the foot of the document, in final position. The actual form in which the date was given, however, was very consistent, and we must conclude that judicial scribes, in Egypt at least, followed some sort of "style sheet" when penning the date.

Element 4: Location

Often the location of the trial is indicated in the *commentarius*, although this is an entirely dispensable element. When the location is given, it follows the date-formula, that is, in fourth position. The location indicated may be a building, such as ἐν τῷ ἱερῷ (in the temple; e.g., *SB* 8261; 154–58 CE); a city, such as ἐν Μέμφει (in Memphis; e.g., *BGU* 347; 171 CE); or merely the tribunal itself, πρὸς τῷ βήματι (before the tribunal; e.g., *P. Ryl.* 77; 192 CE).

---

[20] See ibid., 58.
[21] Ibid., 60.

Element 5: Presence-Phrase

The "presence-phrase" is a term coined by Coles.[22] Coles applied the term primarily to the phrases παρόντων ἐν συμβουλίωι and *cum concilio collocutus* (*dixit*), the latter usually being abbreviated CCC(D). In Appendix 1, the προσελθόντος formula was included in this category. It might have been more appropriate to have included this formula among the participants-formulae, as did Coles, who observed that the "προσελθόντος type formula . . . usually refers to one of the parties (or one side of the parties) only, usually the plaintiff."[23]

When a presence-phrase is given, it normally appears after the location, if indicated, or after the date, if no location is given and the date appears in third position. If both a presence-phrase and a participants-formula are used, Coles found that their relative positions may have significance:

> It seems a possible general distinction that when the "presence" formula precedes the participants it refers to legal advisors of the presiding official or other functionaries, but that when used with reference to persons assisting the participants or other non-official figures (e.g. witnesses) it always follows the "participants" formula.[24]

Following are some examples of presence-phrases:

Δεῖος Ζεύξιδος προσελθὼν εἶπεν·

Dius, son of Zeuxis, having come forward, said . . .[25] (*P. Fouad* 23; 144 CE)

κληθέντος ἐκ βιβλιδίου Εὐδαίμονος Ἑρμαίου, προσελθόντος Διονυσίου καὶ ἀναγνωσθέντος τοῦ ἐπιδοθέντος ὑπὸ αὐτοῦ βιβλιδίου,
Φιλώτας εἶπεν·

Eudaemon, son of Hermaeus, having been summoned by petition, (and) Dionysius having come forward, the petition presented by him having been read, Philotas said . . . (*SB* 7558; 148 CE)

δη]μόσια πρὸς τῷ β[ήματι] παρόντων τῶ[ν ἐνάρ]χων Δίου
γυμ[ν]ασιάρχου . . .

---

[22] Coles, *Reports of Proceedings*, 31.

[23] Ibid., 32n.

[24] Ibid., 33.

[25] I must take issue here with the translation given to this clause by the editors of *P. Fouad* 23: "Dius, son of Zeuxis, came here and made this statement." A more literal translation does not obscure the terse style of the *commentarius*.

there being present at the tribunal from the magistrates in office Dius, gymnasiarch . . . (*P. Ryl.* 77; 192 CE)[26]

Element 6: Participants-Formulae

The participants-formula gives a formulaic statement of the parties involved in the case. When a participants-formula is used, it normally appears after the location, if one is given, or after the date, if it is in third position and no location is indicated.

Coles lists the various types of participants-formulae,[27] but he concluded that

> there does not appear to be any special difference in meaning between these phrases, or the several other variants of the "participants" formula, nor do there seem to be any significant chronological distinctions.[28]

Although Coles is correct that there is no significant difference in meaning between the various formulae, there is a chronological distinction, which may be seen clearly by tracing the "6" in the "Elements of Form" column in Appendix 1. During the first century, the only formula used, with the exception of *P. Oslo* 180, is the "A πρὸς B" type, for example, Πτολέμα πρὸς Ἀπίαν (*SB* 91–96 CE). Moreover, in nearly all these formulae from the first century, the names only are given, without any modifying descriptions or titles.

During the early second century, two things happen to the participants-formula: the descriptions become common and, secondly, other formulae are used in addition to the "A πρὸς B" type. During the second century as a whole, the "A πρὸς B" type is still the most common, but with descriptions added to the participants' names:

> Ἀπολλώνιος φροντιστὴς Μεθυσίου καὶ Ἡρακλείδης Πρωτογένους πρὸς Λεωνίδην γραμματέα βιβλιοφυλάκων.
>
> Apollonius, curator(?) of Methysion, and Herakleides, son of Protogenes, against Leonides, scribe of the keepers of the archives.
>
> (*P. Fam.Teb.* 15; up to 114/15)

Often the "description" is nothing more than the father's name in the geni-

---

[26] See also *P. Teb.* 287; 161–69 CE: [. . . . . βαφέω]ν καὶ γναφέων ἀπὸ τοῦ Ἀρσινοείτου παρόντος Ἑρμί[ου τοῦ ἐγλογιστοῦ τοῦ Ἀρσι]νοείτου [Λονγεῖνος ῥήτ]ωρ εἶπεν· . . .

[27] Coles, *Reports on Proceedings*, 31 n.4; for the phrases themselves, see Appendices 1–2.

[28] Ibid., 31–32.

tive, that is, "X son of Y" (e.g., see the quotation above), but occasionally the description is very elaborate. For example:

Ἰούλιος Θέων τῶν ἱερονικῶν καὶ ἀτελῶν νεωκόρος τοῦ μεγάλου
Σαράπιδος γενόμενος ἀρχιδικαστὴς [ἱερεὺς] καὶ ὑπομνηματογράφος·
[followed by *oratio recta*]
Julius Theon, a victor in the sacred games and exempt from taxation,
neocorus of the great Sarapis, former archidicastes, priest and hypom-
nematographus: (*P. Teb.* 286; 121 – 38)

Another formula which appears during the second century is the "ἐπὶ τῶν κατὰ Χ πρὸς Υ" type. *BGU* 19 (135 CE) gives one such formula:

ἐπὶ τῶν κατὰ Χεναλεξᾶν πρὸς Πετεσοῦχον καὶ Διονύσιον.
in the case of Chenalexas against Petesuchos and Dionysios.

The other forms which the participants-formula might take are: κλη-
θείσης καὶ ὑπακουσάσης or κληθέντος Α πρὸς Β." Combinations of these
formulae also may occur, as in the following example:

[introductory formulae] ἐπὶ τῶν κατὰ Φλαυήσιος Ἀμμούνιος ἐπὶ
παρούσῃ Ταειχήκει θυγατρὶ αὐτοῦ πρὸς Ἥρωνα Πεταήσιος.
. . . in the case of Phlauesis, son of Ammounis, in the presence of his
daughter Taeichekis, against Heron, son of Petaësis. (*P. Oxy.* 237; 186
CE, extract dated 133)[29]

An odd thing happens to the participants-formula during the Antonine period. Of forty-five dated Greek extracts for the period 49 – 137 CE, twenty-three have a participants-formula. Of twenty-nine dated Greek extracts from the reign of Antoninus Pius, only four have a participants-formula. And of nineteen dating to the reign of Marcus and Commodus, none occur, with the exception of the extracts quoted in *P. Oxy.* 237 (186 CE) which are dated 133 and 87 CE. This absence may be only coincidental, due to the chance of survival. The numbers indicate, however, that the tendency—at the least—during the Antonine period was not to use a participants-formula.

During the third century yet another distinction is found. The simple "A πρὸς Β" type apparently went out of vogue and was replaced by the "παρόντος Α πρὸς Β" formula. The participants-formula does occur in

---

[29] See also *BGU* 969; 142 CE?: Ἐπὶ τῶν κατὰ Πανομιέα καὶ Πεθέα ἀμφοτέρους Πεθέως
πρὸς Πασίωνα Χαιρήμονος πρόδικον γυναικὸς ἑαυτοῦ [sic] Ἀθηνόδωρος ῥήτ(ωρ) ὑπὲρ
Πασίωνος εἶπ(εν)·

fourth-century *commentarii*, but the evidence does not permit statistical analysis.

Element 7: Delegation-Phrase

The delegation-phrase, when present, appears near the head of the *commentarius*, either in second position after an extract phrase or in third position after the magistrate's name, the date, or the location. In form, the delegation-phrase remained consistent, as in the following example:

ἐξ ἀναπομπῆς Φλαυίου Τιτιανοῦ τοῦ κρατίστου ἡγεμόνος. (*P. Teb.* 489; 127 CE)

Ἐξ ἀναπομπῆς Ἀτερίου [Νέπ]ω[τ]ος τοῦ κρατίστο[υ ἡγ]ε[μ]όνος... (*MChr.* 84; 124 CE)

The phrase is used in two senses: (1) to denote that a magistrate with *imperium* and *iurisdictio* has "delegated" a case to a subordinate magistrate; (2) as a delegation to a magistrate, as, for example, a delegation from a city to a governor.

Element 8: Ellipsis-Phrase

"Ellipsis-phrase" is my own coinage; Coles refers to such phrases as "phrases of the μεθ' ἕτερα type."[30] Other such phrases found in the *commentarii* are μετ' ἄλλα and μετ' ὀλίγον. The term "ellipsis" is descriptive of how, in my opinion, these phrases function in the *commentarii*. How the ellipsis-phrase was employed by the *commentariensis* will be understood from the following examples:

Ἐξ ὑπομνηματισμῶν Οὐηδίου Φαύστου τοῦ κρατίστου ἐπιστρατήγου. Μεθ' ἕτερα· Φαῦστος σκεψάμενος μετὰ τῶν συνεδρευόντων Ἁρποκρατίωνι στρατηγῶι Θεμίστου καὶ Πολέμωνος μερίδων εἶπεν·

From the *commentarii* of the most excellent epistrategus Vedius Faustus. After some text: Faustus, after considering (the case) beforehand with the council of Harpocration, strategus of the Themistes and Polemon divisions, said ... (*PSI* 1100; 161 CE)

Σουβατιανοῦ Ἀκύλα ἡγεμονεύσαντος (ἔτους) ιε Φααμενὼθ ιϛ. κληθέντων Σαβείνου καὶ Μαξίμου Διονυσίου καὶ ὑπακουσάντων, μεθ' ἕτερα Ἀκύλας εἶπεν·

---

30 Ibid., 48.

(From the *commentarii*) of the former prefect Soubatianus Aquila, (year) 15, Phamenoth 17. Sabinus and Maximus Dionysius having been summoned and having answered (the summons), after some text Aquila said ... (*P. Stras.* 22; 207 CE)[31]

Μεθ' ἕτερα as used in the *commentarii* is given no consistent translation by modern scholars. In *P. Teb.* 286, Grenfell and Hunt translate it as "after other evidence." *P. Oxy.* 3015, edited by P. Parsons, gives "after other matter." The LCL translation of *P. Ryl.* 75 gives "during the course of the proceedings,"[32] but the Rylands editors[33] translate it merely as "&c." The LCL translation of *BGU* 15 gives yet another translation for μεθ' ἕτερα: "extract."[34]

As indicated above, the vast majority of extant *commentarii* are private copies, extracts from an official version. The function of μεθ' ἕτερα and similar phrases is to indicate that the copiest omitted portions of the longer account. Just as modern ellipses points are added by the copiest's hand, so is μεθ' ἕτερα an element alien to the original. Thus these phrases function in a fashion similar to ellipses points in modern quotations; they indicate omission of text. Translations such as "&c." are obscure and "extract" is misleading. The translation "after other evidence" is inadequate as well, since the ellipsis-phrase may occur at any point in a *commentarius*, not necessarily after evidence.

There is no evidence that scribes ever reversed the order of the portions which they extracted from the original version. In addition to being a nonliteral translation, "during the course of the proceedings" is ambiguous. Μετά in the phrase μεθ' ἕτερα is a sequential accusative ("after") rather than a local accusative ("during"). "During" obscures the fact that the copiest has moved forward in the text.

Of the translations quoted above, "after other matter" (Parsons) is the most satisfactory. "After some text" or "after some things" may be suggested for μεθ' ἕτερα and μετ' ἄλλα, even though it is not a strictly literal translation, since it indicates clearly the forward progress of the extract and that the phrase is an alien element. For μετ' ὀλίγον might be proposed "after a little text" for the same reasons. "After a little while" is not at all the probable intent of the copiest, nor is it likely that the scribe who produced the

---

[31] See also *PSI* 1326; ca. 181/83 CE: ... Μακρίνος εἶπεν· ποῦ οὖν ἐπιγέγραπταί σου τὸ ὄνομα ὁμολογήσας δὲ ὅτι ἀναπόγραφός εἰμι· οἱ γονεῖς μου ἐτελεύτησαν μικροῦ μου ὄντος καὶ οὐκ ἀπεγράψαντό με. Μεθ' ἕτερα Μακρίνος εἶπεν· κτλ.

[32] A. S. Hunt and C. C. Edgar, *Select Papyri* (2 vols.; LCL; Cambridge: Harvard University Press, 1963) 2. 201.

[33] J. de M. Johnson, V. Martin, and A. S. Hunt.

[34] Hunt and Edgar, *Select Papyri*, 2. 171.

original would have wished or needed to indicate the passage of time. However the phrases may be translated, they look forward to what follows and do not merely supplement what precedes.

The Body of the Trial

The body of the trial contains a record of the speeches between magistrates and participants, given in *oratio recta*, *oratio obliqua*, and/or narrative abstract. By far the most common form in which discourse was recorded or copied[35] was in one of the following forms:

- a) speaker's name (sometimes accompanied by titles and/or descriptions) followed directly by *oratio recta* ;
- b) speaker's name (sometimes accompanied by titles and/or descriptions) + finite verb of saying (e.g., εἶπεν or ἔφη) followed by *oratio recta*.

The body of the trial normally consists of a monotonous pattern of "X said ... Y said. ..." However, speeches are also recorded in *oratio obliqua* and narrative abstract, and instead of a finite verb of saying, a genitive absolute is occasionally used. The term "summarized discourse" is used below to distinguish discourse recorded in form (a) or (b) above, which are discussed as Elements 11 and 12 below, from other forms of discourse such as *oratio obliqua*.

Element 9: Summarized Discourse and Narrative Abstract

To use the term "summarized discourse" for *oratio obliqua* and other forms of discourse that differ from forms (a) or (b) above might be argued by some to beg a question. As our discussion above has indicated, the vast majority of extant *commentarii* are copies, and the presence of phrases such as μεθ' ἕτερα indicate that copies were not necessarily exact replicas of the exemplar. The form of the exemplar, which would have been either the archival version or a précis produced at the trial, is not known with certainty to us. Did scribes record speeches in a précis form in the first instance and then produce a final version in which summarized discourse was put into *oratio recta* or was the reverse sequence the case? Despite Coles's arguments to the contrary, it seems most probable that at the trial scribes recorded speeches in *oratio recta*, albeit in shorthand, and that *oratio obliqua* and

---

[35] It is not absolutely certain that scribes recorded speeches in *oratio recta* in the first instance: they may have written in a summary form initially and produced a full version later.

other types of "summarized discourse," like "ellipsis phrases," are merely a means of shortening the copy.

There is nothing distinctive about the grammatical structure given to *oratio obliqua* and narrative abstract in the *commentarii*, nor do there seem to be any chronological distinctions. What is important to observe here, for a study of *acta martyrum*, is where these elements may occur and what sorts of materials are recorded therein.

The most common position of summarized discourse and narrative abstract is immediately preceding the first *oratio recta*. Usually the length amounts to a phrase, normally in the genitive absolute, or a sentence or two summarizing preceding events and/or speeches:

> [Introductory formulae]. Κληθέντος ἐκ βιβλιδίου Εὐδαίμονος Ἑρμαίου, προσελθόντος Διονυσίου, καὶ ἀναγνωσθέντος τοῦ ἐπιδοθέντος ὑπὸ αὐτοῦ βιβλιδίου, Φιλώτας εἶπεν· [followed by *oratio recta*]

> Eudaemon son of Hermaeus having been summoned in consequence of a petition, and Dionysios having appeared and the petition presented by him having been read, Philotas said: . . . (*SB* 7558; 173 CE; extract from 148)

> [Introductory formulae]. μεθ᾽ ἕτερα· Φαῦστος σκεψάμενος μετὰ τῶν συνεδρευόντων Ἁρποκρατίωνι στρατηγῶι Θεμίστου καὶ Πολέμωνος μερίδων εἶπεν· [followed by *oratio recta*]

> After some text: Faustus, after holding an inquiry with the council of Harpocration, strategus of the districts of Themistes and Polemon, said: . . . (*PSI* 1100; 161 CE)

> [Introductory formulae]. Στοτοήτιος λέγοντος ἐνκεκληκέναι τοῖς περὶ Σαταβοῦν φόνου ἐπὶ τῶι ἀδελφῶι αὐτοῦ καὶ παρεῖναι τοὺς μαρτυρῆσαι δυναμένους τὸν φόνον καὶ τῶν περὶ Σαταβοῦν ἀποκρειναμένων καὶ πρότερον ἄλλους ὑπὸ αὐτοῦ παρασταθέντας μηδὲν τοιοῦτο μεμαρτυρηκέναι, ὁ στρατηγὸς Στοτοήτι· [followed by *oratio recta*]

> Stotoëtis said that he had accused Satabous and his associates of murdering his brother and that there were present witnesses able to testify to the murder and Satabous and his associates having answered that the witnesses previously produced by him had been able to give no such testimony, the strategus said: . . . (*P. Amh.* 66; 124 CE)

If my discussion of the scribes' use of μεθ᾽ ἕτερα is correct, summarized discourse and narrative abstract are elements which may be found in the official copy,[36] since they are found immediately following μεθ' ἕτερα, as in the quotation from *PSI* 1100 above (narrative in genitive absolute). It is not unlikely, however, that the scribe who produced an extract from the official copy summarized sections of *oratio recta* deemed not relevant to the party who had requested the copy. However, since summarized discourse and narrative abstract could be present in either source, a distinction between official copy and extract cannot be forced.

Normally summarized discourse and narrative abstract merely serve a subsidiary role to the *oratio recta* of the document. That is, portions of the original *commentarius* might be summarized in a copied version, but the important focus of the account was given in *oratio recta*. Summarized discourse and narrative abstract usually provide only a bare-bones context or introduction to the *oratio recta* portion of the account. However, there are variations to this pattern. For example, in *BGU* 347 (171 CE) the entire account is given in narration and summarized discourse, including the κρίσις. A more common variation is to give only the κρίσις in *oratio recta*, as, for example, in *P. Amh.* 64 (107 CE) and *SB* 7601 (135 CE).

Summarized discourse and narrative abstract are employed only as a scribal convenience, that is, they are used principally for one or more of the following purposes:

a) to summarize events and speeches which would otherwise be very lengthy;
b) to summarize legal formalities which preceded the *oratio recta* between the magistrate and the parties;
c) to summarize speeches deemed of secondary importance to the matter at hand.

In other words, summarized discourse and narrative abstract were not employed to give the account a literary flavor, to make the account flow more smoothly, nor to aid the reader in forming a picture of the trial and the emotional atmosphere which existed there. It is very rare to find even a genitive absolute or adverb which give a clue to the emotions present or which break the otherwise monotonous "X said . . . Y said. . . ." Occasionally, however, such elements are encountered. For example, in *P. Ryl.* 77 (192 CE), which is an account of a public session before a strategus:

Ἀμμωνίων Διοσκόρου ὑποτυχὼν εἶπ(εν)· . . .

Ammonion son of Dioscorus, interrupting, said: . . .

The immediately preceding speech was a complete sentence. To indicate that a speaker had interrupted is very rare. Normally the scribe would have

merely recorded "Ammonion son of Dioscorus said . . ."
In this same *commentarius* is recorded an exclamation of the crowd:

τῶν παρεστώτων ἀπὸ τῆς πόλεως ἐπιφωνησάντων· στεφέσθω
Ἀχιλλεὺς κοσμητείαν· μιμοῦ τὸν πατέρα τὸν φιλότιμον τὸν γέροντα
φῶτα.

those from the city standing by cried out, "Crown Achilles as cosmetes;
imitate your father, the munificent, the old champion."[37]

To record such an exclamation is rare, but this is a public session involving
the election of an official, and public acclamation could serve an important
function in such elections. However, it would never be recorded in a *commentarius* that the crowd shouted, for example, "Crucify him!" or "The
Christians to the lions!" The trial is at all times viewed through the eyes and
ears of the recording scribe, and at all times these scribes appear to have
maintained a completely neutral position. This is a point worth noting well.

Element 10: Reading Phrase

Occasionally in the course of a trial the magistrate has a document read.
In the *commentarii* such readings are indicated and usually quoted. The leading verb in the reading phrase is a form of ἀναγιγνώσκω, such as
ἀναγνωσθέντων, or ἀναγνωσθέντος. The transition back to the trial is indicated by μετὰ τὴν ἀνάγνωσιν or other phrases that show the reading is
finished:

ὁ στρατηγός· ἀναγνωσθέτωσαν οἱ ὑπομνηματισμοὶ Κασκελίου
Γεμίνου. Ἀναγνωσθέντων ἐπὶ τοῦ ῑ θεοῦ Τραιανοῦ Μεχὶρ δ . . .

The strategus: "Let the *commentarii* of Cascelius Geminus be read."
When these had been read, dated in the 10th year of the god Trajan,
Mecheir 4 . . . (*P. Fam.Teb.* 19 [118 CE])

Element 11: Oratio Recta of Magistrates and
Element 12: Oratio Recta of Participants

Obviously, for the purposes of this study, the formal pattern exhibited by
the *orationes rectae* between the magistrate and participants of the trial is
very important. Particularly important to notice is the form that is given to
the phrase which introduces *oratio recta*. Concerning these phrases, two elements should be observed: (a) the names, titles, and descriptions of speakers;
and (b) the verb of saying used to introduce the *oratio recta*. In addition, it is

---

[37] Τὸν γέροντα φῶτα here seems to carry more than the literal meaning "the old man." Φώς
is used of heroes in tragedy; see LSJ, *s.v.* φώς, col. 1968b.

important to notice (c) the sorts of questions asked by the magistrate and (d) the length of the speeches allowed to participants.

A. Names, Titles, and Descriptions of Speakers

Coles observed that

> a distinction must be drawn here between the treatment given to the participants and that given to the presiding official. . . . The parties on their first appearance often have descriptive or explanatory details attached to their names, which are subsequently omitted.[38]

Most commonly such explanatory and descriptive details are attached to the participants' names in the participants-formula or in the delegation phrase, wherein the individuals named make their first appearance. However, it is very common that persons not previously named—principally advocates and witnesses—will speak during the course of the trial.[39] The first speech of such persons is often introduced by the person's name modified by descriptive or explanatory details.

Below are examples of introductory phrases from Antonine *commentarii*. The first line in each example below introduces the first *oratio recta* of the account cited:

Ἰουλιανὸς εἶπεν· . . .
Καλλίνεικος· . . .
Ἰουλιανὸς· . . .
Ἰουλιανὸς εἶπεν· . . . (*P. Lond.* 196; 141 CE)

Ἀθηνόδωρος ῥήτ(ωρ) ὑπὲρ Πασίωνος εἶπ(εν)· . . .
Δίδυμος ῥήτ(ωρ) ὑπὲρ Πανομιέως καὶ Πεθέως ἀπεκρείνατο· . . .
Πασίων εἶπ(εν)· . . .
Πανομιεὺς καὶ Πεθεὺς εἶπ(αν)· . . . (*BGU* 969; 142 CE?)

Φιλώτας εἶπεν· . . .
Ἀπολλώνιος νεώτερος εἶπεν· . . .
Φιλώτας εἶπεν· . . .
Ἀπολλώνιος εἶπεν· . . .
Φιλώτας εἶπεν· . . .
Ἀπολλώνιος ὁ νεώτερος εἶπεν· . . . (*SB* 7558; 148 CE)

Φαῦστος σκεψάμενος . . . εἶπεν· . . .
Δῖος νομοφύλαξ εἶπεν· . . .
Φαῦστος εἶπεν· . . .

[38] Coles, *Reports on Proceedings*, 38.
[39] Upon their first appearance, advocates are normally introduced as "X, advocate for Y," and thereafter as "X, advocate."

Ἀρποκρατίων στρατηγὸς εἶπεν· . . .
Φαῦστος ἐπύθετο· . . .
ἀπεκρίνατο· . . .
Φαῦστος εἶπεν· . . .
ἀπεκρίνατο· . . . (*PSI* 1100; 161 CE)

These examples show the simplicity of the phrases (or words) that introduce *oratio recta*. It would appear that scribes modified a speaker's name with explanatory or descriptive details only when it was deemed necessary to identify the speaker. Titles were appended to officials' names, it would seem, merely to identify such persons as officials.

An important distinction must be noted for the presiding magistrate's introductory phrases during the Antonine period. The magistrate is commonly introduced either by name alone or by title alone, but not by both throughout a *commentarius*. As Coles recognized, "In *SB* 5676 (232?) . . . we find for the first time the presiding official given his title formula throughout."[40] That is, not until about the mid-third century did scribes introduce every speech of the magistrate by both his name and title.

B. *Verbs of Saying Introducing Oratio Recta*

For this section, the reader may find it particularly useful to refer to the left side of Appendices 1–3, "Verbs Introducing *Oratio Recta*." As can be seen from Appendix 1, prior to 129 CE scribes consistently used the direct introduction (no verb of saying) to *oratio recta*. An example of such an introduction is:

Οὐίβιος Μάξιμος· Ἔχεις ἐν τοῖς ὑπομνηματισμοῖς μου. (*P. Amh.* 64; 107 CE)

By far the most common pattern prior to ca. 129 was to introduce all *orationes rectae* directly, regardless of speaker and regardless of whether the discourse was a statement, a question, or an answer.

There are only two exceptions to this rule known to me. *P. Yale Inv.* 1528 (63 CE) introduces speeches with εἶπεν or ἀπεκρίνατο—the common pattern after ca. 129—and *SB* 9050 (extract from 100 CE) uses ἀπεκρίνατο to introduce an answer. In both instances, however, the insertion of a leading verb may be due to later copying.

In *SB* 9050 (after 114), a peculiar pattern is encountered: the *orationes rectae* of the magistrate are introduced directly, but the answers and statements of participants are recorded in *oratio obliqua* or in *oratio recta* introduced by a participle of saying. Here arises the question of the mixture of

[40] Coles, *Reports of Proceedings*, 39.

summarized discourse and *oratio recta* within a *commentarius*. It is not uncommon to find the first speech of an account introduced by the participle εἰπόντος but all subsequent speeches introduced by indicatives, such as εἶπεν. Coles lists the following participles that may be used in the genitive absolute to introduce *oratio obliqua*:

λεγούσης, προσειπόντος, ἀποκριναμένου, ἀξιούντων, ἀξιωσάντων, ἀξιουμένης, διαβεβαιωσαμένου (*CPR* I 18), ἀπαγγείλαντος (also *CPR* I 18), φήσαντος (*SB* 7601), προενεγκαμένων (*P. Amh.* 66), and φάσκοντος (M. *Chr.* 372).[41]

The rule here, if indeed one can be found, is that it was exceedingly rare to summarize speeches of the magistrate, and that summarized discourse, when used, tended to be used for the first speech in the *commentarius*. However, *commentarii* such as *SB* 9050 should caution us against applying the latter statement in a rigid fashion; a scribe could intersperse summarized discourse with *oratio obliqua* throughout an account.

About 130 a change begins to take place in the recording of *commentarii*: scribes begin to show a definite preference for using εἶπεν to introduce *oratio recta*. The direct form of introduction is sporadically employed throughout the Antonine period, but after ca. 136 the predominant form of introduction is the εἶπεν-type. The rule for the Antonine period, then, is this: if a scribe chose one form of introduction—usually using εἶπεν as the leading verb—he used only that form of introduction. He might use ἀπεκρίνατο or ἀπεκρείνατο to introduce answers, but he did not mix direct introductions with introductions of the εἶπεν-type.[42]

After ca. 234 scribes began consistently to introduce speeches by means of the abbreviated εἶπεν-type, that is, εἶ⸍, normally transcribed as εἶπ(εν). This abbreviation does occur once earlier—in *BGU* 969 (142 CE?)—but the abbreviation here may be due to later copying of the extract.

Regarding the Latin form of introducing *oratio recta*, although the evidence is meager, the preferred form employed in Latin and bilingual *commentarii* would appear to have been *dixit* and later its abbreviation *d(ixit)*.[43]

C. Questions Asked by the Magistrate

Under the *cognitiones extra ordinem* of the Empire, a single magistrate controlled the entire sequence and outcome of a trial. An a priori conclusion from this fact might be that a magistrate could allow a trial to devolve into

---

[41] Ibid., 41.
[42] There are very few exceptions to this rule. One such exception is *P. London* 196 (141 CE). See also Bisbee, "Acts of Justin," 145–46.
[43] See Appendices 2 and 3.

small talk with participants. The point will be of considerable consequence when we turn to the *acta martyrum*, for there we find magistrates engaging in banter with the *martyrandi*, frequently asking them to elaborate upon their beliefs. Do the *commentarii* provide evidence to corroborate the historical probability of such questions or banter? The answer that we must give to this question is this: probability, no; slight possibility, yes. The magistrates of the *commentarii* remain in utter control of the trial. They do not allow themselves to be maneuvered into asking questions of special interest to one party or the other. The magistrate's line of questioning is typically simple and directly to the point. His sole intention is to ascertain the facts sufficiently to render an equitable judgment. There is little evidence from the *commentarii* under the Empire that would lead us to conclude that an advocate could "throw dust in the eyes of the judge," as Cicero had once boasted.[44] Should the evidence be presented in a roundabout or unclear fashion, magistrates seem to have been quick to get to the heart of the matter. For example, the following case which involves the guardianship of an Antinoite:

Φιλώτας εἶπεν· πόθεν ἦν ὁ κατλιπὼν Εὐδαίμονα ἐπίτροπον
Ἀπολλώνιος νεώτερος εἶπεν· Ῥωμαῖος ὢν κατῴκησεν ἐν Ἰβιῶνι
Πανυκτέρει. Φιλώτας εἶπεν· τοῦτο δικαίως ἀπέλεγεν εἰ ⟨μὴ⟩
Ἀντινοεὺς ἦν ὁ καταστήσας αὐτὸν ἐπίτροπον, ἄλλῳ γὰρ οὐδενὶ
ἀγώγιμός ἐστιν ἐπιτροπεύειν αὐτοῦ τῶν κτημάτων ἢ Ἀντινοεῖ τῶν ἐν
τῇ νομαρχίᾳ. Ἀπολλώνιος εἶπεν· ἀποδίξομεν αὐτοὺς ἀντιλαβο-
μένους τῆς ἐπιτροπῆς καὶ πάντα πεποιηκότας ὡς ἐπιτρόπους. Φιλώτας
εἶπεν· ὅτι μὲν οὐκ ὀφείλι ὁ Εὐδαίμων ἐπιτροπεύειν εἰ μὴ μόνου
Ἀντινοέως κέκριται. εἰ δὲ ἀντελάβετο αὐτῆς τῆς ἐπιτροπῆς, καὶ
κριτὴν καὶ λογοθέτας δώσωι. Ἀπολλώνιος ὁ νεώτερος εἶπεν·
Εὐδαίμων Ἑρμαίου οὐκ ἀντελάβετο . . . . αὐτοῦ ἀντελάβετο.
Φιλώτας εἶπεν· Ἀντινοεύς ἐστιν Ἀντινοεύς ἐστιν ἀπεκρίνατο· ναί, . . .

Philotas said: "What by origin was the person who appointed Eudaemon a guardian?" Apollonius the younger said: "He was a Roman residing at Ibion Panukteris." Philotas said: "He did right to refuse this duty if the person who appointed him guardian was not an Antinoite, for he is not obliged to act as guardian of the property of any person other than an Antinoite belonging to the nomarchy." Apollonius said: "We will prove that they undertook the guardianship and have done all the work of guardians." Philotas said: "It has been decided that Eudaemon is not bound to act as guardian except only for an Antinoite. But, if he undertook the actual guardianship, I will provide a judge and auditors." Apol-

---

[44] Cicero's boast, in a private letter (*apud* Quintilian *Institutio Oratoria* 2.17.21) followed his successful defense of Aulus Cluentius Habitus. See Michael Grant, *Cicero: Murder Trials* (Harmondsworth: Penguin Books, 1975) 19, 119.

lonius the younger said: "Eudaemon son of Hermaeus did not undertake
it, his . . . undertook it." Philotas said: "Is he and Antinoite? Is he an
Antinoite?" He replied, "Yes, . . ." (*SB* 7558; 148 CE)[45]

Philotas' repeated question, "Is he an Antinoite?" is not due to dittography.
It reveals his exasperation that the advocates had allowed the questioning to
center upon the wrong person, Eudaemon, who had not undertaken the guardianship at all.

The extract quoted above is typical of the straightforward question-and-
answer style of the *commentarii*. A typical pattern in this form, when advocates are present, is for the plaintiff's advocate to give an opening speech,
followed by a speech by the defendant's advocate. Thereupon the magistrate
directs a few pertinent questions to one or both advocates and renders his
judgment. It would seem that the preferred course of events, from the
magistrate's point of view at least, was to settle cases in a single sitting,
although cases did at times drag on for months.[46] The secondary sources on
Roman law are oddly silent with regard to the length of trials. The dates
given in the introductory formulae to the *commentarii*, however, indicate that
once a case was brought before a magistrate, it was normally settled in a single session. Cases of longer duration usually involved *appellatio* to a higher
authority—in Egypt appeal from the jurisdiction of the municipal authorities
or epistrategus of a nome to the prefect, the highest authority of the province.[47]

D. Length of Participants' Speeches

Coles remarked that "the recorded utterances of the parties . . . are usually
very brief, as are the reports as a whole, and most of the cases as we have
them would not have taken more than a few minutes to transact, and so brief
a duration seems perhaps improbable."[48] Neither Coles nor any other scholar
to my knowledge has introduced the use of the *clepsydra* (water clock) to
delimit the length of advocates' speeches;[49] it is relevant nevertheless.
According to Pliny the Younger, since the death of Regulus

---

[45] Translation by Hunt and Edgar, *Select Papyri*, 2. 260.
[46] E.g., the case of Dionysia (*P. Oxy.* 237; 186 CE), which lasted well over a year.
[47] Appeal to the emperor was also possible; see Jones, *Criminal Courts*, 95–96; Millar, *Emperor*, 509–15.
[48] Coles, *Reports of Proceedings*, 16.
[49] On the *clypsydra* as a time device, see E. J. Bickermann, *Chronology*, 15–16; H. J. Rose, "Clocks," *OxCD*, 253 col. 2; and Jérôme Carcopino, *Daily Life in Ancient Rome* (New Haven/London: Yale University, 1940) 145–46.

the custom of applying for and granting two water-clocks or one (or even half of one) has gained ground and is generally accepted. Counsel would rather get their speeches over than go on speaking, and judges care more about finishing a case than passing judgment: such is the widespread indifference, idleness, and general disrespect for oratory and its attendant risks. ... Personally, whenever I am hearing a case ... I allow all the time anyone asks for, thinking it rash to predict the length of anything still unheard and to set a time-limit to a trial before its extent is known. ... You will protest that a good deal is said which is irrelevant. That may be, but it is better than leaving out essentials, and it is impossible to judge what is irrelevant without first hearing it.[50]

Pliny was apparently a man of his word, for in another letter he mentions a speech given by him that lasted sixteen *clepsydra*—nearly five hours![51] Speeches of such length lend some credibility to the possibility that Apuleius' *Apology* is not entirely fictitious. The *commentarii*, however, nowhere give evidence for speeches of such duration. We must conclude, then, that either the seemingly verbatim record of the *commentarii* is a fiction or that speeches at trials were indeed of such duration. As Pliny indicated, the length of trials varied from magistrate to magistrate, and the length of speeches from advocate to advocate. But if we are to suppose that Christian editors worked from *commentarii* acquired from the archives through normal channels, then it is not the actual length of trials nor the actual length of speeches delivered, but rather the length of the extracted speeches recorded in the *commentarii* which are of importance to us. With this in mind, we may conclude with the following points regarding the speeches of participants.

First, the opening speeches of participants—which in most trials would be their lengthiest—are usually recorded in summary fashion, as in the *oratio obliqua* below:

> Στοτοήτιος λέγοντος ἐνκεκληκέναι τοῖς περὶ Σαταβοῦν φόνου ἐπὶ τῷ
> ἀδελφῶι αὐτοῦ καὶ παρεῖναι τοὺς μαρτυρῆσαι δυναμένους τὸν φόνον
> καὶ περὶ Σαταβοῦν ἀποκρειναμένων καὶ πρότερον ἄλλους ὑπὸ αὐτοῦ
> παρασταθέντας μηδὲν τοιοῦτο μεμαρατυρηκέναι, ὁ στρατηγὸς
> Στοτοήτι· [followed by *oratio recta*]
>
> Stotoëtis said that he had accused Satabous and his associates of murder-
> ing his brother and that there were present witnesses able to testify to the
> murder and Satabous and his associates having answered that the

---

[50] Pliny *Ep.* 6.2.4–10. Trans. Betty Radice, *Pliny: Letters and Panegyricus* (2 vols.; LCL; London: Heinemann; Cambridge: Harvard University Press, 1969).

[51] Pliny *Ep.* 2.11.14. According to the Roman system, there were three waterclocks to the hour, but as Seneca complained, "it's easier to get philosophers to agree than water-clocks" (*Apocolocyntosis*, 2.2).

witnesses previously produced by him had been able to give no such testimony, the strategus said: . . . (*P. Amh.* 66; 124 CE)

In the trial itself, the speeches of Stotoëtis and Satabous may have lasted several water-clocks—we have no way of knowing for sure.

Second, once these opening speeches have been delivered and the magistrate begins his examination—which is normally recorded in *oratio recta*—the speeches of participants are usually recorded in *oratio recta*. Since these speeches are most often answers to the magistrate's question, their length normally is no more than a sentence or two. Occasionally the recorded speech of a participant will be considerably longer. However, the most common pattern of *orationes rectae* exhibited in the *commentarii* is a rapid succession of single-sentence questions and answers between the magistrate and participants.

Κρίσις

Element 13: Narrative ἐκέλευσεν-*formula*
or κρίσις *given in summarized discourse*

Following the body of the trial there is normally recorded the magistrate's judgment. This judgment is in most cases recorded in *oratio recta*, but occasionally we find the κρίσις given in a summarized form or narrative abstract:

Εἰπόντων ἄσημον αὐτὸν εἶναι Οὔλπιος Σερηνιανὸς ἀρχιερεὺς καὶ ἐπὶ τῶν ἱερῶν σημειωσάμενος τὴν ἐπιστολὴν ἐκέλευσεν τὸν παῖδα περιτμηθῆναι κατὰ τὸ ἔθος. ἀνέγνων.

When they replied that he was without blemish, Ulpius Serenianus, chief priest and superintendent of the temples, signed the letter and ordered the boy to be circumcised according to custom. Read by me. (*BGU* 347; 171 CE)[52]

In addition to this form, we also occasionally find the κρίσις given in a combination of *oratio recta* and summarized discourse, as in the following:

Πακώνιος Φῆλιξ· καθὼς ὁ κράτιστος Τειτιανὸς ἔκρεινεν, πεύσονται τῆς γυναικός· καὶ ἐκέλευσεν δι᾽ ἑρμηνέως αὐτὴν ἐνεχθῆναι, τί βούλεται. εἰπούσης, παρὰ τῷ ἀνδρὶ μένειν, Πακώνιος Φῆλιξ ἐκέλευσεν ὑπομνηματισθῆναι.

Paconius Felix said, "In accordance with the decision of his excellency Titianus, they shall find out from the woman"; and he ordered that she

---

[52] Translation by Hunt and Edgar, *Select Papyri*, 2. 244.

should be asked through an interpreter what she wished. When she had replied "to remain with my husband," Paconius Felix ordered that it be entered in the *commentarius*. (*P. Oxy.* 237; 186 CE; extract from 133)

Element 14: The κρίσις (*in oratio recta*)

According to Coles,

> there is often a . . . differential . . . between the presiding official's pre-liminary utterances and his final decision. Such a differentiation is natural because of the nature of the ὑπομνηματισμοί as a record of the official's activities and not as a judicial record *per se*: thus the κρίσις is the most important factor.[53]

That the *commentarii* are primarily intended as a record of the magistrate's activities is disputable, but Coles's general observation is accurate: the κρίσις does appear to have been the most important element of the *commentarius*, and not, as Niedermeyer asserted, the date. This would have been true for all individuals interested in a particular trial's record.

That the κρίσις is the most important element in many *commentarii* is obvious from the following observations. First, in some *commentarii* the κρίσις is the magistrate's only statement, or it is the only portion quoted from another document.[54] Second, the κρίσις is sometimes the only *oratio recta* of a *commentarius*, with the magistrate's other speeches given in summarized discourse. Third, in several *commentarii*, speeches of the magistrate are introduced by his name alone, but the κρίσις is introduced by name and title.[55] In addition, Coles observes that, although

> it is true that the "dative of addressee" formula is often found elsewhere in the body of a report . . . its use seems to be the prerogative of the presiding official, and in many texts as in P.Flor. 61 it is given only before the final judgment.[56]

The most frequent form in which the κρίσις was recorded was in *oratio recta*, introduced either by only the magistrate's name and/or title (direct introduction) or by the magistrate's name and/or title plus a leading verb,

---

[53] Coles, *Reports of Proceedings*, 49.

[54] E.g., *BGU* 136 (135 CE).

[55] E.g., *P. Phil.* 3 (144?); *P. Fam.Teb.* 15 (up to 114/15); *P. Teb.* 286 (121–38); *P. Teb.* 488 (121/22); *CPR* 1.18 (124).

[56] Coles, *Reports of Proceedings*, 50–51.

most commonly εἶπεν or the abbreviation εἶπ.[57] We may observe the following example of a typical κρίσις:

Ἀκύλας Ἀμμωνίῳ εἶπεν· εἰ διηλλέχεταί τι ἁμαρτημεθὲν καὶ
ἐπέπληξα ἂν· σχεδὸν δὲ ζήτησις οὔκ ἐστιν ὅτι τοῦτο δεῖ
παραφυλάττεσθαι. (P. Oxy. 2341; 208 CE)

Like other *orationes rectae* of the *commentarius*, the κρίσις is normally short and to the point.

Element 15: Concluding Matters

Following the κρίσις in many *commentarii* are found various elements.[58] Of the twenty-four *commentarii* from the Antonine period in which the concluding portion is extant, ten follow the κρίσις with "concluding matter." The most frequent of these matters is the single word ἀνέγνων ("read"), which is a certificate of accuracy, probably roughly equivalent to κατὰ λέξιν ("word for word"), which also occurs in *commentarii*.

P. Fam.Teb. 24 and P. Paris 69

It has been concluded in the discussions above that the vast majority of extant *commentarii* were private copies obtained, usually, by having a scribe produce an extract of relevant portions of the archival original. There are two documents, however, that must be discussed individually because of the special importance that Coles attached to each, namely, *P. Fam.Teb.* 24 and *P. Paris* 69. These documents are treated separately below. The text of each is provided for the reader in the "Texts" section at the back of this study.

P. Fam.Teb. 24 (up to 124)

This text exists in two copies, British Museum 1888 (= B.M.) and Berlin 13992 (= B), which are virtually identical except for a short passage near the end of B.M. 1888. Coles concluded,

> We are perhaps given the extent and form of an original report of proceedings through *P. Fam.Teb.* 24. . . . There is a subscription at the end (l.110) of the British Museum version: Ἀπολώνιος ἀνέγνων τὸν

---

[57] For other forms introducing a κρίσις in *oratio recta*, see the sigla "Elements of Form Present" to Appendix 1; see also Coles, *Reports of Proceedings*, 51.
[58] For a list of these elements, see the sigla to Appendices 1–3.

προκείμενον ὑπομνηματισμὸν ἐν σελίσι τρισὶ ἡμίσει. Both the BM papyrus and the Berlin text are private copies from the official original and this phrase . . . will be a copy of the presiding official's certification of the authenticity of the official record, appended to it originally in his own hand. ἐν σελίσι τρισὶ ἡμίσει (omitted in the Berlin copy) is the mean between the length of the two copies (BM has four cols., B has three). Provided that the columns in the original were of equivalent size, then *P. Fam.Teb.* 24 must almost certainly preserve the original text, a conclusion supported by the fact that the two copies are effectively identical. In this report the majority of the speeches are given in Oratio Obliqua after an introduction with the name of the speaker and a participle in a Genitive Absolute construction, and these speeches read like a précis of what was said: they must then have been given in this summary form in the official document.

I, too, am inclined to believe that *P. Fam.Teb.* 24 preserves the form and extent of an archival version. To the arguments for this conclusion given by Coles above should be added yet another, namely, that this *commentarius* covered a trial of the scribes and keepers of the archives themselves—a trial concerning the cost of repairing and transferring archival records.

P. Paris 69 (232 CE)[59]

It is difficult to know just how much relevance this document has for our analysis of *acta paganorum* and *acta Christianorum*, since it is apparently unique and is dated to a transitional period in *commentarius*-form.[60]

Wilcken called this document an *Amtstagebuch*[61] ("journal of court-days"), that is, a record of the magistrate's daily judicial activities. Coles makes only passing references to *P. Paris* 69, calling it a "clearly original protocol."[62] In discussing the introductory section to *commentarii*, Coles makes the following remarks:

> The "extract" phrase and the specification of the presiding official
> appear to be dispensable features. It seems then plausible that except for
> the prefixing of these latter features the introductory section of the origi-

---

[59] = W.*Chr.* 41 col. 3 lines 17ff. In addition to the brief discussion below, see the (also brief) discussions of Wilcken at W.*Chr.* 41, pp. 59–60 and Coles, *Reports of Proceedings*, 35.

[60] *SB* 5676, which is also dated 232 CE, is the first *commentarius* in which the presiding magistrate is given his title formula when *oratio recta* is introduced. In addition, from the period ca. 130 to ca. 234 scribes used εἶπεν to introduce *oratio recta* but from about the mid-third century they used the abbreviation εἶπ or εἶ.

[61] W.*Chr.*, 59.

[62] Coles, *Reports of Proceedings*, 35.

nal record may generally have been transferred into the copy without modification. Comparison with one clearly original protocol, *P. Paris* 69 ... will support this. The report here will have begun simply with the day of the date formula, followed by the location or possibly directly by the participants; the month from the date formula precedes the first entry in the column of minutes, with above it the year and imperial titles as a heading. In other words, the original or an individual record would not have begun with ὑπομνηματισμοί or ὑπομνηματισμὸς τοῦ δεῖνος. The presence of such a heading (in the plural) as a title to the roll, the *Amtstagebuch* as a whole, would amply explain the derivation of the "extract" phrase; *P. Paris* 69 in fact has such a heading at the top of each column, but we do not have sufficient original material to say how far this format may have been regular or exceptional."

P. Paris 69 is clearly original, but it should not be grouped together with the other documents called "protocols" (= *commentarii* here) by Coles. He is correct that ὑπομνηματισμοί τοῦ δεῖνος appears only at the beginning of the columns in *P. Paris* 69. However, it is not clear that this necessarily has any bearing on scribes' use of extract phrases, for it is not certain, to this writer at least, that *P. Paris* 69 is an original "protocol." It is an *Amtstagebuch*, as both Wilcken and Coles recognized. Unless I have misread him, Coles believes that scribes appended the *caput* of the column to the relevant body of a case when producing extracts (as in the majority of extant *commentarii*). *P. Paris* 69 does not support this conclusion, for the record of individual cases contained therein is even briefer than an extract. The original from which scribes produced extracts must have contained a much fuller record of the *oratio recta* between the magistrate and participants or more substantial summarized discourse and narrative abstract than preserved in the *Amtstagebuch*. The original *commentarius*, whatever its theoretical form, and the *Amtstagebuch* seem to have been related but separately kept documents. If an extract of one of the cases logged in *P. Paris* 69 is ever unearthed, the nature and relationship of the documents will become clear.

Are Extant *Commentarii* Representative?

This question is posed because the vast majority of extant *commentarii* are papyri from Egypt. *Commentarii* from other parts of the Empire are few but, mutatis mutandis, these few survivors indicate that the form of *commentarii* from Egypt is representative of those elsewhere in the Empire. In fact, it is most probable that the form of *commentarii* used in Egypt was adopted from the form used in Rome. Coles noted that there is a complete difference in style between reports of proceedings[63] in papyri from Ptolemaic Egypt and such reports from Roman time, reports of proceedings in Oratio Recta not being found before the first century A.D. In the normal Ptolemaic form the declarations of the parties are given in narrative form and are followed by a decision expressed in Oratio Obliqua. . . . Because of the deficiencies in our material we cannot provide a closely-documented date for this transition in style, but it seems likely to have been a result of the political transition. There is evidence to suggest that the reporting of proceedings in Oratio Recta may have been adopted in Rome, through the development of a Latin shorthand system, at any rate by the middle of the first century A.D.; if this is correct, the question will be whether the emergence of this style in Egypt was simply a formal imitation of the method adopted by the central administration, or whether it may have been adopted more purposefully through the parallel availability of a shorthand system for Greek.[64]

If the reader compares *commentarii* from other provinces of the Empire with those from Egypt, it will be seen that the things done mutatis mutandis are primarily two: (1) nearly all of the *commentarii* from Egypt are written in Greek, whereas those from other regions might be Latin or bilingual as well as Greek; (2) the laws and magistrates found in Egyptian *commentarii* are very often peculiar to Egypt itself. In addition, it is likely that the trial in Roman Egypt was a humbler affair than in Rome and the other provinces. This last point would appear, from the meager evidence, to have relevance only with regard to the length of rhetors' speeches. From a form-critical perspective, these differences are minor. *Commentarii* from all regions can be form-critically dissected into the four main sections: (1) introductory formulae; (2) body of the account; (3) κρίσις; and (4) concluding matters. The particular elements of form—descriptions of speakers, manner of introducing *oratio recta*, etc.—are also analogous.

---

[63] "Reports of proceedings" = *commentarii* in the present study.
[64] Coles, *Reports of Proceedings*, 9–10.

3

Commentarii and
the Acts of the Pagan Martyrs

Chapter Two was an analysis of true *commentarii*. The present chapter is a form-critical comparison between the *acta paganorum* and the documents analyzed there. The term *acta paganorum* which is often used in this study is meant to be both broader and less prejudicial than the term *Acta Alexandrinorum* but narrower in scope than *Exitus inlustrium virorum*. Although the *Acta Alexandrinorum* are the most important of the *acta paganorum*, our concern here is with any account of a pagan martyr's trial and death that bears resemblances to *commentarius*-form.

The method employed here renews many of the topics of discussion between the historical and history-of-religions schools during the late nineteenth and early twentieth century.[1] The sole concern here, however, is to demonstrate how form criticism of the *acta paganorum* may provide a means of delineating historical from ahistorical in the acts. If the comparison does not actually succeed in detecting the historical substratum, it will in most instances help to determine the degree of probability that a certain account, or portions of an account, did or did not ultimately derive from a *commentarius*.

---

[1] Musurillo (*Pagan Martyrs*, Appendix IV) gives a fine survey of the history of scholarship on the *acta paganorum*. See also Manlio Simonetti, "Qualche osservazione a propositio dell'origine degli Atti dei martiri," *REA* 2 (1956) 39–57.

66   *Acts of Martyrs and Commentarii*

The initial discoveries of *acta paganorum* among the great papyrological finds in Egypt caused great excitement in the academic circles of Europe. At first, scholars such as Ulrich Wilcken, Theodor Mommsen, and von Premerstein considered the *acta* to be extracts from ὑπομνηματισμοί, that is, *commentarii*.[2] Dissenting opinions were voiced almost immediately by those such as Théodore Reinach,[3] Adolf Deismann,[4] Adolf Bauer,[5] and Richard Reitzenstein,[6] who regarded the accounts as tendentious or fictitious. Other scholars, such as E. von Dobschütz[7] and A. Momigliano,[8] regarded the acts as outright anti-Semitic propaganda.[9] According to Musurillo, the undoubted authority on *acta paganorum*, the "historical approach initiated by Wilcken—whose intuitions were so often right—is still dominant among recent scholars."[10]

After much historical, text, and literary criticism of the individual fragments that comprise the *Acta Alexandrinorum*, Musurillo devotes a short section to a discussion of the *commentarius*-form:[11]

> In the various protocols extant in the documentary papyri we may note, in general, the following elements:
>
> (a) The κεφάλαιον (*caput*). This often contains a statement of the type of the document (e.g., whether an excerpt from official archives or merely a copy); next there is often the date; and then the names of the persons involved in the case (e.g., ὁ δεῖνα πρὸς τὸν δεῖνα) and the name of the official before whom the case was tried.
>
> (b) *The record of the speeches*
>
> 1. The name of the official presiding, often with his title, is usually given; also the names of the parties involved and the

---

[2] See Wilcken, "Alexandrinische gesandtschaften vor Kaiser Claudius," *Hermes* 30 (1895) 496ff.; Mommsen, *Römisches Strafrecht* (Leipzig: Dunker & Humboldt, 1899) 690; and von Premerstein, "Commentarii," 737.

[3] "Nouveaux documents relatifs aux juifs d'Egypte," *REJ* 37 (1898) 224.

[4] *Die Hellenisierung des semitischen Monotheismus* (Leipzig: Teubner, 1903).

[5] Bauer, "Heidnische Märtyrerakten," *ArchP* 1 (1901) 29–47.

[6] Reitzenstein, *Ein Stück hellenistischer Kleinliteratur* (NAWG; Göttingen: Vandenhoeck & Ruprecht, 1904) 309–32.

[7] Von Dobschütz, "Jews and Antisemites in Ancient Alexandria," *AJT* 8 (1904) 728–55, esp. 738ff.

[8] Momigliano, *Claudius: The Emperor and His Achievement* (Oxford, 1934) 35.

[9] Musurillo notes, however, that "granting the presence of anti-Semitic motifs, it is to be doubted whether anti-Semitism is really a primary factor in the *Acta Alexandrinorum*. In the few fragments in which the Jews are concerned (*Acta Isidori, Herm., Paul.*), anti-Semitism is not so much a propaganda motif of the *Acta* literature as an authentic reflection of the actual situation at Alexandria" (*Pagan Martyrs*, 263).

[10] Ibid., 260.

[11] Ibid., 249–50.

rhetors representing them.
2. The words of the official are usually (though not always) given in direct discourse; but often the speeches of the parties involved are given in indirect discourse. See, for example, BGU 114, 388; Mitteis, *Chrest.* 84; *P. Oxy.* 237.
3. A variety of verbs are used to introduce the speeches (e.g. εἶπεν, ἀπεκρίνατο, προσέθηκεν), or the verb may be simply omitted.
4. Except when dealing with the speeches of rhetors, the testimony is usually brief. The more "literary" expressions and particles are rare. The remarks of the persons involved are usually brief, prosaic, and businesslike. Introductory or narrative sections are reduced to a minimum.

(c) The κρίσις of the presiding magistrate, usually very briefly.
In addition, we sometimes find
(d) The σφραγίς, the magistrate's official approval of the report (e.g., ἀνέγνων), and
(e) The ὑπογραφή of the court-scribe or copyist (e.g., ἔγραψα).

Musurillo's analysis of the form of *commentarii* is more accurate than that of Delehaye, but it is surprisingly brief and general. That Musurillo did not devote more attention to the *commentarii* is surprising because of his conclusions regarding the relationship between the *Acta Alexandrinorum* and *commentarii* (which he calls "protocols"):[12]

> With regard to the relationship between the *Acta Alexandrinorum* and the protocols, we may, by way of summary, reduce the fragments to the following general categories:
>
> i. Those that adhere more strictly to the protocol form: *Max.* II, *A. Hermiae, Paul.* (and its derivative, BGU 341), and, to a lesser extent, *P. Giss.*
> ii. The rhetorical fragments: PSI, *Diog., Max.* I, and perhaps BGU 588, *P. Fay.*, and *P. Ryl.*
> iii. Documents that have been reworked and fictionized in varying degrees, viz. (a) the *Acta Isidori, Athen.*, and, to a greater extent, (b) *Herm.*, and the *Acta Appiani.*
> iv. Documents not based on protocols: *P. Oxy.* 1089.
> v. Documents of dubious classification: *P. Fay., P. Oslo., P. Bour.*, and *P. Aberd.*
> vi. Documents probably not to be classed with the *Acta Alexandrinorum: P. Fouad,* PRUM, *P. Erl.*, and *Heracl.*

[12] Ibid., 251–52.

Of these fragments, therefore, it would appear that those listed under
"ii" were in some way associated with the speeches delivered at the
actual hearings and perhaps partly based on the rhetors' private
copies; those under "i" and "iii (a)" (and *Heracl.*) were undoubtedly based on private copies of the official protocols; those under "iii
(b)" probably derive only partly and indirectly from written documents; and "iv" (P. Oxy. 1089) was perhaps based on oral tradition.

In Chapter Two, the formal differences between *commentarii* of different
periods were taken into account. The editors of the *Acta Alexandrinorum*
employed a literary genre whose dramatic setting was the court room and
whose outward form was the *commentarius*-form. The question for the historian is whether a particular account did in fact derive from an authentic
commentarius. Once the question has been asked, the interlocking wheels of
the various means of criticism—textual, historial, literary, form, redaction—
begin to turn. What is learned by means of one type of criticism will facilitate the application of a second method, and what is learned by the second
method will in turn facilitate application of the first method.

Here we are concerned with the application of form criticism, as defined
in the Introduction. The dramatic date of many of the *Acta Alexandrinorum*
has been determined, providing a terminus a quo, and the scribal hand can
usually be dated within fifty years or so, providing a rough terminus ad quem.
In most cases the period between the termini is about one hundred fifty years,
from the mid-first to the late second or early third century. As indicated in
Chapters One and Two, there are discernible formal differences between
commentarii of the mid-first century and those of the late second century.
Let us say, for example, that account X looks like it may be derived from a
commentarius. However, account X has a dramatic date ca. 50 CE but the
commentarius-form of the account is that of a late second-century *commentarius*. This suggests that account X is either outright fiction and that
commentarius-form has been consciously chosen by the author, or that a later
editor has "up-dated" the *commentarius*-form of an older version. If the
application of form criticism has determined that account X is not based upon
a *commentarius* but merely assumes the form, the form may suggest the date
of writing. Form criticism will further be used to explore the writer's social
context. If it is determined that account X is an edited version of a *commentarius*, form and redaction criticism will be used to learn more about the editorial changes and to suggest possible readings of the original text.

Tabular Analysis of *Acta Alexandrinorum*

In the table that follows, the various fragments of the *Acta Alexandrinorum*
are outlined in sigla notation according to elements of form, as is done with

commentarii in Appendices 1 – 3 to this study. In order to analyze the accounts in this fashion, it was initially assumed that each account derived from a *commentarius*. The subsequent application will then use the data to explore questions regarding authenticity and editorial emendation.

Perhaps the following example of "sigla notation" will help the reader to make sense of the table:

Text	Sigla Notation and Explanation
ἔφη Λάμπων τῷ Ἰσιδώρῳ·	12nPU* = *oratio recta* of participant introduced by participants name, leading verb ἔφη + dative of addressee, and regarded as non-*commentarius*-form by this writer.

Sigla to Column "Elements of Form"

1   Extract phrase: (a) ἀντίγραφον
                      (b) ἀντίγραφον ὑπομνηματισμοῦ
                      (c) ἐξ ὑπομνηματισμῶν
                      (d) ὑπομνηματισμοί
                      (e) ἐκ τῶν ῥηθέντων
                      (f) ἄλλου or ἄλλου ὁμοίως
                      (g) other

2   Presiding magistrate(s): n = name   t = title

3   Date formula

4   Location: (a) ἐν location;
                (b) πρὸ βήματος ἐπὶ (τοῦ) βήματος πρὸς τῷ βήματι
                (c) ἐν τῇ αὐλῇ

5   Presence phrase: e.g., παρόντων ἐν συμβουλίῳ
                       παρερχομένου προσελθών ἐντυχόντων followed by
                       name(s) and/or description (=δ) or title

6   Participants formula: n = name   δ = description   t = title
    (a) Α πρὸς Β; (b) ἐπὶ τῶν κατὰ . . . κατὰ/πρὸς . . .
    (c) κληθείσης καὶ ὑπακουσάσης/κληθέντος καὶ (μὴ) ὑπακούσαντος
    (d) Α διὰ/ὑπὲρ Χ ῥήτορος (e) παρόντος Α πρὸς Β

7   Delegation phrase: e.g., ἐξ ἀναπομπῆς

8   "Ellipsis" phrase: e.g., μεθ' ἕτερα μετ' ἄλλα/ὀλίγον

9   Summarizing *oratio obliqua* and/or narrative abstract

10 Reading phrase: e.g., ἀναγνόντος ἀναγνωσθέντων
                      ἀναγνωσθέντος μετὰ τὴν ἀνάγνωσιν followed
                      (usually) by quotation

11 *Oratio recta* of magistrate(s)

12 *Oratio recta* of participants

13   Narrative ἐκέλευσεν-formula or κρίσις given in *oratio obliqua*

14   Κρίσις: name and/or title of magistrate + *oratio recta* introduced by:
          (a) no verb (direct introduction); (b) εἶπεν/εἶπ
          (c) ἀπεφήνατο (d) ἀπεφήνατο οὕτως/κατὰ λέξιν
          (e) ὑπηγόρευσεν ἀπόφασιν, ἢ καὶ ἀνεγνώσθη κατὰ λέξιν
          οὕτως ἔχουσα (f) dative of addressee

15   Concluding matters: (a) ἐξῆλθεν ὁ δεῖνα ὑπηρέτης
                    (b) ἀνέγνων (c) ὑπογραφή/ἔγραψα
                    (d) ἐξεδόμην/ἐξέδωκα τὰ ὑπομνήματα
                    (e) σεσημείωμαι
                    (f) (magistrate's name) ἐκέλευσεν/εἶπεν
                    ὑπομνηματισθῆναι
                    (g) summary of penalties exacted or summary of action
                    taken at the magistrate's order, introduced, e.g.,
                    ἐστιν δὲ τὰ ὀφειλόμενα

Additional sigla and abbreviations to "Elements of Form" column

Verbs introducing *oratio recta*

A	ἀπεκρείθη		N	ἐπύθετο
B	ἀπεκρείνατο		O	ἔφασαν
C	ἀπεκρίνατο		P	ἔφη
D	ἀπεκρ(ίνατο)		Q	ἐφώνησαν
E	ἀποκρίνεται		R	ἐφώνησεν
F	εἶπαν		S	λέγοντος
G	εἶπεν		T	direct (no introductory verb)
H	εἶπ(εν)		U	dative of addressee
I	εἶποσιν		V	λέγων
J	εἰπόντος		W	λέγει
K	εἰποντων		X	φησιν
L	ἐπιφώνησαν		Y	dixit
M	ἐπιφωνησάντων		Z	respondit

Miscellaneous sigla and abbreviations:

≡   fragmentary
±   very fragmentary or missing
?   when following an element = my conjecture
( )   elements contained within an element
[? ?] conjectured sequence
*   form of element unlike form found in *commentarii*

Analysis of *Acta Alexandrinorum* According to Form

(The dates given in parentheses after the *acta* are the dramatic dates; other relevant data are given in the footnotes.)

Acta Alexandrinorum	Magistrate	Elements of Form Present
PSI 1160 (ca. 30 BCE)[13]	καῖσαρ	±, (12), 11tG, ±
P. Oxy. 1089 (38 CE)[14]		±, 9*, (11nG, 11nG?)*, ±
P. bibl.univ.Giss. 46 (37 CE)[15]	καῖσαρ	± (fragmentary throughout), [?11ntT?], 12G, [?11ntG?], 11δ (ἡρώτων), 12nP, [?11P?], ±, 12nG, ±, 13, ±
Acta Isidori (41 – 53 CE)[16]		
Rec. A[17]	καῖσαρ	≡ [?9*?], 9*, 3, 3*, 2nt, 6nt*, 5δ*, 12n (ἔλεγεν Musurillo; λέγων Bell)*, 11tT, 9*, 11ntT, ±, 12nTU, 11ntT, 12nT, 11ntT, 12nT, 12nPU*, 14nta, ±
Rec. B[18]	(καῖσαρ)	±, [?4?], 5*, 12n(ἤρξατο λέγων)*, 11tT, 9*, 11ntT, 12nT*, 11ntT, ±
Rec. C[19]	(καῖσαρ)	±, 12n (name of speaker on line alone)*, 12n (name of speaker on line alone)*, 12n (name of speaker on line alone)*, ±

---

[13] *PSI* 1160: published in 1929; "written in an early Roman hand" (Musurillo, *Pagan Martyrs*, 83), perhaps ca. Tiberius? Provenance unknown. The dramatic date, 30 BCE, relates to a delegation before Octavian who were hoping to retain their βουλή.

[14] *P. Oxy.* 1089: published in 1911; provenance Behnesa. Hand dated probably to third century (Grenfell and Hunt). On the dramatic date, see Musurillo, *Pagan Martyrs*, 93 – 97.

[15] *P. Giss.* 46: published in 1939. Hand dated to late second or early third century. On the dramatic date, see Musurillo, *Pagan Martyrs*, 106 – 12.

[16] *Acta Isidori*: on the dramatic date, see Musurillo, *Pagan Martyrs*, 118 – 33.

[17] *Acta Isidori* recension A: *Chrest.* 14; published in 1895. Hand dated to late second or early third century; provenance unknown.

[18] *Acta Isidori* recension B: *P. Lond. Inv.* 2785; published in 1839. Hand probably early third century.

[19] *Acta Isidori* recension C: *P. Berol. Inv.* 8877. Hand dated to late second or early third century.

Acta Diogenis (ca. 71 – 75?)[20]	(καῖσαρ)	≢, (12), ≢
Acta Hermiae (79 – 81)[21]	(καῖσαρ)	≢, 11ntT, 12nT, 11ntT, ≡ [?12nT, 11ntT?], ≢
P. Oxy. 3021 (1st century)[22]	αὐτοκρ	≢, 9*, ≡ [?12, 11?], ≢
P. Oxy. 2339[23]		≢, 11*, 9*, 13*, ≢
Acta Maximi (ca. 107)[24]	(καῖσαρ)	≢, (12), (reading)*, (12), 12ntT, 12ntT, ≢
Acta Hermaisci (ca. 111?)[25]	(καῖσαρ)	≢, 9*, 11H*, ≢ [11], 12nH, 11tH, 12nH, 11tH, 12nT, 9*
Acta Pauli et Antonini (ca. 117?)[26]		
Rec. A[27]	καῖσαρ	9*, 10*, 11*, ≢, 11tTU, 12δ ('Iου- δαῖοι)T, 11tT, 12δT, 11nT, 11nT, 14ta, ≢

[20] *Acta Diogenis: P. Oxy.* ined. Hand dated to second half of second century. On the dramatic date, see Musurillo, *Pagan Martyrs*, 141 – 42.

[21] *Acta Hermiae: P. Harr.* ined.; C. H. Roberts, *JRomS* 39 (1949) 79 – 80. Hand dated to mid-second century. On the dramatic date, see Musurillo, *Pagan Martyrs*, 147 – 48.

[22] First published in 1974, and was not yet available to Musurillo.

[23] *P. Oxy.* 2339; published in 1954 (apparently not known to Musurillo). The editors of this text, E. Lobel and C. H. Roberts, write: "The subject is clearly a trial before some Roman authority; there are probably four defendants, one of them a woman. They are no ordinary proceedings, as the references to war and crucifixion show; nor does the form of the report suggest the familiar précis of legal proceedings. These considerations, together with certain stylistic features (cf. the frequent asyndeton and a vocabulary which is not that of the ordinary papyri) as well as the Alexandrian background to the proceedings ... might suggest that in 2339 we have a private copy of part of the *Acta Alexandrinorum*; against this should be set the documentary appearance of the text, which has all the appearance of a copy of contemporary proceedings, and ... the absence of any allusion to an emperor. In the absence of further evidence the question is best left open" (*ad loc.*). It is almost certainly to be counted among the *Acta Alexandrinorum* and in Musurillo's category iii, "documents that have been reworked and fictionized," or iv, "documents not based on protocols."

[24] *Acta Maximi: P. Oxy.* 471 (published in 1903; mid- to late second century hand) + *Griech. lit. Pap.* n. 42. On the dramatic date, see Musurillo, *Pagan Martyrs*, 152 – 57.

[25] *Acta Hermaisci: P. Oxy.* 1242; published in 1914. Hand dated to late second or early third century. On the dramatic date, see Musurillo, *Pagan Martyrs*, 162 – 70.

[26] *Acta Pauli et Antonini*: on the dramatic date, see Musurillo, *Pagan Martyrs*, 181 – 86.

[27] *Acta Pauli et Antonini* recension A: *P. Louvre* 2376 (published 1865) + *P. Lond. Inv.* I (published in 1893). Musurillo: "Both the date and style of recension A of the *Acta Pauli* would incline one to believe that it is not far removed from the authentic *procès-verbal*; it has, however,

Rec. B[28]		±, ≡ [?11tT, 12δT, 12nT?], ±
Acta Athenodori[29]	καῖσαρ	±, 11tT, 12nT, 11tT, 12nT*, 11tT, 12nT, ≡, 11tT, 12nT, 9, ±
Acta Appiani (ca. 190)[30]	αὐτοκρ	±, 12nG, 11tG, 12nG, 11tT, 12nT, 11tT, 9*, 12nG*, ≡, 9*, 12nG*, 9*, 11tG, 12nT*, 11tT, 12nT, 13, 12nG*, 11tT, 12nT, 11tT, 9*, 12n(ἀνεβόησεν), 9*, 12tV, 11tT, 12tT, 11tT, 9*, 12nG, 11tT, 12nT, 11tT, 12nT, 11tT, 12nT, 11tT, 12nT, ±

Application of Method

Musurillo noted[31] that only in Recension A of the *Acta Isidori* (col. ii lines 1ff.) do we have anything in the *Acta Alexandrinorum* that resembles a *caput* of a *commentarius*. The *Acta Diogenis* and *Acta Hermaisci* also show traces of lines that perhaps may have resembled the form of a *caput*. In the majority of the *acta*, the initial lines of the first column are unfortunately missing. This is the case with *PSI* 1160, *P. Oxy.* 1089, *P. Giss.* 46, *Acta Maximi*, and *Acta Appiani*, all of which may or may not have had *capites*. Neither the *Acta Pauli* nor *Acta Athenodori* had *capites*, and it is improbable that the *Acta Hermiae* did. This being the case, emphasis must be placed upon the *caput* of the *Acta Isidori* and upon the extant portions of the other *acta*.

There are three recensions of the *Acta Isidori*, called A, B, and C by Musurillo. The texts of Recensions A and B partially overlap, and the application of form-critical method according to *commentarius*-form provides some insights into the possible relationship of these two recensions.

---

been abridged and obviously revised in accordance with the Alexandrian sympathies of the author(s)'' (*Pagan Martyrs*, 188).

[28] *Acta Pauli et Antonini* recension B: *BGU* 341; published in 1895; provenance Fayyûm. Hand dated to the late second or early third century.

[29] *Acta Athenodori: P. Oxy.* 2177; published in 1941. Hand dated to third century. Dramatic date difficult to determine (perhaps reign of Trajan or Hadrian).

[30] *Acta Appiani: P. Yale Inv.* 1536 (published in 1936) + *P. Oxy.* 33 (published in 1898). Hands dated to first half of the third century. Dramatic date under the rule of Commodus (177–92), perhaps to the period of his "reign of terror."

[31] *Pagan Martyrs*, 250.

74   Acts of Martyrs and Commentarii

Recension A ""consists of two fragments from different parts of the same
roll (BGU 511 + *P. Cairo* Inv. 10448 = *Chrest.* 14). It is written in an oval,
upright bookhand of the semi-literary variety.''[32] The hand is late second or
early third century. Recension B (*P. Lond. Inv.* 2785) is written in semi-
cursive. The hand is from the early third century. Below is the text and
translation of Recension A, as given by Musurillo, with a collation of the
overlapping portion of Recension B which corresponds to portions of column
ii in Recension A:

Recension A, column i (*P. Cairo Inv.* 10448)

1   [Ἰσίδ]ωρον. Ταρκύνιος
    [συνκλητικὸς...   Καίσ]αρι ἀναστὰς
    [   ].τον ὅλην τὴν
    [   ]ον ποιήσεις
5   [ὑ]πὲρ πατρίδος
    [   ]μεν ὑπὲρ
    [ἠγω]νίζετο, δίκαιον ἦν
    [ἀναστὰς] δὲ Ἀουϊόλαος συνκλη-
    [τικὸς   ἐστ]ιν ὁ ἄνθρωπος καὶ
10 [ἀγω]γ[ί]ζετα[ι]. διὸ ἐρωτῶ
    [   ].τω τοῦτο τὸ ἅπαξ
    [   ]. τοῦ τηλικούτου
    [π]ολὺ προσηκούσης
    [   ]ς, εἰ μὴ οὗτοι παρε-
15 [   ]ν συμβουλίῳ
    [   ] ἐκάθισεν. ἐκλήθησαν
    [Ἀλεξανδρέων πρέσ]βεις, καὶ μετετάξατο
    [ὁ αὐτοκράτωρ εἰς αὔ]ριον ἀκοῦσαι αὐτῶν.
    [ιγ Κλαυδίου Καίσα]ρος Σεβαστοῦ
20 [   ] Παχὼν ε.

Recension A, Column ii (*BGU* 511)
Recension B, Column i (*P. Lond. Inv.* 2785)

Rec. A, ii.1   ἡμέρα [δε]υτ[έ]ρα· Παχὼ[ν ϛ.]
Rec. A, ii.2   ἀκούει Κλαύδιος Καῖσα[ρ τὸ τοῦ Ἰσιδώρου]
Rec. A, ii.3   γυμνασιάρχου πόλεως Ἀ[λεξανδρέων]
Rec. A, ii.4   κατὰ Ἀγρίππου βασιλέω[ς ἐν τοῖς -]

Rec. A, ii.5   λιανοῖς κήποις, συνκα[θημένων αὐτῷ]
Rec. B, i.1   [.........-λια]νοῖς [κή]ποις συν[καθημένων αὐτῷ

Rec. A, ii.6   συνκλητικ[ῶ]ν εἴκο[σ]ι, π[ρὸς δὲ τούτοις]
Rec. B, i.2   σ]υνκλητι[κῶ]ν κ̄,

[32] Ibid., 117. For secondary literature on the *Acta Isidori*, see ibid., notes to pp. 117–23.

Rec. A, ii.7	ὑπατικῶν δέκα ἕξ, πα[ρουσῶν δὲ καὶ]
Rec. B, i.2-3	ὑπατι|[κῶν δέκα ἕξ ὁμ]ιλουσῶν δὲ
Rec. A, ii.8	τῶν ματρωνῶν εἰσ.[τὸ τοῦ]
Rec. B, i.3-4	ματρωνῶν Ι [εἰσ........] τὸ τοῦ
Rec. A, ii.9	Ἰσ[ι]δώρου. Ἰσίδωρ[ο]ς ἐν πρ[ώτοις ἔλεγεν·]
Rec. B, i.4-6	Ἰσιδώρου.— Ι [ὁ δὲ Ἰσίδωρος πρ]ῶτον λόγον ἤρξατο, λέ|γων·
Rec. A, ii.10	κύριέ μου Καῖσαρ, τῶν γονά[των σου δέομαι]
Rec. B, i.6-7	κύριέ μου Καῖσ]αρ, τῶν γονάτων σου δέ|ο[μαι
Rec. A, ii.11	ἀκοῦσαί μου τὰ πονοῦν[τα τῇ πατρίδι.]
Rec. B, i.7-8	ἀκοῦσαί μ]ου τὰ πονοῦντα τῇ πα|[τρίδι.
Rec. A, ii.12	ὁ αὐτοκράτωρ· μερίσω σο[ι ταύτην τὴν]
Rec. B, i.8	Κλαύδιος] Καῖσαρ· μερίζω σοι τὴν
Rec. A, ii.12-13	ἡ|μέραν. συνεπένευ[σαν καὶ οἱ συν|καθήμενοι]
Rec. B, i.8-9	ἡ|[μέραν. συνεπένευσα]ν καὶ οἱ συνκαθήμενοι
Rec. A, ii.14	[π]άντες σ[υνκλητικοὶ]
Rec. B, i.10	||[πάντες συνκλητικοί,]
Rec. A, ii.15	εἰδότες ὁποῖο[ς ἐσ]τιν ἀ[νὴρ ὁ Ἰσίδωρος.]
Rec. B, i.10-11	εἰδότες οἷός ἐστιν ἀνὴρ |[ὁ Ἰσίδωρος.
Rec. A, ii.16	Κλαύδιος Καῖ[σαρ· μηδὲν]
Rec. B, i.11-12	Κλαύδι]ος Καῖσαρ· μηδὲν ὑπερθε|[......
Rec. A, ii.17	κατὰ τοῦ ἐμοῦ [φίλου εἴης· ἄλλους γάρ]
Rec. B, i.12	τοῦ ἐμοῦ] φίλου εἴης. καὶ γὰρ ἄλλους
Rec. A, ii.18	μου δύο φίλ[ους ἀνήρηκας ἤδη·]
Rec. B, i.13	||[...... μου δύο φί]λους ἀνήρκας·
Rec. A, ii.19	Θέωνα ἐξηγη[τὴν καὶ Ναίυιον ἔπαρχον]
Rec. B, i.13-14	Θέων[α |γὰρ ἐξηγητὴν καὶ Να]ίυιον ἔπαρχον Αἰγύπτου
Rec. B, i.15	[τὸν καὶ ἡγεμονεύ]σαντα τῆς Ῥώμης τῆς
Rec. B, i.16	[παρεμβολῆς ἤδη ἀν]ήρηκας, καὶ τοῦτον τὸν
Rec. B, i.17	[ἄνδρα διώκεις. Ἰσίδ]ωρος· κύριέ μου Καῖσαρ, τί
Rec. B, i.18	[μέλει σοι ὑπὲρ Ἀγρίπ]που Ἰουδαίου τριωβολείου
Rec. B, i.19	[................]λαι. Κλαύδιος Καῖσαρ· τ[ί]
Rec. B, i.20	[φὴς αὐθαδέστατος] εἶ πάντων ἀνθρώπων
Rec. B, i.21	[ca. 18 ἐ]κείνη εἰρηκέναι.—
Rec. B, i.22	[Ἰσίδωρος·.........] οὐκ ἀρνήσομαι κα-
Rec. B, i.23	[ca. 20]υ ἡσυχάζει—
Rec. B, i.24	[ca. 20]ερ τύψας ειχ[
Rec. B, i.25	[ca. 20] Ὀλύμπιε Καῖ-
Rec. B, i.26	[σαρ,]σου
Rec. B, i.27	]ην

Recension A, Column iii (*P. Cairo Inv.* 10448)

1 (40)   [...]ε πρέσβεα[...........] ἡ πατρίς.
[Λά]μπων τῷ Ἰσ[ιδώρῳ ......] ἐφεῖδον
[ἤδη] τὸν θάνατ[ον ..... Κλαύ]διος Καῖσαρ·
[πολ]λούς μου φίλους ἀπέκτ[ει]νας, Ἰσίδωρε.

5 (45)   [Ἰσί]δωρος· βασιλέως ἤκουσα τοῦ τότε
[ἐπ]ιτάξαντος. καὶ σὺ λέγε τίνος θέλεις
[κα]τηγορήσ῾ω῾. Κλαύδιος Καῖσαρ· ἀσφαλῶς
[ἐ]κ μουσικῆς εἶ, Ἰσίδωρε· Ἰσίδωρος·
[ἐγ]ὼ μὲν οὔκ εἰμι δοῦλος οὐδὲ μουσικῆς

10 (50)   [υἱ]ός, ἀλλὰ διασήμου πόλεως [Ἀ]λεξαν-
[δρ]εί[ας] γυμνασίαρχος. σὺ δὲ ἐκ Σαλώμη[ς]
[τ]ῆς Ἰουδα[ίας] υἱ[ὸς [ἀπό]βλητος. διὸ ῾καὶ῾ ἀπο[.]
.ειας ἐπ[...]ατη[..]ως. ἔφη Λά[μπ]ων
[τ]ῷ Ἰσιδώρῳ· τί γὰρ ἄλλο ἔχομεν ἢ παρα-

15 (55)   [φ]ρονοῦντι βασιλεῖ τόπον διδόναι
[Κ]λαύδιος Καῖσαρ· οἷς προεκέλευσα
[τ]ὸν θάνατον τοῦ Ἰσιδώρου καὶ Λάμπων[ος]

Translation: Recension A
Column i, lines 16–19

The Alexandrian envoys were summoned and the emperor postponed
their hearing until the following day. The fifth day of Pachon, in the
(thirteenth?) year of Claudius Caesar Augustus . . .

Column ii

The sixth day of Pachon: the second day. Claudius Caesar hears the case
of Isidorus, gymnasiarch of Alexandria, *v.* King Agrippa in the . . . gardens. With him sat twenty senators (and in addition to these) sixteen
men of consular rank, the women of the court also attending . . . Isidorus' trial.

Isidorus was the first to speak: "My Lord Caesar, I beseech you to
listen to my account of my native city's sufferings."

The emperor: "I shall grant you this day."

All the senators who were sitting as assessors agreed with this, knowing the kind of man Isidorus was.

Claudius Caesar: "Say nothing . . . against my friend. You have
already done away with two of my friends, Theon the exegete and . . ."

Column iii

Lampon to Isidorus: "I have looked upon death . . ."

Claudius Caesar: "Isidorus, you have killed many friends of mine."

Isidorus: "I merely obeyed the orders of the emperor at the time. So
too I should be willing to denounce anyone *you* wish."

Claudius Caesar: "Isidorus, are you really the son of an actress?"

Isidorus: "I am neither slave nor actress's son, but gymnasiarch of
the glorious city of Alexandria. But you are the cast-off son of the

Jewess Salome! And therefore . . ."
Lampon said to Isidorus: "We might as well give in to a crazy
Emperor."
Claudius Caesar: "Those whom I told (to carry out) the execution of
Isidorus and Lampon . . ."[33]

Musurillo includes the *Acta Isidori* in the category of "documents that have
been reworked and fictionized in varying degrees" but which were
"undoubtedly based on private copies of the official protocols." Let us
assume, then, that either one of the recensions or a prototype no longer extant
was based upon a private copy of the official *commentarius*. If the discussion
of private copies in Chapter One was accurate, the form of such a private
copy, normally produced by a legal scribe, will have conformed to the
commentarius-form discussed in Chapter Two.

The dramatic date of the *Acta Isidori* is the reign of Claudius.[34] Thus at
the outset our form-critical approach will be to compare the recensions with
commentarii of the first century. However, since the terminus ad quem is the
early third century (the date of the hands), we must be alert for indications of
second- and early third-century *commentarius*-form and for editorial harmon-
ization with contemporary stylistic preferences.

The ten *commentarii* dating to the first century analyzed in Appendix 1 all
begin with an extract phrase. The preferred form of extract phrase appears to
have been ἀντίγραφον ὑπομνηματισμοῦ (used in 5 out of 10). The lacuna
of Rec. A, col. i.1 certainly does not allow for this reconstruction, and the
extant]ωρον rules out the other extract phrases used during the first
century—ἀντίγραφον, ἐξ ὑπομνηματισμῶν or the magistrate's name in the
genitive. Rec. A, col. i.16–col. ii.9 bears some resemblances to the *caput* of
a *commentarius*. The date formula is not stylistically objectionable. Nor is
the participants formula τὸ τοῦ Ἰσιδώρου . . . κατὰ Ἀγρίππου. . . ." However, the form is perhaps closer to that of the *Amtstagebuch*. *Commentarii*
record single sittings and Rec. A, ii.1's ἡμέρα [δε]υτ[έ]ρα is more appropriate to the *Amtstagebuch*, as is the present tense ἀκούει of ii.2. However, if
our sole representative of *Amtstagebücher*, *P. Paris* 69, is typical of that
genre, each column would have begun with ὑπομνηματισμοί τοῦ δεῖνος, and
neither Rec. A nor Rec. B does this.

Column i of Rec. B seems to begin with a location phrase: [. . .λια]νοῖς
[κή]ποις. Neither Musurillo nor apparently any other editor of the *Acta Isidori* attempted to fill the lacuna. Rec. A is of no help, since only -λιανοῖς is

[33] Text and translation from Musurillo, *Pagan Martyrs*, 18ff.
[34] The majority of the secondary literature on the *Acta Isidori* seems to be devoted to determining the precise year (see Musurillo, ibid., 117ff.). Here the general date "reign of Claudius"
is sufficient.

preserved there also. Millar believes that "it is probable that this [garden] was the Horti Lucullani on the Mons Pincius, laid out by Lucullus in about 60 BC. . . . In Plutarch's time they were counted among the most luxurious of imperial gardens."[35] Perhaps the text read ἐν (τοῖς) Λυκυλ(λ)ιανοῖς κηποῖς. B's "*caput*" is not entirely objectionable according to *commentarius*-form, but it, like Rec. A, contains the doubtful reference to συνκλητικῶν, ὑπατικῶν and ματρωνῶν being in attendance. These *dramatis personae*, "twenty senators . . . sixteen men of consular rank, [and] the women of the court," are unlikely to have been recorded in either a *commentarius* or an *Amtstagebuch*. Of a similar nature is the intrusive comment that πάντες συνκλητικοὶ εἰδότες ὁποῖος / οἷός ἐστιν ἀνήρ ὁ Ἰσίδωρος (A ii.14-15; B i.10-11). It is more probable that an Alexandrian editor, not necessarily A's or B's, has supplied these lines, either from imagination or from memory of eyewitness accounts (assuming the trial did occur).

Rec. B's abbreviation κ̄ is probably earlier than A's εἴκοσι, and this and other textual differences, for example, A's πα[ρουσῶν (ii.7) versus B's ὁμιλουσῶν (i.3), indicates that at least one of the editors worked partially from memory and perhaps was copying from an oral reading. A ii.12's μερίσω versus B i.8 μερίζω and A ii.15's ὁποῖος versus B i.10's οἷός may also be explained in this fashion.

Although Rec. A has a formally more acceptable *caput* than that of B, there are indications—if an origin from a *commentarius* is accepted—that Rec. B is the earlier or less edited of the two recensions. The opening lines of Rec. A, which have no parallel in Rec. B, appear to be a narrative of non-*commentarius*-form. There is B's κ̄ (i.2) versus A's εἴκοσι already mentioned above. The rule "longer is later" probably applies to A's addition πρὸς δὲ τούτοις (ii.6). Second-century *commentarius*-form allows for the first *oratio recta* to be introduced by a participle. According to second-century form, Rec. B's λέγων (i.6) would be possible, although the addition ἤρξατο is improbable. The verb leading to Rec. A's opening discourse is missing. Bell supplied the lacuna with ἤρξατο λέγων from B. Musurillo objected that Bell's reading is "too long for the lacuna" and supplied simply πρ[ώτοις ἔλεγεν.[36]

However, the evidence from the first century indicates that scribes then introduced the first *oratio recta*, as they did *orationes rectae* in general, directly (without a leading verb), as for example the scribe of *P. Oxy.* 37 (49 CE) did: Ἀριστοκλῆς ῥήτωρ ὑπὲρ Πεσούριος followed immediately by the first *oratio recta*. The first discourse of Rec. A seems to be introduced with a

---

35 Millar, *Emperor*, 23.
36 Musurillo, *Pagan Martyrs*, 20.

leading verb and near the end, at iii.13, a discourse is introduced by ἔφη. All other *orationes rectae* of Rec. A are introduced directly. One might theorize at this point that the editor of Rec. A has taken the *commentarius*, added a prologue and (probably) an epilogue, but has retained the body of the trial containing *oratio recta* with few modifications. But the body of Rec. A also shows some non-*commentarius*-forms. *Commentarius*-form of all periods seems to have reserved the dative of addressee for speeches of magistrates alone.[37] The editor of Rec. B, with one possible exception,[38] did not use the dative of addressee. The editor of Rec. A, however, twice uses the dative of addressee to introduce a participant's speech, both times Lampon to Isidorus (Λάμπων τῷ Ἰσιδώρῳ; iii.2; iii.14). These speeches are triply suspicious. The first objectionable feature is the dative of addressee used with a participant's speech. Second, these are discourses between participants, which is not likely in a *commentarius*. Third, the remarks contained in the speeches are almost certainly editorial, especially iii.14: "Lampon said to Isidorus: 'We might as well give in to a crazy Emperor.'" This speech, following the fragment of iii.2 ("I have looked upon death . . .") are no doubt meant to depict the Alexandrian envoys opposition to a tyrant and disdain for death, both common motifs in *exitus*-literature.

The following may be conjectured from the brief analysis of recensions A and B above:

1) Both A and B contain many signs of editing; neither is simply a copy of a *commentarius*.
2) Rec. B is probably earlier than Rec. A.
3) Rec. B is either an edited version of a *commentarius* or of a recension no longer extant.
4) Rec. A is either an edited version of a *commentarius*, of B, or of a recension no longer extant.
5) If the recensions are not ultimately derived from a *commentarius*, the editors attempted, with some degree of success, to mimic *commentarius*-form.

---

[37] In the *commentarii* analyzed in Appendix 1, the use of dative of addressee is rare, occurring only in connection with a few of the magistrates' speeches (never of participants) in *P. Mil.Vogl.* 25 (126/127), *P. Mil.Vogl.* 27 (128/129), *BGU* 19 (135 CE), and *SB* 8246 (340 CE).

[38] Col. ii.36 (see text in Musurillo, *Pagan Martyrs*, 22).

4

Commentarii and
the Acts of the Christian Martyrs

In Chapter Two, the forms of true commentarii were analyzed. Chapters Four through Seven are form-critical studies that compare the acta Christianorum to the forms described in there. No attempt is made here to make definitive statements about all of the acta Christianorum but rather to show how a knowledge of commentarius-form and Formgeschichte, with an accompanying form-critical analysis according to that form provide many useful insights.

The Canon of Second-Century
Acta Christianorum

Scholarship, from the earliest work by the Bollandists in the seventeenth century up to the present, has separated the acta Christianorum into two groups labelled "authentic" and "inauthentic." The publications of collections of "authentic texts" and lists of texts regarded as authentic have for informs and purposes created a "canon" of "authentic" acta. Of the acts which might date before the end of the second century, G. Rubbach,[?] Oscar von

---

[?] On the work of the Bollandists, see Hippolyte Delehaye L'oeuvre des Bollandistes à travers trois siècles (Société des Bollandistes, 1920; English translation 1922; Anzeigable Marryrologium (4th ed.; Tübingen: Mohr-Siebeck, 1965).

4

Commentarii and
the Acts of the Christian Martyrs

In Chapter Two, the forms of true *commentarii* were analyzed. Chapters Four through Seven are form-critical studies that compare the *acta Christianorum* to the forms described in there. No attempt is made here to make definitive statements about all of the *acta Christianorum* but rather to show how a knowledge of *commentarius*-form and *Formgeschichte* with an accompanying form-critical analysis according to that form provide many useful insights.

The "Canon" of Second-Century
Acta Christianorum

Scholarship, from the earliest work by the Bollandists in the seventeenth century up to the present,[1] has separated the *acta Christianorum* into two groups labelled "authentic" and "inauthentic." The publications of collections of "authentic texts" and lists of texts regarded as authentic have for intents and purposes created a "canon" of "authentic" acts. Of the acts which might date before the end of the second century, G. Ruhbach,[2] Oscar von

---

[1] On the work of the Bollandists, see Hippolyte Delehaye, *L'oeuvre des Bollandistes à travers trois siècles* (Brussels: Société des Bollandistes, 1920; English translation 1922).

[2] *Ausgewählte Märtyrerakten* (4th ed.; Tübingen: Mohr-Siebeck, 1965).

Gebhardt,[3] Adolf von Harnack,[4] H. Lietzmann,[5] René Aigrain,[6] Giuseppi Lazzati,[7] B. Altaner–K. Stuiber,[8] Hippolyte Delehaye,[9] Timothy D. Barnes,[10] Herbert Musurillo[11] and others have now pruned the "canon" to the following seven acts:

Acts	Extant MSS
Martyrdom of Polycarp	*apud* Eusebius *Hist. eccl.* 4.15.3ff. and
	six Greek MSS (Ps.-Pionius)[12]
Acts of Carpus, Papylus and Agathonicê	one Greek MS, one Latin MS[13]
Martyrdom of Ptolemaeus and Lucius	*apud* Justin Martyr *2 Apology* 2
Acts of Justin and Companions	six Greek MSS[14]
Martyrs of Lyons	*apud* Eusebius *Hist. eccl.* 5.1.3–5.2.8
Acts of the Scillitan Martyrs	three Latin MSS, one Greek MS[15]
Martyrdom of Apollonius	*apud* Eusebius *Hist. eccl.* 5.21 and
	one Greek MS, one Armenian MS[16]

The *Acts of Pionius* were sometimes included in this list, since Eusebius (*Hist. eccl.* 4.15.46–47) included them among the *acta Christianorum* written during the reign of Marcus Aurelius (161–180), but they are today

---

[3] *Acta Martyrum Selecta: Ausgewählte Märtyreracten* (Berlin: Alexander Duncker, 1902).

[4] *Geschichte der altchristlichen Literatur bis Eusebius* (3 vols.; 1904; reprinted Leipzig: Hinrichs, 1958).

[5] "Martyrs," PW 14 (1930) 2048.

[6] *L'hagiographie: Ses sources, ses méthodes, son histoire* (Poitiers: Bloud & Gay, 1953) 209–10.

[7] *Gli sviluppi della letteratura sui martiri nei primi quattro secoli* (Torino: Società editrice internazionale, 1956).

[8] *Patrologie* (7th ed. rev. K. Stuiber; Freiburg im Bresgau: Herder, 1966) 91–92.

[9] *Les passions des martyrs.*

[10] "Pre-Decian *Acta Martyrum.*"

[11] *Christian Martyrs.*

[12] Extant MSS: Codex Parisinus graecus 1452 (10th cen.); Codex Hierosolymitanus sancti Sepulchri I (9th/10th cen.); Codex Baroccianus 238 (11th cen.); Codex Chalcensis Mon. 95 (11th cen.); Codex Vindobonensis graecus eccles. iii (11th cen.); Codex Mosquensis 150 (13th cen.).

[13] Extant MSS: Codex Parisinus graecus 1468 (12th cen.); Codex latinus 4 of the Library of Bergamo (11th cen.).

[14] Extant MSS: Codex Parisinus graecus 1470 (890 CE); Codex Cantabrigiensis add. 4489 (8th/9th cen.); Codex Hierosolymitanus sancti Sepulchri 6 (9th/10th cen.); Codex Vaticanus graecus 1667 (10th cen.); Codex Hierosolymitanus sancti Sepulchri 17 (12th cen.); Codex Vaticanus graecus 1991 (13th cen.).

[15] Extant MSS: Codex Musei Britannici II. 880 (9th cen.); Codex Vindobonensis latinus 377 (11th cen.); Codex Ebroicensis 37 (13th cen.); Codex Parisinus graecus 1470 (9th cen.).

[16] Extant MSS: Codex Parisinus graecus 1219 (11th/12th cen.); a fifth-century MS published by the Mekhitarist Fathers, *Armenian Lives of the Saints* (Venice: Institut des Mekhitaristes, 1874) 1. 138–42.

generally assigned to the Decian period.[17]

Most scholars believe that the earliest *acta Christianorum* originated as copies of *commentarii* or as letters written by contemporaries of the events. To my knowledge, no scholar doubts the ''authenticity'' of the *Acts of Justin*, but in my own study of the early recensions (A and B) of these *acta*, I concluded that these acts are not simply a copy of the official records with a prologue and epilogue attached. Rather,

> both recensions have been edited to a greater or less extent throughout. In some respects the *Acts of Justin* still conform to *commentarius* style: the simple *oratio recta* between the prefect and the accused, the general absence of parenetic and eulogistic material, the absence of narrative framework, and the predominant use of εἶπεν as the introductory verb. But in other respects the acts differ from *commentarius* style: the absence of introductory formulae, the absence of an extract phrase, the predominant use of Rusticus's name and title throughout, the absence of descriptive introductions for the accused, speeches introduced by the present indicative and/or participle, the questionable κρίσις, and the absence of concluding matters. In addition, the non-Justinian *apologia* (2.5 – 7) and the difficulties involving Rusticus's questions in 2.1 and 4.8 arouse the suspicion that entire sections of the acts have been interpolated or substantially edited. Despite these differences and difficulties, it is probable that the *Acts of Justin* are ultimately derived from the *commentarius* of Justin's trial, but within the so-called ''authentic'' portion of the acts (the *oratio recta*), no speech manifesting any of these differences or difficulties should be accepted without question as the ipsissima verba of the *commentarius*.[18]

Nevertheless, the *Acts of Justin* are regarded as ''authentic.''

All scholars, as far as I know, regard the *Martyrdom of Polycarp* in one form or another as being the authentic account (a letter) of a contemporary, written very shortly after Polycarp's martyrdom. But, as the discussion of the *Martyrdom of Polycarp* in Chapter Six will show, there is much debate about whether Eusebius's version is a more authentic text than the manuscript tradition (Ps.-Pionius), and whether one or both versions have been edited at various stages.

We must ask ourselves, What have scholars meant by an authentic account? By what criteria are the labels ''authentic'' and ''inauthentic'' afixed? It is extremely doubtful whether any of the ''canonized'' acts is completely ''authentic,'' if by ''authentic'' is meant ''the original, unedited

---

n. 24See Musurillo, *Christian Martyrs*, xxviii
[18] Bisbee, ''Acts of Justin,'' 157.

account." It is also doubtful that we possess the original text of any letter written by an eyewitness, or the text of an initially edited *commentarius*. In transmitting *acta Christianorum*, martyrologists, from the earliest times it would appear, often, perhaps even usually, did not resist the temptation to edit. Perhaps the community of scholars defines an "authentic account" as a text that is not necessarily the historical original but is demonstrably derived from a historical original. If so, authenticity is a matter of degree. Many texts, it cannot be doubted, rest upon no historical foundation and are pure fiction, written long after and quite removed from the facts. Other texts that in fact may rest upon historical originals are (conveniently) rejected as "inauthentic" because of the degree of editorial revision thought or known to be present. Thus a text that has demonstrable readings from the fifth century may contain "katachronistic" readings from the second century. It is only a matter of degree whether the community of scholars calls such a text "a fifth-century text containing readings from the second century" or "a second-century text that has been edited in the fifth century." If texts are treated as "wholes," without regard for editorial layers and the dating thereof, the danger of incorrectly reconstructing history from anachronistic data is great. Of this danger, the community of scholars is well aware. But the community has not always been sufficiently concerned about the danger of ignoring "katachronistic" data in rejected texts (those omitted from collections of texts and lists of authentic texts), and of unwittingly discarding historical residua of data such as descriptions of persons and events, traditional but ancient legends, and discourses.

This is especially true when discussions of origins are involved. The modern scholar who places texts as wholes into the categories "authentic" and "inauthentic" misunderstands the nature of ancient Christian literature. The redaction critic recognizes that Christian writers consciously reworked older materials to meet new needs.

> The redaction critic . . . pays closest attention to what distinguishes the work before him from the earlier material on which it is based. He observes how that material has been arranged or rearranged, how a new setting for a traditional unit gives it new meaning, in what ways the author inserts new themes, how he comments on the older material in editorial asides and transitional passages, and so forth. In ways such as these the particular interests of the author are allowed to stand out and to be seen as functions of his own historical situation, illuminating how his *Sitz im Leben* has changed from that of the earlier source or tradition.[19]

As indicated in the general Introduction, the consensus of scholarship to date

---

[19] R. T. Fortna, "Redaction criticism, NT," *IDBSup*, 733.

is that the earliest "authentic" *acta Christianorum* are the *Martyrdom of Polycarp* (died 155 – 177), the *Martyrdom of Ptolemaeus and Lucius* (*apud* Justin 2 *Apology* 2; before 160), and the *Acts of Justin* (died 162 – 167). If the accounts named above are indeed the earliest, the path of "retrojectories" for the genre can be traced back only to about the mid-second century. This is indeed extraordinary when we consider the emphasis that Christians came to place on martyrs and martyrdom. If the path of retrojectory is traced according to dramatic dates of accounts alone, without regard for scholarship's opinion about "authenticity" and date of writing, there are several Christian writings that might vie for the title "earliest of the genre." The most important of these are Matt 27:11 – 26 par.; Acts 6:12 – 7:58; 18:12 – 16; 25:1 – 12. In addition, accounts such as the *Acts of Peter*, the *Acts of Paul and Thecla*, and the *Acts of Ignatius*, which are usually disregarded because they contain "legendary material" should be considered. What Helmut Koester wrote regarding the *Acts of Peter* and *Acts of Paul* is well worth quoting here:

> Their [*Acts of Peter* and *Acts of Paul*] relationship to the canonical Acts of the Apostles is peculiar. If they indeed knew Acts—and this possibility cannot be excluded—they still tried to create a completely different image of Peter and Paul on the basis of the great store of legends about them that Luke had also used for his work. For the authors of both books, the two apostles belong together ... the two apostles stand together as martyrs. The older tradition of the two martyrs Peter and Paul that Luke had suppressed, and that had appeared for the first time in *1 Clement* and Ignatius was thus brought back into use by these two books. The composition of the reports of these martyrdoms seems to have drawn on older traditional narratives. We know that such reports existed in written form in an earlier period, as is evident in Acts 6 – 7, where Luke uses a written source containing a report of the martyrdom of Stephen. We should be careful, in any case, not to view such stories about the death of the apostles, and legends about the miraculous deeds, as merely products of the pious interests of a later period. On the contrary, their origin is best explained on the basis of the immediate reaction to the martyr's death. The *Martyrdom of Polycarp* was written immediately after the bishop's death, yet it by no means lacks miraculous features. We could go even one step further. Not only did such stories circulate early as isolated narratives, they were soon composed into cycles of written stories.[20]

It is not the contention here that the texts listed above are necessarily or even probably contemporaneous to the events described. The questions of origins,

[20] Koester, *Introduction to the New Testament*, 2. 325 – 26.

oral traditions, and of genres other than the *commentarius*-form demand more attention than space permits in this study. A few questions will be posed and some answers attempted in the discussions that follow, but a full treatment of "trajectories" will have to wait for a subsequent study.

Nevertheless, a few points in passing should be made with regard to the mutual influences of Scripture and *acta Christianorum*. First, such accounts of the trial of Jesus as Matt 27:11–26 par. that probably do not derive from a *commentarius* but that bear superficial resemblances to *commentarius*-form must be analyzed because they may have influenced the forms given to later *acta Christianorum*. Koester wrote that

> The model for the passion narrative . . . is the Christian kerygma of Jesus' suffering, death, and resurrection which earlier had been called "gospel" by Paul (1 Cor 15:1–5). . . . Literary models are absent, unless one assumes that Jewish stories of martyrdom had already developed into a distinct literary genre; but that is uncertain (despite IV Maccabees). Yet, Christian experience of martyrdom has certainly influenced the later development of Jesus' passion narrative, especially in the gospels of John and Luke.[21]

We should not exclude the possibilities that a *commentarius* may lie at the base of a tradition or that *commentarius*-form could have influenced the form given to oral traditions about the trials of martyrs—Jesus' trial included.

In the *acta Christianorum* it is evident that the Scriptures were the principal literature of the martyrs. Any quotation from Scripture used by the martyrs, however, must be understood against the background of the contemporary social context. As the society's general understanding of a concept such as the afterlife changed, so too did its understanding of what was meant by words found in older writings. What the author of John's Revelation intended by the souls of "martyrs" residing under the altar is not necessarily the same thing that is understood by later generations. However, and this is important to note, the Scriptures and *acta Christianorum* provided for the Christian communities a "canonical" view of existence that tended to shade out competing conceptions. For example, ancient society had many concepts of the abode of the dead, but only certain ones of these concepts were reconcilable with Scripture. The formations of canons of Scriptures thus become critical events in the development of Christianity. According to Dibelius, "the first step was taken towards the construction of a canon when it became the regular custom in public worship to read aloud Christian writings along-

---

[21] Koester, "Literature, early Christian," *IDBSup*, 555.

side of sacred books of the Old Testament."[22] Against the background of what has just been said, a passage such as Matt 10:16–39 could, and probably did, exert an immense influence upon catholic Christianity's "canonical view" toward the Empire and martyrdom. The *acta Christianorum*, we know, were read at the yearly commemorations of the martyr's death.[23] But for the Christian community, what was important was not which *written accounts* were authentic but rather which *martyrs* were authentic. To the Christian community, the *acta* of an authentic martyr were *de facto* authentic. At least one function of the *acta*, then, was to demonstrate the authenticity of the martyr. It cannot be doubted that they also served the functions of propaganda, polemic, and edification.

Tabular Analysis of *Acta Christianorum*

In the table below, the "canonical" second-century *acta Christianorum*, and several other "accounts" that bear resemblances to *commentarius*-form, are analyzed according to the elements of form described in Chapter Two.[24]

First- and Second-Century *Acta Christianorum*
Elements of Form Present

Account	Magistrate	Elements of Form Present
Matt 27:11–26	ἡγεμόνος	5*, 11t (ἐπηρώτησεν . . . λέγων), 12nP*, 9*, 11nWU, 9*, 11nGU, 9*, 11nGU, 12F*, 11nWU, 12 (λέγουσιν)*, 11P*, 12 (ἔκραζον λέγοντες)*, 9*, 11nV*, 12 (ἀποκριθεὶς πᾶς ὁ λαὸς εἶπεν)*, 13*
Mark 15:1–15	Πιλᾶτος	9*, 11n (ἐπηρώτα + acc. of addressee)*, 12 (ἀποκριθεὶς αὐτῷ λέγει)*, 9*, 11n (ἐπηρώτα αὐτὸν λέγων)*, 9*, 11n (ἀπεκρίθη αὐτοῖς λέγων)*, 9*,

[22] Martin Dibelius, *A Fresh Approach to the New Testament and Early Christian Literature* (1936; reprinted Westport, CT: Greenwood, 1979) 20–21.

[23] E.g., see the quotation from Cyprian on p. 10 above. See also Eric Waldram Kemp, *Canonization and Authority in the Western Church* (Oxford: Oxford University, 1948) 10–12, 16; W. H. C. Frend, *The Donatist Church: A Movement of Protest in Roman North Africa* (Oxford: Oxford University, 1952); Victor Saxer, *Morts martyrs reliques en afrique chrétienne aux premiers siècles: les témoignages de Tertullien, Cyprien, et Augustin à la lumiére de l'archéologie africaine* (Paris: Éditions Beauchesne, 1980).

[24] For explanation of the sigla and of sigla analysis, see pp. 71–72 above and pp. 179–81 below. The data relevant to the individual manuscripts are given on p. 84 above.

88   Acts of Martyrs and Commentarii

11n (ἀποκριθεὶς ἔλεγεν αὐτοῖς)*, 12 (ἔκραξαν)*,
11n (ἔλεγεν αὐτοῖς)*, 12 (ἔκραξαν)*, 13*

Luke 23:1–25	Πιλᾶτος	9*, 12 (ἤρξαντο … λέγοντες), 11n (ἠρώτησεν αὐτόν λέγων)*, 12 (ἀποκριθεὶς αὐτῷ ἔφη)*, 11n (εἶπεν πρὸς …)*, 12 (λέγοντες ὅτι …), 9*, 11n (εἶπεν πρὸς …)*, 12 (ἀνέκραγον … λέγοντες)*, 9*, 12 (ἐπεφώνουν λέγοντες)*, 11 (εἶπεν πρὸς …)*, 9*, 13*
John 18:28–19:16	Πιλᾶτος	4*, 3*, 9*, 11nX*, 12 (ἀπεκρίθησαν καὶ εἶπαν αὐτῷ), 11nGU, 12 (οἱ Ἰουδαῖοι) FU*, 9*, 4, 5*, 11nGU, 12nA, 11nA, 12nA, 11nGU, 12nA, 11nWU*, 9*, 11nWU*, 12 (ἐκραύγασαν … λέγοντες)*, 13*, 9*, 12 (ἔλεγον)*, 11nWU*, 9*, 11WU*, 12δ/t (ἐκραύγασαν λέγοντες)*, 11nWU*, 12 (ἀπεκρίθησαν αὐτῷ οἱ Ἰουδαῖοι), 9*, 11WU*, 9*, 11WU*, 12nAU, 9*, 12 (οἱ Ἰουδαῖοι ἐκραύγαζον λέγοντες)*, 9*, 4, 3*, 11WU*, 12 (ἐκραύγασαν), 11nWU*, 12 (ἀπεκρίθησαν οἱ ἀρχιερεῖς)*, 13*
Acts 6:12–7:58	ἀρχιερεύς	9*, 2*, 9*, 12 (λέγοντας), 9*, 11tG, 12P* [long apology], 9*, 12G*, 9* (13*)
Acts 18:12–16	ἀνθυπάτος	2nt, 6nδ, 4, 12 (λέγοντες ὅτι …)*, 9*, 11n (εἶπεν πρὸς …)*, 9*/13*
Acts 25:1–12	Φῆστος	9*, 11X*, 9*, 4b, 6nδ, 9*, 12n (ἀπολογουμένου ὅτι [ἡγεμόνος] 9*, 11X*,…)*, 9*, 11nAUG*, 12nG*, 9, 14n (ἀπεκρίθη)
Acts of Peter	Ἀγρίππα	The "trial" consists of two sentences only: ταῦτα τοῦ Πέτρου λαλοῦντος καὶ τῶν ἀδελφῶν πάντων κλαιόντων, ἰδοὺ στρατιῶται τέσσαρες αὐτὸν παραλαβόντες ἀπήγαγον τῷ Ἀγρίππᾳ. κἀκεῖνος διὰ τὴν νόσον αὐτοῦ ἐπ᾽ αἰτίᾳ ἀθεότητος ἐκέλευσεν αὐτὸν σταυρωθῆναι (§ 7).
Acts of Paul and Thecla	ἡγεμόνος	(§§ 16–21): 3, 12n (κραυγῇ μεγάλῃ εἶπεν), 12nn (εἶπον + dat. of addr.), 9*, 5*, 11tVU, 12nV [apology], 13, 9*, 5, 3, 9*, 5*, 3, 9*, 2 (ὁ δὲ ὄχλος … ἐβόα)*, 9*, 9/5 (συμβούλιον ποιήσας ἐκάλεσεν τὴν Θέκλαν), 11V*, 9*, 12nδ (λέγουσα)*, 9*, 13, 15*; (§§ 37–38): 2t*, 5*, 11GU, 12 (ἡ δέ)G*

[apology], 9, 11 (καὶ εἶπεν)*, 12 (ἡ δὲ εἶπεν)*, 9*,
14t (ἐξέπεμψεν ... ἄκτον λέγων)

Antonine Acts of Ignatius	Τραϊανός	1/2?, 3*, 5*, 9*, 3*, 9*, 5*, 11nT, 12nG, 11nG, 12nC, 11nG, 12nG, 11nG, 12nG, 11nG, 12nG, 14nc, 9*, 3, 9*
Roman Acts of Ignatius	Τρϊανός	3, 5nδ*, 9*, 2t, 5, 4, 11 (φησιν πρός αὐτόν)*, 12nG, 11nG, 12nG, 11nG, 12nG, 11 (ἡ σύγκλητος εἶπεν), 12nG, 11nG, 12nG, 11nG, 12nG, 11nG, 12nG, 11nG, 12nG, 11nG, 12nG, 11nG, 12nG, 11nG, 12nG, 11nG, 12nG, 11nG, 12nG, 11nG, 12nG, 11nG, 12nG, 11nG, 12nG, 11nG, 12nG, 11nG, 12nG, 11nG, 12nG, 11nG, 12nG, 11 (ἡ σύγκλητος εἶπεν), 12nG, 11nG, 12nG, 11nG, 12nG, 11nG, 12nG, 11nG, 12nG, 11nG, 12nG, 11nG, 12nG, 11nG, 12nG, 11nG, 12nG, 11nG, 12nG, 11nG, 12nG, 11nG, 11 (ἡ σύγκλητος εἶπεν), 12nG, 3 [cf. *Amtstagebuch*]/2n/5/4 (τῇ τρίτῃ ἡμέρᾳ ὁ Τραϊανὸς προσκαλεσάμενος τὴν σύγκλητον καὶ τὸν ἔπαρχον πρόεισιν ἐπὶ τὸ ἀμφιθέατρον, συνδραμόντος καὶ τοῦ δήμου τῶν Ῥωμαίων), 9*, 5, 9*, 11 (ἔφη πρὸς αὐτόν)*, 12nG, 14nb, 12 (θεασάμενος ὁ μακάριος ἔφη πρὸς τὸν δῆμον)*, 11nV*, 12nG, 9*, 3
Mart. Polycarp 9.2 – 11.2[25]	ἀνθύπατος	9*, 11V, 9*, 12G, 9*, 11tS, 12nP, 9*, 11S, 12C 11tP, 12nG, 11tG, 12G, 11T*, 12nG
Mart. Carpus Greek Rec.	ἀνθύπατος	4, 5*, 9*, 12P*, 11tG, 12nG, 9*, 11tP, 9*, 12nG, 11tG, 12nG, 11tG, 12nG, 11tG, 12nG, 9*, 11tV, 12W, 11tG, 12nG, 12* (ἐβόησεν λέγων), 11tG, 12nG, 11tG, 12nG, 13*, 9*, 12* (ἔλεγον), 12G*, 9*, 12nG*, 12* (προσηύξατο λέγων), 9*, 12*, 12* (ἐβόα λέγων), 12G*, 9*, 12* (λέγοντες), 9*, 12* (ἐβόησεν εἰποῦσα), 9*
Mart. Carpus Latin Rec.	proconsul	5*, 2, 11tY, 12nZ, 11tY, 12nY, 11tY, 12nY, 11tY, 12nZ, 11tY, 12nZ, 13*, 12* (*dicebat*), 13*, 11Y, 12nZ, 11tY, 12nZ, 11tY, 12nZ, 11tY, 12nZ, 9*, 11tY, 12nZ, 13*, 11tY, 12nZ, 13*, 9*, 12* (*dixerunt*), 12Z*, 9*, 12n* (*dicebat*), 9*, 12Y*, 9*,

[25] Pseudo-Pionus 9.2 – 11.2 = Eusebius *Hist. eccl.* 4.15.18 – 24.

		12Y*, 9, 11tY, 12Z, 9, 11tY, 12nZ, 14tY, 9*, 12* (*exlamauiti*), 9*, 5*, 4, 3*, 2*
Mart. Ptolemaeus	(ἔπαρχος)	9*, 13*, 9*, 12nP*, 9*, 11P, 9*, 13*
Acts of Justin Rec. A.	ἔπαρχος	3*, 5*, 2*, 9, 11tGU, 12nG, 11ntG, 12nG, 11ntG, 12nG, 11ntG, 12nG, 11ntG, 12nG, 11ntG, 12nG, 11nG, 12nC, 11ntGU, 12nG, 11ntG + acc. of addr., 12nG, 11ntGU, 12nG, 11ntGU, 12nG, 11ntG, 12nG, 12nG, 11nG, 12nG, 12nG, 11nG, 12nG, 11ntW + dat. of addr.*, 12nG, 11ntGU, 12nG, 11tW + dat. of addr.*, 12nG, 11ntG, 12nG, 11ntG, 12nG, 14ntc, 9*
Acts of Justin Rec. B.	ἔπαρχος	3*, 9*, 5*, 2*, 9, 4b, 11ntG + acc. of addr., 12nG, 11ntG, 12nG, 11ntG, 12nG, 11ntG, 12nG, 11ntG, 12nG, 11ntG, 12nG, 11ntG, 12nG, 11ntGU, 11ntG + acc. of addr., 12nG, 11ntGU, 12nδC, 11ntGU, 12nG, 11ntG, 12nG, 12nG, 11nG, 12nG, 12nG, 11ntG, 12nG, 11ntW + dat. of addr.*, 12CV*, 11ntGU, 12nG, 11tW + acc. of addr.*, 12nG, 11ntG, 12nG, 11ntG, 12nG, 11ntG, 12nG, 14ntcV*, 9*
Acts of Justin Rec. C.	ἔπαρχος	3*, 2*, 5*, 4*, 9*, 12 (εἶπον)*, 11W*, 12 (ἔφη ὁ ἅγιος)*, 11tT*, 12T*, 11tP*, 12T*, 11tG*, 12W*, 9*, 11t (φησι)*, 12X*, 12X*, 11tW*, 12P*, 11tP*, 12T*, 9*, 11 (εἶπε)*, 12 (ἀντέφησεν)*, 11G + acc. of addr.*, 12T*, 11*, 12n (ἀπελογήσατο), 11tG*, 12T*, 13*, 14*, 9*, 3*, 9*
Mart. Lyons		[narrated entirely]
Acts of Scillitans	*proconsul*	3, 4, 5, 11ntY, 12nY, 11ntY, 12nY, 11nY, 12nY, 11ntY, 12nY, 11ntY, 12nY, 12nY, 12nY, 12nY, 11ntY + dat. of addr., 12nY, 11ntY, 12nY, 11ntY, 12nY, 11ntY, 12nY*, 14nt (*recitauit*), 12nY, 12nY, 14nt, 9*
Mart. Apollonius	ἀνθύπατος	3*, 2*, 5*, 11ntG, 12nG, 11ntG, 12nδG, 11ntG, 12nG*, 11ntG, 9*, 10, 11ntG, 12nG, 11ntG, 12nG, 11ntG, 12nδG, 11ntG, 12nG, 11ntG, 12nG, 12nδG, 12nG, 11ntG, 12nG, 11ntG, 12nG, 11ntG, 13*, 12nδG, 9*, 3*

Application of Method to Jesus' Trial

The secondary literature on any one verse of the passion narrative is enormous, and no attempt has been made here to converse with secondary writers.[26] Nor will any attempt be made to explain the relationships of the Gospel accounts to each other. The Gospel parallels are analyzed here primarily because of the possible formal influence that they may have exerted upon later *acta Christianorum*. New Testament scholarship has shown, of course, that oral tradition lies at the base of the Gospel accounts, but the possibility that *commentarius*-form exerted an influence upon the forms given to traditions regarding Jesus' trial should not be discounted a priori.

To begin our form-critical comparison of Matt 27:11 – 26 par. with *commentarii*, we must assume that, like other trials before Roman magistrates, there would have existed a *commentarius* of Jesus' trial before Pilate. Such a *commentarius*, we also assume, would have resembled *P. Oxy.* 37 (49 CE), which is representative of first-century *commentarius*-form.[27] The full text of *P. Oxy.* 37, which records a trial concerning the kidnapping and subsequent death of a foundling, is given at the back of this study, but the condensation below clearly reveals the form:

	Element	Text
Caput	extract phrase	Ἐξ ὑπομ[ν]ηματισμῶν
	magistrate	Τι[βερίο]υ Κλαυδ[ίο]υ Πασίωνος στρατη(γοῦ).
	date formula	(ἔτους) ἐνάτ[ο]υ Τιβερίου Κλαυδίου Καίσαρος
		Σεβαστοῦ Γερμανικοῦ Αὐτοκ[ρά]τορος, Φαρμοῦθι γ̄.
	location	ἐπὶ τοῦ βήματος,
	participants	[Π]εσοῦρι[ς] πρὸς Σαραεῦν.
Body	oratio recta	Ἀριστοκλῆς ῥήτωρ ὑπὲρ Πεσούριος· [*oratio recta*].
of the Trial	oratio recta	Σα[ρα]εῦς· [*oratio recta*].
	oratio recta	Θέων· [*oratio recta*].
κρίσις		ὁ στρατηγός· [judgment given in *oratio recta*].
Concluding Matters		[none given]

None of the forms given to Jesus' trial in the Gospel accounts can be said to resemble either the form outlined above or any of the *commentarius*-forms of

---

[26] I will, however, point the reader to A. N. Sherwin-White's lecture on "the trial of Christ in the synoptic gospels" in idem, *Roman Society and Roman Law in the New Testament* (Oxford: Clarendon, 1963) 24 – 47.

[27] See Chapter Two and Coles, *Reports of Proceedings*, on *P. Oxy.* 37 as a representative *commentarius*. For other *commentarii* of the first century, see Appendix One below.

92 Acts of Martyrs and Commentarii

later periods.[28] We need not tarry very long here, for nearly every element of the Gospel accounts can be rejected in a formal analysis.

Caput

In none of the Gospel accounts do we find the formal elements of a *caput*. We do not find even the faintest traces of an extract phrase, presiding magistrate's formula, a true date formula, presence phrase or participants formula. Nor do we find other telltale traces of *residuum commentarii* such as ellipsis phrases or reading phrases. The only Gospel that gives anything resembling a *caput* is John. John 18:28, Ἄγουσιν οὖν τὸν Ἰησοῦν ἀπὸ τοῦ Καϊάφα εἰς τὸ πραιτώριον· ἦν δὲ πρωΐ, gives a location and time, but both elements are of non-*commentarius*-form. The time is not a true date formula and ἦν δέ would arouse our suspicions in any case. The form of the location is to be rejected because it is the object of ἄγουσιν . . . εἰς. Both the third person plural and the present indicative of the verb are highly improbable, as is the preposition εἰς. In the *commentarii*, if a verb is used with the location phrase, it is normally given in the genitive absolute. John 19:13–14 also gives a location and time:

Ὁ οὖν Πιλᾶτος ἀκούσας τῶν λόγων τούτων ἤγαγεν ἔξω τὸν Ἰησοῦν καὶ ἐκάθισεν ἐπὶ βήματος εἰς τόπον λεγόμενον Λιθόστρωτον, Ἑβραϊστὶ δὲ Γαββαθά. ἦν δὲ παρασκευὴ τοῦ πάσχα, ὥρα ἦν ὡς ἕκτη.

Ἐπὶ βήματος by itself would be acceptable, but it is followed by the highly improbable prepositional clause εἰς . . . Γαββαθά. The date is again given in a form that would not be found in a *commentarius*.

Body of the Trial

Here, in the *oratio recta* sections, we might expect the analysis to get trickier, but in fact a form-critical comparison of the speeches given in the Gospel accounts with *commentarius*-forms reveals that nearly every speech

---

[28] The form of the *commentarius* of Jesus' trial perhaps resembled the following:

From the *commentarii* of Pontius Pilate, governor. The [year] of Tiberius Caesar Augustus, [month and day]. Caiaphas, high priest of the Jewish religion having accused Jesus, a Jew, of treason, Jesus appeared before the tribunal. Pilate: "Do you call yourself king of the Jews?" Jesus: "As you say." Pilate: "Don't you understand the severity of the charges that have been brought against you? Do you have anything to say in your defense?" When Jesus made no reply, Pilate: "Since Jesus has been charged with and found guilty of treason, he is to be scourged and taken outside the city to be crucified."

can be rejected. Rather than go through all of the speeches of the Gospel accounts one by one, which is impractical and unnecessary, a few general observations will be made and then the form-critical reasons for rejecting a few specific speeches will be given.

In a first-century *commentarius*, we would expect speeches to be introduced by the speaker's name alone or the name plus a description and/or title followed directly by *oratio recta*, although εἰπόντος was occasionally used to introduce *oratio recta* in first-century *commentarii*.[29] The first speech of a speaker is often accompanied by some sort of description of that speaker. The Gospel writers could hardly have chosen a more diverse or more improbable group of leading verbs to introduce their *orationes rectae*; to use any verb of saying at all is nonstandard for the first century. John does show a definite preference for λέγει and λέγοντες, but, to my knowledge, neither verb form is ever used to introduce *oratio recta* in any of the extant *commentarii* from any period.[30] Moreover, the Gospel writers frequently use two verbs of saying concurrently, e.g., ἀποκριθεὶς ἔλεγεν and ἔκραζον λέγοντες. Such concurrent use is not employed in the *commentarii*.

A specific example that we will notice briefly is Mark 15:4: ὁ δὲ Πιλᾶτος πάλιν ἐπηρώτα αὐτὸν λέγων· [*oratio recta*]. Copulative phrases such as ὁ δέ, or even καί connecting the flow of action, and adverbs such as πάλιν and οὕτως are not found in the introductory clauses to *oratio recta* in the *commentarii*; the style is terse and far removed from literary pretense. The accusative of addressee, here ἐπηρώτα αὐτόν, is to my knowledge never used in the *commentarii*. Moreover, ἐπηρώτα is not a leading verb used in the *commentarii*, and the combination with the participle λέγων is even more improbable.

Κρίσις

The Gospels give Pilate's judgment as follows:

Matt 27:26: Τότε ἀπέλυσεν αὐτοῖς τὸν Βαραββᾶν, τὸν δὲ Ἰησοῦν φραγελλώσας παρέδωκεν ἵνα σταυρωθῇ.

Mark 15:15: Ὁ δὲ Πιλᾶτος βουλόμενος τῷ ὄχλῳ τὸ ἱκανὸν ποιῆσαι ἀπέλυσεν αὐτοῖς τὸν Βαραββᾶν, καὶ παρέδωκεν τὸν Ἰησοῦν φραγελλώσας ἵνα σταυρωθῇ.

29 E.g., in *SB* 9050 (after 114; *commentarii* from 100 and 114).
30 Λέγοντος is seldom used as a leading verb in *commentarii*. See, e.g., *SB* 9050 (after 114; *commentarius* from 114 CE).

Luke 23:24–25:   Καὶ Πιλᾶτος ἐπέκρινεν γενέσθαι τὸ αἴτημα αὐτῶν·
                  ἀπέλυσεν δὲ τὸν διὰ στάσιν καὶ φόνον βεβλημένον εἰς
                  φυλακὴν ὃν ᾐτοῦντο, τὸν δὲ Ἰησοῦν παρέδωκεν τῷ
                  θελήματι αὐτῶν.

John 19:16:   Τότε οὖν παρέδωκεν αὐτὸν αὐτοῖς ἵνα σταυρωθῇ.

None of these sentences is in *commentarius*-form. The copulas τότε, ὁ δέ, and καί would not occur in the κρίσις of a *commentarius*. When the κρίσις is given in narrative form, the magistrate's judgment is simply stated, without histrionics or revelation of motive or intent.

The question of why Jesus' trial assumes the forms it does in the Gospel accounts will be studiously avoided here. Likewise avoided is any attempt to relate the forms of the trials of Eleazar and the seven brothers given in 2 Macc 5–15 and 4 Macc 6–7 to any of the *acta Christianorum*, important as the association may in fact be. It was only at a late point in the research for this study that the *Acts of Peter* and *Acts of Paul and Thecla* were added to the tabular analysis above. However, the relationship of those acts to each other and to the "canonical" *acta Christianorum* pose many intriguing questions, although any attempt to explore those relationships will have to wait for a subsequent study. Nevertheless, it may here be observed, before proceeding to the *Acts of Justin*, that although the *Acts of Peter* (which show no influence of *commentarius*-form) have been used by the *Acts of Paul*, the form given to Paul's and Thecla's trials in the *Acts of Paul and Thecla* (see the tabular analysis above) has almost certainly been influenced by *commentarius*-form.

5

The Acts of Justin Martyr

The *Acts of Justin* have long enjoyed a privileged position among the so-called authentic *acta Christianorum* and are perhaps the best of the Christian *acta* upon which to demonstrate our form-critical methodology.[1] Scholars have long accepted the *Acts of Justin* as based upon the *commentarius* from the trial of Justin Martyr and six of his students before Q. Iunius Rusticus, the *praefectus urbi* from 163 to 168 CE.[2] Typical is the opinion of Otto Bardenhewer: "Apart from the beginning and the end, these brief acts, apparently unknown to Eusebius, are a copy of the official records."[3] Likewise Johannes Quasten: "These acts are very valuable, because they contain the official court proceedings."[4] Of similar opinions are Rudolf Freudenberger,[5] Adolf

---

[1] This chapter is a reworking of my earlier study, "The Acts of Justin Martyr: A Form-Critical Study," *Second Century* 3 (1983) 129–57.

[2] On Rusticus see George H. Williams, "Justin Glimpsed as Martyr among His Roman Contemporaries," in Alexander J. McKelway and E. David Willis, eds., *The Context of Contemporary Theology: Essays in Honor of Paul Lehmann* (Atlanta: John Knox, 1974) 109–12; and Rudolf Freudenberger, "Die Acta Justini als historisches Dokument," in Karlmann Beyschlag, et al., eds., *Humanitas-Christianitas: Walter v. Loewenich zum 65 Geburtstag* (Witten: Luther, 1968) 25.

[3] Bardenhewer, *Patrologie* (Freiburg: Herder, 1901) 201.

[4] Quasten, *Patrology* (3 vols.; Utrecht-Antwerp: Spectrum, 1975) 1. 178.

[5] "Die Redaktion dieser Akten in ihrer ältesten Form stammt zwar auch schon aus der Zeit nach dem Frieden zwischen Staat und Kirche, sie ist aber vom älteren Corpus, der protokollartigen Wiedergabe des Verhörs, leicht abzulösen, Überschrift, Einleitung (Kap 1) und Epilog (Kap 6) geben sich durch ihre Terminologie, bes. durch die Wendung 'hoi hagioi martyres' als Erzeugnisse des 4. Jahrhunderts zu erkennen" (Freudenberger, "Acta Justini," 24).

von Harnack,[6] and Hippolyte Delehaye.[7] Scholars have accepted the *Acts of Justin* as essentially a copy of the *commentarius* primarily because their methodologies have led to that conclusion. However, as will be seen below, when historical and text criticism are supplemented by form and redaction criticism, we find that the *Acts of Justin* are not simply a copy of the *commentarius* with a prologue and epilogue attached; these acts have been edited throughout.

Moreover, there are three distinct recensions of these *acta*. Scholars have placed the *Acts of Justin* in the category "authentic," but which recension is authentic, or most authentic? But before this question can be answered, a prior question must be answered: Are any of these recensions in fact verbatim extracts of, or ultimately derived from, the *commentarius*? Form criticism is better suited to answering this question than is historical criticism, for how can it be known that an account is an authentic copy until it is known what an authentic account looked like? The question sounds ridiculous, but scholars have long assumed, without proving, that these acts are a copy of the *commentarius* with a prologue and epilogue attached. The assumption, as has been indicated, is mistaken. Lazzati was closer to the truth when he concluded that we cannot reconstruct the original text of any *commentarius* from our extant acts.[8] However, a thorough comparison of the *acta* with *commentarii* will prove instructive for a knowledge of what should, could, and could not have been in the original text. In turn, this will tell us in what ways the earliest redactor(s) is likely to have edited the text.

The text-critical studies of Franchi de' Cavalieri,[9] F. C. Burkitt,[10] and Giuseppe Lazzati[11] were able to separate the manuscripts into the three recensions of the *Acts of Justin*, now commonly known as A (short), B (middle), and C (long).[12] The precise textual relationship between the recensions, and especially between A and B, has proven to be a more difficult puzzle to solve. Employing the method that "the most ancient text is the most brief

---

[6] "[The acts] bear the stamp of authenticity, one must say, and certainly almost every word rests upon the protocol of the trial" (Harnack, *Geschichte der altchristlichen Literatur bis Eusebius* [3 vols.; Leipzig: Hinrichs, 1958] 2/1. 282 n. 2).

[7] Delehaye (*Les passions des Martyrs*, 87) states that the value of the *Acts of Justin* has never been seriously contested.

[8] Lazzati, *Gli sviluppi della letteratura sui martiri*, 91–92.

[9] "Note agiografiche," *Studi e Testi* 8 (1902) 33–36.

[10] "The Oldest MS of St Justin's Martyrdom," *JTS* 11 (1909) 61–66.

[11] "Atti di S. Giustino," 473–97.

[12] Texts and translations of the three recensions may be found in Musurillo, *Christian Martyrs*, 42–61. The codices of A and B are as follows: Recension A: P = Codex Parisinus graecus 1470 (890 CE). Recension B: C = Codex Cantabrigiensis add. 4489 (8th/9th cen.); H = Codex Hierosolymitanus sancti Sepulchri 6 (9th/10th cen.); V = Codex Vaticanus graecus 1667 (10th cen.) and its copy Vaticanus graecus 655 (16th cen.).

and in it the literary elaboration is minimal," and maintaining that there was an "absence of every element of parenetical character" in recension A, Lazzati concluded that the general relationship of the three recensions was as follows:

> The first text [rec. A], the most ancient, goes back to a period of peace, as one may conclude from the beginning, but which could also be placed, and probably is placed, before the conclusion of the persecutions; the second text [rec. B], a reworking of the first, is probably of the fourth century; the third text [rec. C] is later, perhaps much later, even than the fourth century.[13]

Musurillo was less certain about the relationship between A and B than was Lazzati:

> Although the relationship between the shorter and the middle versions is still not completely clear, it would seem more likely that the middle version does indeed derive from the tradition of the shorter one.[14]

Recension C, the longest of the three, is without doubt much later than A and B, and the present chapter will treat it only in passing.

Analysis of Recensions A and B

Caput

If the *Acts of Justin* were a verbatim copy of the *commentarius,* we would expect to find something like the following as the *caput*:

> From the *commentarii* of Q. Iunius Rusticus, prefect of the city (of Rome), year 5 (?) of Antoninus and Verus the lords Augusti, (month, day), were arraigned (names and probably brief descriptions of the defendants).

Instead, we find the following:

Rec. A:
Μαρτύριον τῶν Ἁγίων Ἰουστίνου, Χαρίτωνος,
Χαριτοῦς, Εὐελπίστου, Ἱέρακος, Παίονος, Λιβεριανοῦ,
καὶ τῆς Συνοδίας αὐτῶν.

---

[13] Lazzati, *Gli sviluppi della letteratura sui martiri*, 119.
[14] Musurillo, *Christian Martyrs*, xviii.

Ἐν τῷ καιρῷ τῶν ἀνόμων προσταγμάτων τῆς εἰδωλολατρείας συλληφθέντες οἱ μνημονευθέντες ἅγιοι εἰσήχθησαν πρὸς τὸν τῆς Ῥώμης
ἔπαρχον Ῥούστικον.

The Martyrdom of Saints Justin, Chariton,
Charito, Euelpistus, Hierax, Paeon, Liberian,
and their Community.

In the time of the lawless commands of idolatry, the aforementioned
saints were arrested and arraigned before Rusticus, the urban prefect of
Rome.

Rec. B:

Μαρτύριον τῶν Ἁγίων Μαρτύρων Ἰουστίνου, Χαρίτονος,
Χαριτοῦς, Εὐελπίστου, Ἱέρακος, Παίονος, καὶ Λιβεριανοῦ.

Ἐν τῷ καιρῷ τῶν ἀνόμων ὑπερμάχων τῆς εἰδωλολατρείας προστά-
γματα ἀσεβῆ κατὰ τῶν εὐσεβούντων Χριστιανῶν κατὰ πόλιν καὶ
χώραν ἐξετίθετο, ὥστε αὐτοὺς ἀναγκάζεσθαι σπένδειν τοῖς ματαίοις
εἰδώλοις. συλληφθέντες οὖν οἱ μνημονευθέντες ἅγιοι ἄνδρες εἰσήχθησαν πρὸς τὸν τῆς Ῥώμην ἔπαρχον ὀνόματι Ῥούστικον.

The Martyrdom of the Holy Martyrs Justin, Chariton,
Charito, Evelpistus, Hierax, Paeon, and Liberian.

In the time of the lawless defenders of idolatry, impious commands were
posted publicly against the pious Christians in town and country alike, so
as to force them to pour libations to the empty idols. Therefore, the
aforementioned saints were arrested and arraigned before the urban prefect of Rome, who was named Rusticus.

The period to which one dates these introductions is important, but
difficult to determine with any certainty. To whatever date one assigns the
earlier introduction, so too will a title be dated, since the reference
"aforementioned" in the introductions must refer to a title containing the
martyrs' names. This, in turn, is important as possible evidence for the date
at which Justin and his companions were regarded as "holy martyrs," and
we should not assume that "holy martyrs" must date to the fourth or
succeeding centuries. The possibility must not be ruled out, moreover, that
"holy martyrs" is a later interpolation to an earlier, no longer extant, form of
the titles.

Scholars have long thought that B's preface must derive from the period
after the Decian persecution ca. 251 CE, which was the first empirewide persecution directed specifically against the Christians. This conclusion is based
principally on the assumption that there is no evidence of "impious commands posted publicly against the pious Christians in town and country
alike" before Decius. The introductions to A and B may date to the fourth
century, but there are difficulties with such a late date.

First of all, after the Constantinian victory, Christian editors laid increasing emphasis upon the sufferings of the martyrs and less emphasis on the dialogue. What dialogue that remained tended towards *oratio obliqua* and narrative, and away from *oratio recta*. These tendencies are lacking in both A and B. Moreover, as we shall see below, the date of the martyrdom is lacking in A and B—interpolated in C—and this would be remarkable if fourth-century editors had been responsible for the interpolated introductions. Perhaps a case can be made for a date during the peace that preceded the Decian persecution.

To begin with, Paul Keresztes has argued that the troubled years of plague and impending war ca. 167 may have resulted in an edict for empirewide sacrifice intended to restore the *pax deorum*.[15] Such an edict, if in fact one was issued, would not have been directed specifically at the Christians, but they would have felt it so. The martyr mentality was one that intensely desired and believed that the "prophecies" of Matthew 10 would come true in the present. The fact is that no matter how much the apologists denied it, the martyr mentality was often guilty of treason, for it regarded the Roman Empire as Satan's puppet, and accordingly many of the Christians actively sought to tear it down, even if it meant throwing themselves headlong into the machinery of the empire.

B's reading need not refer to a universal edict, however. As Mason Hammond has observed, under Antoninus and Marcus, "generally so mild and humane, the policy of persecuting the Christians seems first to have become widespread and the failure to offer sacrifice to the emperor's statue, used sporadically as a test since Pliny's day, to have become a regular test for disloyalty which exposed recalcitrants to prosecution for treason."[16] It is certainly the sacrifice test to which the "impious commands" refer. As Hammond indicates, governors such as Pliny employed the sacrifice test to determine the loyalty of a person accused or suspected of treason. Local magistrates had considerable powers for the purpose of keeping the peace—powers which seem to have included *ius gladii*.[17] In short, B's reading may refer to the command to sacrifice issued in a province by a governor, and not a universal edict of the emperors.

Justin was tried in Rome, however, and here the emperor's oversight of the city and its environs was primarily the responsibility of the *praefectus urbi*.[18] As prefect of the city, Rusticus had the *imperium,* and there can be little doubt that he exercised it whenever he thought Marcus's welfare was at

[15] Keresztes, "Marcus Aurelius a Persecutor?" *HTR* 61 (1968) 321 _41.

[16] Hammond, *Antonine Monarchy*, 211.

[17] See Garnsey, "Criminal Jurisdiction," 51 – 59.

[18] The *praefectus urbi* had a 100-mile jurisdiction; see Jones, *Criminal Courts*, 95.

stake. Marcus Aurelius greatly admired his Stoic tutor, Rusticus, as can be seen from his encomium to him in the *Meditations* (1.7). M. Cornelius Fronto wrote to Marcus that Rusticus "would gladly surrender and sacrifice his life for your little finger."[19] That Rusticus might perceive Justin's teaching to be a threat to the emperor and empire is not difficult to imagine.

Many scholars, however, point to the hatred that the Cynic philosopher Crescens had for Justin, which, it is thought, resulted in Crescens' accusing Justin before the magistrate.[20] Under the *cognitiones extraordinaria*, a trial could result from any charge that the magistrate felt was worth prosecuting: *maiestas, flagitia, illicita collegia*, or some equally vague crime. Crescens may be Justin's *delator*, but it is also possible that Justin landed in court as a result of a refusal to sacrifice to the emperors and the gods.

Whatever the exact historical situation, the sacrifice test is required of the Christians in both recensions, A 5.6 and B 5.4 and 5.8. These sections of the acts are regarded by scholars as deriving from the *commentarius* and not as later interpolations. The additional phrase of B's introduction ("posted publicly") indicates that B's editor had a more heightened sense of the cosmic battle / earthly battle between *Christus victor* / *Chrisitanus victor* and Satan / Roman Empire than did A's editor. This does not necessarily indicate a date much later than recension A: a Tatian or a Tertullian would have written in terms equally as strong as B's.

In any case, B's introduction is later than A's. Both introductions obviously derive from a period of peace, perhaps to the post-Constantinian peace, perhaps to the period of sporadic, local persecution preceding the Decian persecution. The syntax of A's reference to Rusticus, τὸν τῆς Ῥώμης ἔπαρχον Ῥούστικον, indicates an early date when readers might still remember Rusticus. The addition of ὀνόματι in B indicates a later date when readers no longer would remember him. The textual similarities of the introductions show that either B is derived from A or that both A and B are descended from a prototype no longer extant; A's introduction cannot have derived from B's.

Neither recension A nor B give a date for the martyrdom—not in the introductory formulae, which are missing, nor in the appended epilogue. Recension C gives the date as 1 June in the epilogue, but this is far from historically certain: the traditional celebration dates for Justin's martyrdom are 1 June (Greek and Maronite); 13 April (Roman); 31 March and 11 August

---

[19] Marcus Cornelius Fronto *Correspondence* 2. 37.

[20] Justin *2 Apology* 3; Tatian *Address to the Greeks* 19; but see Abraham J. Malherbe, "Justin and Crescens," in Everett Ferguson, ed., *Christian Teaching: Studies in Honor of LeMoine Lewis* (Abilene, TX: Abilene Christian University Bookstore, 1981) 312–27.

(Coptic).[21] It appears that the earliest editors of the *Acts of Justin* were not concerned with the yearly commemoration of Justin's martyrdom, at least not in the sense understood from the mid-third century on. If they had been thus concerned, they would have dutifully recorded the day and month of the event. Plutarch's account of Cato the Younger's suicide shows Cato reading Plato's *Phaedo* (*Cato* 66–71)—a genre similar in many respects to the *Acts of Justin*—as a preparation for death.[22] Even the uneducated Christian would have known something about pagan ideology/theology regarding philosophers' suicides and the deaths of heroes and gods, and especially is this so in the social context of the Second Sophistic.[23] As is well known, the second-century Empire showed a marked predilection for antiquity and archaism. Atticists looked back to the Athens of the fifth century BCE, and there towered the figure of Socrates. The influence of Socrates—that is, of Plato's *Apologia*, *Crito*, and *Phaedo* in addition to popular stories about Socrates—upon Christian martyrology cannot be doubted.[24] Perhaps Tatian or another of Justin's students has written a *Phaedo* (i.e., the *Acts of Justin*) for his own "Socrates."

With regard to form, the *Acts of Justin* bears many more similarities to the *commentarii* than they do to the philosophical *exitus*-literature. The earliest editors of the *Acts of Justin*, however, seem to have shared common concerns with Plato and the Stoics in their desire to record the *ultima verba* of their teachers and philosophical exemplars and in their demonstration that death, even by suicide, was preferable to compromising one's philosophy or religion. In these things the *Acts of Justin* share more in common with the *exitus*-literature than they do with other acts of the martyrs, whose concerns are more to demonstrate the "glorious" deaths of the martyrs and to record the day and month of their deaths in order that their commemorations might be celebrated by the church.

[21] On the problem of the date, see Grant, *Eusebius*, 115.

[22] See Ramsay MacMullen, *Enemies of the Roman Order: Treason, Unrest, and Alienation in the Empire* (Cambridge, MA: Harvard University Press, 1966) 46–94; Manlio Simonetti, "Qualche osservazione a propositio dell'origine degli Atti dei martiri," *REA* 2 (1956) 39–57.

[23] On the Second Sophistic see G. W. Bowersock, *Greek Sophists in the Roman Empire* (Oxford: Clarendon, 1969); and Albin Lesky, *A History of Greek Literature* (New York: Crowell, 1966) 827–59.

[24] See, e.g., Ernst Benz, "Christus und Sokrates in der alten Kirche (Ein Beitrag zum altkirchlichen Verständnis des Märtyrers und des Martyriums)" *ZNW* 43 (1950/51) 195–223.

Body of the Trial

The body of the trial, the reader will recall, comprises everything between the introductory formulae and the judgment of the presiding magistrate. Following the prologues quoted above, recensions A and B continue with Rusticus's first question and Justin's answer:

Rec. A	Rec. B
2.1 Ὧν εἰσαχθέντων	2.1 Ὧν εἰσαχθέντων πρὸ τοῦ βήματος Ῥούστικος
ὁ ἔπαρχος Ἰουστίνῳ εἶπεν· τίνα βίον βιοῖς;	ἔπαρχος εἶπεν πρὸς Ἰουστῖνος· Πρῶτον πείσθητι τοῖ θεοῖς καὶ ὑπάκουσον τοῖς βασιλεῦσιν.
2.2 Ἰουστῖνος εἶπεν· Ἄμεμπτον καὶ ἀκατάγνωστον πᾶσιν ἀνθρώποις.	2.2 Ἰουστῖνος εἶπεν· Ἄμεμπτον καὶ ἀκατάγνωστον τὸ πείθεσθαι τοῖς προσταχθεῖσιν ὑπὸ τοῦ σωτῆρος ὑμῶν Ἰησοῦ Χριστοῦ.
2.1 After they had been arraigned, the prefect said to Justin "What sort of life do you lead?"	2.1 After they had been arraigned before the tribunal, Rusticus the prefect said to Justin: "First of all, you must obey the gods and submit to the emperors."
2.2 Justin said: "Blameless and without condemnation before all men."	2.2 Justin said: "Blameless and without condemnation is the obedience to the commands of our savior Jesus Christ."

At first glance, it would seem that the original redactor inserted the clause "After they had been arraigned" to form a bridge to the *oratio recta* between Rusticus and the martyrs, and that at a later date the prepositional phrase "before the tribunal" had been added by B's redactor to establish the setting. However, the genitive absolute ὧν εἰσαχθέντων, or the like, is very true to the *commentarius*-form.[25] This indicates a possibility that A's reading is authentic. But judging strictly from the *commentarii,* B's addition πρὸ τοῦ βήματος ("before the tribunal") may also be authentic, since the place of the trial is usually indicated, and the phrase "before the tribunal" is one such

[25] See, e.g., *P. Ryl.* 75 (late 2d cen.); *P. Teb.* 287 (161–69 CE); *P. Oxy.* 40 (2d cen.); and *P. Fouad* 23 (144 CE).

indication found in the *commentarii*.[26] Hence there are two possible explanations for the relationship between ὧν εἰσαχθέντων (A 2.1) and ὧν εἰσαχθέντων πρὸ τοῦ βήματος (B 2.1): (1) B is an interpolation of A that mimicked *commentarius*-style, or (2) A and B are independently derived from a prototype, possibly being the *commentarius* itself.

We turn now to a thorny problem, namely, that Rusticus opened the trial with a question in A and a demand in B. Musurillo suggested that Rusticus's question "What sort of life do you lead?" (Rec. A) may have been "intended to allow the philosopher a loophole from which to escape the ultimate penalty, which hinges finally on the martyrs' refusal to offer sacrifice."[27] This is possible, perhaps, but I find this doubtful, since the only "loophole" Rusticus would have allowed was a demonstration of loyalty, that is, performance of the sacrifice.

In attempting to answer whether A's question or B's demand is the more original, it must be recognized that neither the *commentarii* nor a knowledge of Roman criminal law will provide much assistance. As indicated in Chapter One, Roman criminal law, in stark contrast to civil law, was a vague and never systematically defined entity. The *cognitio extra ordinem* of the empire was conducted before a single magistrate, normally a prefect, without a jury or prescribed *cursus*. The course of the trial, the questions asked, and the judgments or punishments delivered were normally determined solely by the presiding magistrate, although magistrates often did attempt to follow legal precedent.[28]

In pre-Decian acts of the martyrs, trials are normally opened with one of two concerns:

1) a demand to sacrifice/swear allegiance to the emperors and the gods: *Martyrdom of Polycarp* 9.2; *Martyrdom of Carpus* 2 (Latin recension); *Acts of Justin* (B 2.1; C 1.4); *Martyrdom of Ignatius* 2; *Acts of Phocas* 3(?); *Acts of the Scillitan Martyrs* 2(?); *Martyrdom of Perpetua* 6.3; *Martyrdom of Pionius* 3.2(?);

[26] See, e.g., *SB* 7601 (12 July 135); *P. Strass.* 179 (176–80 CE); and *P. Ryl.* 77 (192 CE). For examples of other indications of place in *commentarii*, see Chapter Two above. The phrase πρὸ τοῦ βήματος in B does not seem to be an editorial imitation of the Gospels or Acts, which do not use the preposition πρό to modify βήματος (ἐπὶ βήματος: John 19:13; ἐπὶ τοῦ βήματος: Matt 27:19, Acts 12:21, and 18:12; ἀπὸ τοῦ βήματος: Acts 18:16; ἔμπροσθεν βήματος Acts 18:17). Neither *imitatio Christi* nor *imitatio Pauli* were on the editors' minds when they wrote the *Acts of Justin*; imitation of Socrates, perhaps.

[27] Musurillo, *Christian Martyrs*, xix; cf. Luigi Franco Pizzolato, "Christianesimo e mondo in tre passiones dell' età degli Antonini," *Studia Patavina* 23 (1976) 515.

[28] As, e.g., it is to be seen in the famous letter of Pliny to Trajan regarding the prosecution and punishment of Christians (Pliny *Ep.* 10.96). On this letter, see esp. E. J. Bickermann, "Trajan, Hadrian and the Christians," *RivFil* 96 (1968) 290–315.

2) the question "Are you a Christian?": *Martyrdom of Ptolemaeus* 12; *Martyrs of Lyons* 1.8 – 10; *Martyrdom of Apollonius* 1; *Acts of Eugenia* 14(?). Exceptions: "What is your name?" (*Martyrdom of Carpus* 2, Greek recension); "What sort of life do you lead?" (*Acts of Justin*, A 2.1).

In many of the post-Decian acts, the magistrate's first utterance is "What is your name?" (e.g., *Martyrdom of Conon*; *Acts of Maximilian*; *Martyrdom of Julius the Veteran*; *Martyrdom of Dasius*) and not a command to perform sacrifice. In sum, how a trial began was determined by the individual magistrate, and no strong argument can be made for the priority of one opening against another opening.

In the case of the *Acts of Justin*, it would be essential to know how Justin landed in court before arguing for the priority of Rusticus's opening question in Rec. A. The nature of the charge in A is less certain than in B, where it is apparently refusal to sacrifice that has brought Justin to trial. Almost certainly Rusticus had been advised of the charges against Justin and his companions and had consulted with his *consilium* regarding the charges and legal precedent. If these charges originated with a *delator*, such as Crescens, they will not have been "refusal to sacrifice," but "Justin is a Christian" or "Justin commits treason against the emperors and the gods," etc. A scribe might have preceded Rusticus's opening question in A with μεθ᾽ ἕτερα or a genitive absolute that summarized Rusticus's consultation with the *consilium*.

Rusticus's vague question "What sort of life do you lead?" (Rec. A) may be a euphemism for a question that Pliny seems to have asked, namely, "Do you Christians practice Thyestean banquets and Oedipean intercourse as is charged?" It may be an editorial, apologetic device leading to Justin's answer. Rusticus's belligerent attitude in B, however, would not be unexpected of this Stoic prefect. The government made repeated attempts to dissuade Christians from their fanatic drive to "commit suicide," and the Rusticus of B may merely be expressing his disdain for the *contumacia* or *parataxis* of the Christians.[29] But we cannot analyze Rusticus's personality: the texts must suffice.

As presented above, no strong argument can be made for the priority of A 2.1 over against B 2.1 based upon historical criticism. Redaction criticism, however, may provide a solution. In Justin's answer (2.2), the presence of ἄμεμπτον καὶ ἀκατάγνωστον in both A and B makes it certain that they are related to each other or to a prototype. Whether B's longer reading is the *lectio difficilior* is arguable. It is rather the literary structure of B that is suspicious. B's editor has apparently restructured Rusticus's question as a demand in order to heighten the "we-they" perspective of the martyr church.

---

[29] See Anthony Birley, *Marcus Aurelius* (Boston: Little, Brown, 1966) 210.

The "mirroring" of πείσθητι (B 2.1) with πείθεσθαι (B 2.2) and προσ-τάγματα (B 1.1) with προσταχθεῖσιν (B 2.2) give B an enhanced literary color that is lacking in A. These repetitions coupled with Rusticus's demand and the later interpolation πανάθλιε ("wretched fellow"; B 2.4) are structured specifically to heighten the antipathy between the martyrs and the magistrate, between the forces of God and those of Rome, Satan's puppet. Thus it is probably safe to assume that B 2.1–2 is later than A 2.1–2 and that B is derived from A or a prototype.

Before proceeding further in the texts, there are two elements of general commentarius-form that should be discussed, namely, descriptions of speakers and verbs introducing oratio recta.

Descriptions of Speakers

In the commentarii a distinction is usually made between the description of defendants, advocates, witnesses, etc., and that of the presiding magistrate. On their first appearance, the former commonly have identifying details added to their names. Subsequent speeches are merely introduced by the speaker's name alone or name plus introductory verb. In the Acts of Justin, however, the Christians are introduced from the outset by name and verb only, without descriptive references. The absence of any such descriptive materials indicates that either the court scribe decided to forego such descriptions or that a Christian editor omitted such references. The latter is more probable, since the Christian community would have found such descriptive material either superfluous or offensive, depending upon that of which such descriptions consisted. On the other hand, the speeches of the martyrs in recensions A and B are never introduced by "the saint said" or by the addition of "saint" to the martyr's name, as is the case, for example, in recension C and in the later recensions of the Acts of the Scillitan Martyrs. The two phenomena—absence of both descriptions and "saint"—when taken together probably indicate editing at a rather early date.

In the commentarii the names and titles of the presiding magistrate are normally given in the introductory formulae. Any orationes rectae of the magistrate are thereafter introduced by either his name or title, but not by both.[30] The magistrate is introduced by title-formula throughout a commen-

---

[30] Cf. Delehaye: "The name of the magistrate is followed by his title, which is repeated each time throughout. . . . The names of the accused are not accompanied by any qualification" (Les Passions des martyrs, 126–27). This conclusion is true of the fourth-century acta Christianorum but not of late second-century commentarii.

tarius for the first time ca. 232 CE.[31]
In the *Acts of Justin*, the prefect is introduced thus:

	Rec. A	Rec. B
ὁ ἔπαρχος	2 times	1 time
Ῥούστικος	4 times	1 time
Ῥούστικος ἔπαρχος	14 times	19 times

Although the figures for B indicate a greater degree of revision than A, A's predominant use of the name and title throughout must also arouse our suspicions. If we assume derivation from a *commentarius*, have Christian editors after 232 CE harmonized the form with current scribal style? If so, this may indicate that the "period of peace" during which the introductions were written was post-Decian rather than pre-Decian, or that the acts have been edited during both periods.

Introductory Verbs

As indicated in Chapter Two, a study of verbs introducing *oratio recta* proves particularly helpful in a form-critical approach to the *acta Christianorum*. To summarize briefly the relevant material there, in the *commentarii* dating before 135 CE, *orationes rectae* were introduced directly with no verb of saying. Between 135 and 234 CE the vast majority of *commentarii* introduce *orationes rectae* by εἶπεν and its antithesis ἀπεκρίνατο; a few *commentarii* still employ the direct introduction during this period. From 234 CE on scribes consistently use the abbreviations εἶπ and ἀπεκρ instead of εἶπεν and ἀπεκρίνατο. What is to be noticed is that if a scribe chose εἶπεν to introduce *oratio recta*, he consistently used that expression throughout the *commentarius*. In the *acta Christianorum*, however, such consistency is usually lacking, as can be seen from the pre-Decian accounts tabulated.

By comparison with the inconsistency found in recension C and in the *Martyrdom of Polycarp*, recensions A and B fare rather well. But the monotonous repetition of εἶπεν would have been easily mimicked by the Christians, and caution must be used when constructing arguments from the consistent use of εἶπεν in a martyr account. However, when two or more recensions are extant and one or more of these recensions is dominated by one form of introductory verb, those speeches that are introduced by exceptional forms are rendered suspect. Recension C of the *Acts of Justin* is a good example of the extent to which the εἶπεν form could deteriorate through retelling and rewriting. As applied to A and B, recension A (4.8; 5.1) and B (4.8; 5.1) each introduce two speeches by the present tense, λέγει, and in

---

[31] See Appendices 1–3 and Coles, *Reports of Proceedings*, 39.

Introductory Verbs to *Oratio Recta*
in Pre-Decian Acts of the Martyrs

Texts	Direct	εἶπεν	εἶπον	ἔφη	φημί	λέγει	λέγοντος	λέγων	φήσαντος	ἀπεκρίνατο	ἀπεκ. λέγων	ἀπελογήσαντο
Mart. Ignatius	8								1			
Mart. Polycarp Eusebius	1	4		3	1			2	1			
Pseudo-Pionius	1	5		2	1			2	1		1	
Mart. Carpus (Gk Rec.)		17		3		1			1			
Mart. Ptolemaeus and Lucius				2						1		
Acts of Justin Rec. A		37						2		1		
Rec. B		38						2		1	1	
Rec. C	7	4	1	4	3	3						1
Mart. Apollonius		26										

each instance the reading is suspect. Recension B also introduces a speech by a combination of the indicative plus participle: ὁ δὲ ἀπεκρίνατο λέγων (4.8). These speeches will be discussed below.

To return to the texts, from 2.4 on, we need only take note of a few differences between A and B. Especially important among these differences are the creedal statements of A 2.5–7 and B 2.5–7:

Rec. A

2.5 Ῥούστικος ἔπαρχος εἶπεν·
Ποῖόν ἐστι δόγμα; Ἰουστῖνος
εἶπεν· Ὅπερ εὐσεβοῦμεν εἰς
τὸν τῶν Χριστιανῶν θεόν, ὃν
ἡγούμεθα ἕνα τούτων ἐξ ἀρχῆς

δημιουργὸν τῆς
τοῦ παντὸς κόσμου ποιήσεως,

Rec. B

2.5 Ῥούστικος ἔπαρχος εἶπεν·
Ποῖόν ἐστι δόγμα; Ἰουστῖνος
εἶπεν· Ὅπερ εὐσεβοῦμεν εἰς
τὸν τῶν Χριστιανῶν θεόν, ὃν
ἡγούμεθα ἕνα τούτων ἐξ ἀρχῆς
ποιητὴν καὶ
δημιουργὸν τῆς

καὶ
θεοῦ παῖδα Ἰησοῦν Χριστόν,
ὃς καὶ προκεκήρυκται ὑπὸ τῶν
προφητῶν μέλλων παραγίνεσθαι
τῷ γένει τῶν ἀνθρώπων σωτηρίας
κῆρυξ καὶ διδάσκαλος καλῶν
μαθημάτων.
2.6
μικρὰ δὲ
νομίζω λέγειν πρὸς τὴν αὐτοῦ

θεότητα, προφητικήν τινα
δύναμιν ὁμολογῶν,
2.7 ὅτι προκεκήρυκται περὶ
τούτου ὅν ἔφην νῦν υἱὸν θεοῦ
ὄντα. ἴσθι γὰρ ὅτι ἄνωθεν
προεῖπον οἱ προφῆται περὶ τῆς
τούτου ἐν ἀνθρώποις γενομένης
παρουσίας.

2.5 The prefect Rusticus said:
"What belief do you mean?" Justin
said: "The belief that we piously
hold regarding the God
of the Christians,
whom alone we hold to be
craftsman of the whole
world from the beginning,

and also regarding Jesus Christ,
the child of God,
who was foretold by the
prophets as one who was to come
down to mankind as a herald
of salvation and a teacher
of good doctrines.

2.6 What I say is insignificant when
measured against his godhead,
acknowledging the power of prophecy,
2.7 for proclamation has been made
about him whom I have just now
said to be the Son of God. For know
you that in earlier times the prophets
foretold his coming among men."

πάσης κτίσεως, ὁρατῆς τε καὶ
ἀοράτου, καὶ κύριον
Ἰησοῦν Χριστὸν παῖδα θεοῦ,
ὃς καὶ προκεκήρυκται ὑπὸ τῶν
προφητῶν μέλλων παραγίνεσθαι
τῷ γένει τῶν ἀνθρώπον σωτηρίας
κῆρυξ καὶ διδάσκαλος καλῶν
μαθημάτων.
2.6 κἀγὼ ἄνθρωπος ὢν
μικρὰ
νομίζω λέγειν πρὸς τὴν αὐτοῦ
ἄπειρον
θεότητα, προφητικήν τινα
δύναμιν ὁμολογῶν,
2.7 ὅτι προκεκήρυκται περὶ
τούτου ὅν ἔφην νῦν θεοῦ υἱὸν
ὄντα. ἴσθι γὰρ ὅτι ἄνωθεν
προεῖπον οἱ προφῆται περὶ τῆς
τούτου παρουσίας γενομένης
ἐν ἀνθρώποις.

2.5 The prefect Rusticus said:
"What belief do you mean?" Justin
said: "The belief that we piously
hold regarding the God of
of the Christians,
whom alone we believe to have been
the maker and creator of the entire
world from the beginning,
both visible and invisible;
also regarding the Lord Jesus Christ,
the child of God,
who was also foretold by the
prophets as one who was to come
down to mankind as a herald
of salvation and a teacher
of good doctrines.
2.6 Now I, being but a man, realize
that what I say is insignificant when
measured against his infinite godhead,
acknowledging the power of prophecy,
2.7 for proclamation has been made
about him whom I have just now
said to be the Son of God. For know
you that in earlier times the prophets
foretold his coming among men."

According to Musurillo, "Justin's *apologia* seems to belong to an early stage in the development of the tradition, emanating perhaps from Justin's own school or circle. Here it is not always true that the shortest version is necessarily the earliest one."[32] That is, creedal statements are especially susceptible to later editing by those who want to "bring them up to date." Thus a shorter statement might be interpolated to include elements originally not present, as has happened in recension C, where Justin is even made to call Mary θεοτόκος! Longer statements, on the other hand, might be purged of those elements that sounded unorthodox to the later ear.

Concerning the *apologia* of A and B, the first difference to notice is δημιουργὸν τῆς τοῦ παντὸς κόσμου ποιήσεως (A 2.5) and δημιουργὸν τῆς πάσης κτίσεως, ὁρατῆς τε καὶ ἀοράτου (B 2.3). Regarding the latter phrase, Adalbert Hamman has observed:

La comparaison des deux recensions permet de conclure que le *textus receptus*, sous la poussée de l'usage liturgique, a fini par substituer à la formulation primitive et originelle, celle quie se récitait dans le Credo: "créateur ... des choses visibles et invisibles." Le cas est classique. ... L'addition "des choses visibles et invisibles" est suspect, parce qu'elle ne parait dans les symboles qu'au IVᵉ siècle.[33]

"Visible and invisible," of course, is already used in the Christological hymn of Col 1:15–23 and by Ignatius (*Smyrn.* 6.1; *Trall.* 5.2; *Rom.* 5.3), but with a different theological emphasis than the *apologia* of B. During the fourth century, πάντων ὁρατῶν τε καὶ ἀοράτων ποιητήν, or the like, suddenly appears in the *regulae fidei* of Eusebius of Caesarea, Cyril of Jerusalem, Epiphanius, the Niceno-Constantinopolitan creed, the *Apostolic Constitutions*, and others.[34] Certainly "visible and invisible" is an interpolation in B, but it is unlikely to date as late as the fourth century. The theological emphases and wording of both A and B reflect a date earlier than Eusebius and Nicaea. For instance, we would expect πατέρα παντοκράτορα to be interpolated in the fourth century and υἱός to be substituted for the older παῖς. However, the *apologia* of both A and B bear scarcely more resemblance to the many creedal statements found in Justin's writings. Typical of such statements are the following:

[32] Musurillo, *Christian Martyrs*, xix.
[33] Hamman, "La Confession de la foi dans les premiers actes des martyrs," in Jacques Fontaine and Charles Kannengiesser, eds., *Epektasis: Mélanges Patristiques offerts au Cardinal Jean Daniélou* (Paris: Éditions Beauchesne, 1972) 100, 102.
[34] See Philip Schaff, *The Creeds of Christendom* (New York: Harper & Brothers, 1877) 11–39.

Our teacher of these things is Jesus Christ, who also was born for this purpose, and was crucified under Pontius Pilate, procurator of Judaea, in the times of Tiberius Caesar; and that we reasonably worship him, having learned that he is the Son (υἱόν) of the true God himself, and holding him in the second place, and the prophetic Spirit in the third. . . . (*1 Apol.* 13)

For in the name of this very Son of God and first-begotten of all creation (υἱοῦ τοῦ θεοῦ καὶ πρωτοτόκου πάσης κτίσεως), who was born through the virgin and became a man destined to suffer, and was crucified under Pontius Pilate by our people, and died, and rose again from the dead, and ascended into heaven . . . (*Dial.* 85.2)

J. N. D. Kelly observed that "the majority of confessions found in St Justin exhibit the familiar three-clause ground-plan. It is indeed remarkable how deeply the pattern was imprinted on his mind."[35] If Justin did give an *apologia* at his trial, it more likely resembled those quoted above than it did either A or B. In general, the characteristic order, emphases, and brevity of Justin's confessions are lacking or obscured in both A and B.

Moreover, both contain terms and phrases almost certainly not used by Justin. For instance, both recensions use παῖς for "Son" whereas Justin himself invariably used υἱός.[36] Παῖς is at the same time ancient and non-Justinian. Both recensions refer to Jesus as a κῆρυξ, which Justin never did in his extant writings. The use of ποιήσεως (A 2.5) versus ποιητήν (B 2.5) is difficult to assess. On the one hand, ποιητήν is much more characteristic of Justin than is ποιήσεως as a description for God, but as was seen above, ποιητήν is the form most commonly used during the fourth century. It may be that ποιητήν and ὁρατῆς τε καὶ ἀοράτου entered B's text together. But neither παντὸς κόσμου ποιήσεως (A) nor ποιητὴν . . . πάσης κτίσεως (B) is likely to have originated with Justin. In the creedal statements of his writings, Justin describes God's creative role as follows:

1 Apol. 46.5:	τοῦ πατρὸς πάντων καὶ δεσπότου θεοῦ
1 Apol. 58.1:	τὸν ποιητὴν τῶν οὐρανίων καὶ γηΐνων ἁπάντων θεόν
	. . . τὸν δημιουργὸν τὸν πάντων
1 Apol. 61.3:	τοῦ πατρὸς τῶν ὅλων καὶ δεσπότου θεοῦ
1 Apol. 61.10:	τοῦ πατρὸς τῶν ὅλων καὶ δεσπότου θεοῦ
1 Apol. 65.3:	τῷ πατρὶ τῶν ὅλων
1 Apol. 67.2:	τὸν ποιητὴν τῶν πάντων

He rebuked Marcion, who "teaches his disciples to believe in some other

---

35 Kelly, *Early Christian Creeds* (London: Longmans, Green, 1950) 71.
36 E.g., *1 Apol.* 6, 13, 31, 65, 67; *Dial.* 85.

god greater than the creator [τοῦ δημιουργοῦ] . . . and to deny that God is the maker of the universe [τὸν ποιητὴν τοῦδε τοῦ παντὸς θεόν] . . .'' (*1 Apol.* 26.5). It would appear, then, that neither A nor B's description of God very closely resembles Justin's own descriptions.

Even those phrases and emphases found in A and B that are characteristic of Justin are not entirely above suspicion. For example, προκεκήρυκται ὑπὸ τῶν προφητῶν (2.5) is characteristic of Justin,[37] but it is traditional and appears in many *regulae fidei*. Also typical of Justin is his description of Jesus as διδάσκαλος (2.5),[38] but this is modified by καλῶν μαθημάτων, which Justin never does in his extant writings.

The relationship of A 2.5−7 to B 2.5−7 is difficult, if not impossible, to discern precisely. B contains several interpolations absent from A, such as ὁρατῆς τε καὶ ἀοράτου (2.5), κύριον (2.5), and ἄπειρον (2.6), and these indicate a date later than A. However, Rusticus's question, "What belief do you mean?'' may itself be an interpolation that sets up Justin's *apologia*, and in this case, neither *apologia* derives from the trial. If Justin did give an *apologia* at the trial, neither A nor B preserves its probable text; both have been redacted and behind both lies a prototype—or prototypes. Rec. A may be derived from the *commentarius* itself, whether or not the *apologia* as a whole is an interpolation, since the interpolation could originate with A's editor. B may derive from A or from a prototype.

From 2.7 we move to the interesting but perplexing problem of Justin's meeting place:

Rec. A	Rec. B
3.1 Ῥούστικος ἔπαρχος εἶπεν·	3.1 Ῥούστικος ἔπαρχος εἶπεν·
Ποῦ συνέρχεσθε Ἰουστίνος εἶπεν·	Ποῦ συνέρχεσθε Ἰουστίνος εἶπεν·
Ἔνθα ἑκάστῳ προαίρεσις καὶ	Ἔνθα ἑκάστῳ προαίρεσις καὶ
δύναμίς ἐστιν πάντως γὰρ νομίζεις	δύναμίς ἐστιν πάντως γὰρ νομίζεις
κατὰ αὐτὸ	ἐπὶ τὸ αὐτὸ
δυνατὸν	
συνέρχεσθαι ἡμᾶς πάντας	συνέρχεσθαι ἡμᾶς πάντας
	Οὐχ οὕτως δέ, διότι ὁ θεὸς τῶν
	Χριστιανῶν τόπῳ οὐ περιγράφεται,
	ἀλλ᾿ ἀόρατος ὢν τὸν οὐρανὸν
	καὶ τὴν γῆν πληροῖ καὶ πανταχοῦ
	ὑπὸ τῶν πιστῶν προσκυνεῖται
	καὶ δοξάζεται.
3.2 Ῥούστικος ἔπαρχος εἶπεν·	3.2 Ῥούστικος ἔπαρχος εἶπεν·
Εἰπέ, ποῦ συνέρχεσθε, ἢ εἰς	Εἰπέ, ποῦ συνέρχεσθε, ἢ εἰς

[37] E.g., *1 Apol.* 61.10; *Dial.* 78.6; 84.2; 91.4; 106.1.
[38] E.g., *1 Apol.* 6; 13.

τίνα τόπον

3.3 Ἰουστῖνος εἶπεν· Ἐγὼ
ἐπάνω μένω
τοῦ Μυρτίνου
Βαλανείου παρὰ πάντα τὸν
χρόνον ὃν ἐπεδήμησα τὸ δεύτερον
τῇ Ῥωμαίων πόλει· οὐ
γινώσκω δὲ ἄλλην τινα συνέλευσιν
εἰ μὴ τὴν ἐκεῖ. καὶ εἴ
τις ἐβούλετο ἀφικνεῖσθαι παρ᾽
ἐμοί, ἐκοινώνουν αὐτῷ τῶν
τῆς ἀληθείας λόγων.
3.4 Ῥούστικος εἶπεν·
Οὐκοῦν
Χριστιανὸς εἶ Ἰουστῖνος
ἀπεκρίνατο·
Ναί, Χριστιανός εἰμι.

πoῖον τόπον
ἀθροίζεις τοὺς μαθητάς σου

3.3 Ἰουστῖνος εἶπεν· Ἐγὼ
ἐπάνω μένω
τινὸς Μαρτίνου τοῦ Τιμιοτίνου
Βαλανείου καὶ παρὰ πάντα τὸν
χρόνον ὃν ἐπεδήμησα τὸ δεύτερον
τῇ Ῥωμαίων πόλει οὐ
γινώσκω ἄλλην τινα συνέλευσιν
εἰ μὴ τὴν ἐκεῖ. καὶ εἴ
τις ἐβούλετο ἀφικνεῖσθαι παρ᾽
ἐμοί, ἐκοινώνουν αὐτῷ τῶν
τῆς ἀληθείας λόγων.
3.4 Ῥούστικος ἔπαρχος εἶπεν·
Οὐκοῦν λοιπὸν
Χριστιανὸς εἶ Ἰουστῖνος
εἶπεν·
Ναί, Χριστιανός εἰμι.

The prefect Rusticus said,
"Where do you meet?" Justin
said, "Where each decides and
is able. Do you think we all
are able to meet in the same
place?"

The prefect Rusticus said,
"Where do you meet?" Justin
said, "where each decides and
is able. Do you think we all
are able to meet in the same
place? But it is not so, since the God
of the Christians is not circumscribed
by place, but being invisible he fills
heaven and earth and is worshiped and
glorified by the faithful everywhere."

3.2 The prefect Rusticus said,
"Tell me, where do you meet,
in what place?"

3.2 The prefect Rusticus said,
"Tell me, where do you meet,
in what place do you gather together
your disciples?"

3.3 Justin said, "I am staying above
the bath of Myrtinus during the entire
period of this second sojourn in the
city of the Romans; I do not know any
other meeting place but there. And if
anyone wishes to come to me there, I
share with him from the words of
truth. 3.4 Rusticus said, "Are you a
Christian then?"

3.3 Justin said, "I am staying above
the bath of a certain Martinus, son of
Timiotinus, and during the entire
period of this second sojourn in the city
of the Romans I have not known any
other meeting place but there. And if
anyone wishes to come to me there, I
share with him from the words of
truth. 3.4 Rusticus said, "And so you
are a Christian hereafter?"

The difficulty here, for historical interests, involves the difference between
"the bath of Myrtinus" (A) and "the bath of a certain Martinus, son of

Timiotinus'' (B). In a note to recension B, Musurillo remarked that ''the reference to Justin's living quarters here, as in Recension A, seems to be corrupt, and no suggestion has yet been satisfactory.''[39] B's reference to the bath is the *lectio difficilior* but, I would say, not necessarily corrupt. B's editor may have preserved the difficult reading whereas A's editor did not. By the omission, A's editor created another problem: Rusticus's question in A 3.4 is an illogical response to Justin's answer in 3.3. In A Justin tells Rusticus where he has been living, but without any reference to his being a Christian, whereupon Rusticus asks, ''Are you a Christian then?'' In recension B, on the other hand, Justin had referred to the ''God of the Christians'' in 3.1. Moreover, Rusticus's question in B 3.4 makes more sense with the additional word λοιπόν than does A 3.4 without it, since Rusticus no doubt knew that Justin was a Christian before the trial even began. In B he shows concern over whether Justin intends to remain a Christian, which is identical to Pliny's known concern: if they persist in their profession of the name, they will be executed.

A 3.1–4 is obviously corrupt; B 3.1–4 is not. This indicates that either (1) B's editor realized the difficulty in A and attempted to correct it; or (2) B preserves the longer reading of a prototypical account, whereas in the process of abridging the *commentarius* or a prototype, A's editor created an illogical sequence of questions and a garbled reference to Justin's meeting place.

The *oratio recta* between Rusticus and the martyrs in the remainder of the texts is unremarkable, with the exception of Hierax's reply:

Rec. A	Rec. B
4.8 Ῥούστικος ἔπαρχος Ἱέρακι λέγει· Οἱ σοι γονεῖς ποῦ εἰσιν Ἱέραξ εἶπεν·	3.1 Ῥούστικος ἔπαρχος τῷ Ἱέρακι λέγει· Οἱ σοι γονεῖς ποῦ εἰσιν ὁ δὲ ἀπεκρίνατο λέγων· Ὁ ἀληθινὸς ἡμῶν πατήρ ἐστιν ὁ Χριστὸς καὶ μήτηρ ἡ εἰς αὐτὸν πίστις· οἱ δὲ ἐπίγειοί μου γονεῖς
Ἐτελεύτησαν. ἐγὼ δὲ ἀπὸ ἱκανοῦ χρόνου τῆς Φρυγίας ἀπεσπάσθην.	ἐτελεύτησαν, καὶ ἐγὼ ἀπὸ Ἰκονίου τῆς Φρυγίας ἀποσπασθεὶς ἐνθάδε ἐλήλυθα.
The prefect Rusticus says to Hierax: ''Where are your parents?'' Hierax said: ''They are dead. It is a considerable time since I was	The prefect Rusticus says to Hierax: ''Where are your parents?'' and he answered saying: ''Christ is our true father, and our faith in him is our

39 Musurillo, *Christian Martyrs*, 49 n. 8.

dragged off from Phrygia."

mother. My earthly parents have passed away. I came to Rome because I was dragged off from Iconium in Phrygia."

Lazatti and Freudenberger found both A and B suspect here. Certainly Lazatti is correct in recognizing B's ὁ δὲ ἀπεκρίνατο λέγων as a later literary expansion.[40] But Rusticus's question in both recensions is introduced by the present indicative λέγει rather than the aorist εἶπεν as would have been in the *commentarius*. This may be an indication that Rusticus's question itself has been edited.

Freudenberger found the Atticizing phrase τῆς Φρυγίας ἀπεσπάσθην (A) suspect. He also found B suspect because, properly speaking, Iconium was in Lycaonia, not Phrygia; he added, however, that "in phrygischer Sprache bestätigt."[41] His suggestion was that Ἰκονίου was a scribal error for ἱκανοῦ.[42]

B's reference to Christ as father and *pistis* as mother is an interesting problem. Although A's reading is shorter, B's is the *lectio difficilior* and seems an improbable interpolation. To my knowledge, the close connection of Christ as father and *pistis* as mother as stated in B is a *hapax legomenon*. The ἐκκλησία is most frequently the referent of "mother" in patristic literature.[43] However, *pistis* is called mother by Polycarp (*Phil.* 3.2–3), Hermas (*Vis.* 3.8.2–5), Clement of Alexandria (*Strom.* 2.5), Chrysostom (*Serm. on John* 33.1; *Serm. on Rom.* 2.6), and Cyril of Alexandria (*Comm. on John* 11.5).[44] God, of course, is the normal referent of "father." Christ, however, is called father in the *Acts of Thomas* (97), the *Acts of Matthaias* (3), and in Theodoret's *Commentary on Isaiah* (9.5). In Gnostic literature, of course, is found a close association between Christ, or one of his many likenesses, in some sort of fatherly role with Pistis as his female counterpart (*Eugnostos the Blessed* [NHC 3,3] 81.21–82.6).

[40] Lazzati, "Atti di S. Giustino," 483.

[41] Freudenberger, "Acta Justini," 27.

[42] Ibid., 28.

[43] See Joseph C. Plumpe, *Mater Ecclesia: An Inquiry into the Concept of the Church as Mother in Early Christianity* (Washington, D.C.: The Catholic University of America, 1943).

[44] An interesting parallel, shown to me by George H. Williams, is found in Kathleen McVey's translation of "The Life of Severus of Antioch by Robert Bishop of the Arabians": "He [Severus] earnestly desired to receive baptism there and also to become, he, too, a signed one among the lambs of the house of God. For this Mother had still not been acquired by him, because in the country of his people, they used to baptize none except [grown] men" (McVey, "The *memra* on the Life of Severus of Antioch Composed by George, Bishop of the Arab Tribes" [Ph.D. diss., Harvard University, 1977] 95).

Plumpe has shown that Μήτηρ Πίστις was a precedent of Μήτηρ Ἐκκλησία.[45] If B's reading is an interpolation, it is likely to have been an early one. Moreover, the Gnostic sound of Hierax's answer makes it an unlikely interpolation, unless the interpolator had Gnostic inclinations. If this were the case, we would expect other evidences of such inclinations in the account. If we must choose between A and B, priority must be given to A, since Hierax's answer in B is introduced by ὁ δὲ ἀπεκρίνατο λέγων and not εἶπεν. However, in B 5.8 the editor added λέγων to ἀπεφήνατο, apparently feeling that ἀπεφήνατο alone did not properly introduce the *oratio recta* that followed. According to *commentarius*-form, either εἶπεν or ἀπεκρίνατο could introduce Hierax's reply (4.8). It is possible that the text from which B's editor worked had had ἀπεκρίνατο, to which he added λέγων.

Κρίσις

In the *commentarii*, the κρίσις is the most important factor, and often when an earlier *commentarius* is quoted in a later *commentarius*, it is only the κρίσις that is quoted. The judgment may be recorded in *oratio obliqua* or, more often, in *oratio recta* introduced by the magistrate's name or title plus εἶπεν. Notice the κρίσις of the *Acts of Justin:*

Rec. A	Rec. B
5.6 Ῥούστικος ἔπαρχος ἀπεφήνατο·	5.8 Ῥούστικος ἔπαρχος ἀπεφήνατο λέγων·
Οἱ μὴ βουληθέντες ἐπιθῦσαι τοῖς θεοῖς,	Οἱ μὴ βουληθέντες θῦσαι τοῖς θεοῖς καὶ εἶξαι τῷ τοῦ αὐτοκράτορος προστάγματι,
φραγελλωθέντες ἀπαχθήτωσαν	μαστιγωθέντες ἀπαχθήτωσαν, κεφαλικὴν ἀποτιννύντες δίκην
τῇ τῶν νόμων ἀκολουθίᾳ.	κατὰ τὴν τῶν νόμων ἀκολουθίαν.
The prefect Rusticus passed judgment:	The prefect Rusticus passed judgment, saying:
"Those who have refused to sacrifice	"Those who have refused to sacrifice
to the gods, having been scourged, are	to the gods and to yield to the

45 Plumpe, *Mater Ecclesia*, 19.

to be led away in accordance with the laws."

emperor's edict, having been flogged, are to be led away and be beheaded in accordance with the laws."

B is obviously the later of the two readings here. To begin with, αὐτο-κράτορος in the singular is a historical blunder, since Lucius Verus was coemperor until his death in 169. Moreover, B's combination of finite verb plus participle to introduce the judgment would be later than A's finite verb alone. However, according to *commentarius*-form, we should expect the κρίσις to be introduced by εἶπεν or a genitive absolute, although an introduction by ἀπεφήνατο is also possible, as, for example, is found in *P. Oxy.* 706 (ca. 115).

If the text from which B's editor worked was A, or resembled A, it is understandable why he felt the need to interpolate a word or two into the judgment. Musurillo translated the judgment as follows: "Those who have refused to sacrifice to the gods are to be scourged and executed in accordance with the laws."[46] The legal meanings of ἀπάγω are given in LSJ as "bring before a magistrate and accuse" and "carry off to prison," but do not include "execute" among its meanings.[47] G. W. H. Lampe gives "lead away, carry off, met., of death" as a meaning of ἀπάγω.[48] B's editor apparently felt that ἀπαχθήτωσαν was too vague and therefore added that they were led away to be beheaded, making it clear that the martyrs were indeed martyred.

Concluding Matters

Following the κρίσις there is often a sentence or two of concluding matters in the *commentarii*. In some *commentarii* is found the phrase ἐξῆλθεν ὁ δεῖνα ὑπηρέτης, "the (titles and name) went out."[49] In the *Acts of Justin*, the words immediately following the κρίσις are οἱ δὲ ἅγιοι μάρτυρες δοξάζοντες, ἐξελθόντες ... (A 6; B 6.1). Recensions A and B, then, have no concluding section from the *commentarius*, unless ἐξελθόντες is a remnant of ἐξῆλθεν ὁ δεῖνα ὑπηρέτης.

46 Musurillo, *Christian Martyrs*, 47.
47 LSJ, *s.v.* ἀπάγω, IV. 2, 3.
48 Lampe, *A Patristic Greek Lexicon* (Oxford: Clarendon, 1974) *s.v.* ἀπάγω, 1.
49 The precise meaning of this phrase is unclear.

Conclusions

Throughout this chapter I have alluded to the possibility that recension B derives from a prototypical account and not from recension A. In order to prove the existence of such a prototype, it would be necessary to demonstrate conclusively that at least one reading in B is earlier than the corresponding reading of A. The form-critical method we have employed here has led to at least four readings—2.1; 2.5–7; 3.1–4; 4.8—in which a separate, but not necessarily earlier, text tradition can be argued for A and B. Normally, it is preferable to discuss extant texts and not hypothetical ones, and since the *commentarius* itself is no longer extant, a dogmatic answer cannot be given to the question of the textual relationship of A to B. The application of method is often a subjective process, and for this reason I have preferred to present evidence that allows for the formation of individual conclusions. Unless the individual concludes that one of B's readings is earlier than A's, it must be said that B derives from A.

Lazzati dated the editing of recension A "before the conclusion of the persecutions" and recension B "probably to the fourth century."[50] Others, such as Freudenberger, would date the editing of both recensions to the fourth century, based principally upon the wording of the prologues.[51] I have attempted to show that the prologues need not date so late as is commonly assumed and that there are difficulties with dating either recension as late as the fourth century. Especially relevant to this question are the absence of a dramatic date and the early form of the creedal statements. The reference to Rusticus in A's prologue may indicate quite an early date for one editing. The predominant use of Rusticus's title throughout both recensions perhaps indicates another editing ca. the mid-third century, but I would not date the final editing of either A or B beyond the late third century.

It is commonly assumed that the *Acts of Justin* are "a copy of the official records with a prologue and epilogue attached." Clearly this is not so. Both recensions have been edited to a greater or lesser extent throughout. In some respects the *Acts of Justin* still conform to *commentarius* form: the simple *oratio recta* between the prefect and the accused, the general absence of parenetic and eulogistic material, the absence of narrative framework, and the predominant use of εἶπεν as the introductory verb. But in other respects the acts differ from *commentarius* form: the absence of introductory formulae, the absence of an extract phrase, the predominant use of Rusticus's name and title throughout, the absence of descriptive introductions for the accused, speeches introduced by the present indicative and/or participle, the

---

[50] Lazzati, *Gli sviluppi della letteratura sui martiri,* 119.
[51] Freudenberger, "Acta Justini," 24–31.

questionable κρίσις, and the absence of concluding matters. In addition, the non-Justinian *apologia* (2.5–7) and the difficulties involving Rusticus's questions in 2.1 and 4.8 arouse the suspicion that entire sections of the acts have been interpolated or substantially edited. Despite these differences and difficulties, it is probable that the *Acts of Justin* are ultimately derived from the *commentarius* of Justin's trial, but within the so-called "authentic" portion of the acts (the *oratio recta*), no speech manifesting any of these differences or difficulties should be accepted without question as the ipsissima verba of the *commentarius*.

6

The Martyrdom of Polycarp

The *Martyrdom of Polycarp* is an extremely important account, since it is commonly regarded, along with the *Acts of Justin*, as the earliest of the "authentic" *acta Christianorum*, and many theories about the origins of the Christian concepts of martyrdom and related topics are based upon the assumption that it is a historical account. The precise date is important for several reasons. A date during the reign of Antoninus Pius (138–61) rather than during the reign of Marcus Aurelius (161–80) has several ramifications for studies of the persecutions. Whether the *Martyrdom of Polycarp* is earlier than the *Acts of Justin* is important for studies on the origins and development of the genre *acta Christianorum*, since the possibility of influence exists.

The Date of Polycarp's Martyrdom

Much of the secondary literature on the *Martyrdom of Polycarp* has been devoted to ascertaining the precise date of Polycarp's martyrdom. The date has been a topic of hot debate among scholars of the acts. Arguments for the

---

[1] Lightfoot, *Apostolic Fathers*, 1. 629–702; C. H. Turner, "The Day and Year of St. Polycarp's Martyrdom," *Studia Biblica* 2 (1890) 105; Timothy D. Barnes, "A Note on Polycarp," *JTS* 18 (1967) 433–37.

[2] Musurillo, *Christian Martyrs*, xiii. Barnes states ("Pre-Decian *Acta Martyrum*," 512):

"The precise date of Polycarp's death is not easy to determine, although some degree of certainty is attainable if the correct method of inquiry is followed. First, Eusebius must be disregarded. Although he assigns Polycarp's death to the reign of Marcus Aurelius, it

dates 155/56,[1] 157/58 or 158/59,[2] 166/67,[3] and 177 have been given.[4] Musurillo argues,

> If we assume that Ignatius's final passage through Smyrna occurred during the last years of Trajan's reign (when Polycarp was already bishop), it would seem correct to infer that Polycarp's martyrdom at the age of 86 would have taken place close to the last quarter of the second century, but the precise date has been widely controverted. Eusebius (*Hist. eccl.* 15.1) places it in the reign of the Emperor Marcus Aurelius, and most scholars, like H. von Campenhausen, would incline towards 166/7. But the correct solution would seem to hinge on the date of the proconsul mentioned in 21 (if this is to be regarded as historical), L. Statius Quadratus. For if Quadratus is really the man who had been *consul ordinarius* in 142 (*PIR* iii. 640), then it is impossible to believe that twenty-five years had elapsed since his consulate. Thus an earlier date, e.g. 155/6, would seem more plausible.[5]

Grant has perhaps solved the puzzle:

> The next martyr to be discussed [by Eusebius in the *Chronicle*] was the Roman apologist Justin, whose death, dated in 156/7, was ascribed to the plotting of a Cynic named Crescens. Justin had convicted him as a glutton and an impostor. The language comes from the remarks of Justin's disciple Tatian, explicitly quoted in the *Church History* (4.16.9) but obviously known during the composition of the *Chronicle*. In preparing

---

is unlikely that he possessed any reliable evidence, since he also dates the Decian *Passion of Pionius* to the same period. Secondly, chap. 21 of *Martyrdom* must be assessed. It gives two contradictory statements for the year: that Philippus of Tralles was high-priest and that Statius Quadratus was proconsul of Asia. Philippus was high-priest of Asia no later than 149/50, while no conceivable argument could put Quadratus's proconsulate earlier than 153/4. But the notice about Philippus may easily be a mistaken inference from 12.2. Hence the posing of a dilemma points to a definite year. Either the Christians of Smyrna forgot the name of the proconsul who condemned Polycarp, or he was L. Statius Quadratus (*consul ordinarius* in 142). If the former is the case, it becomes difficult to credit any Christian tradition, however early. If the latter, an argument is available from the known careers of Roman senators. In the Antonine age, no man is attested holding one of the senior proconsulates (Asia and Africa) a mere twelve years after his consulate: an interval of thirteen years is very rare, while fourteen appears to be the normal minimum and fifteen and sixteen are common. In the present state of our evidence, therefore, 154/5 is excluded for the proconsular year of Polycarp's death, while 155/6 is possible, and 156/7 perhaps the most probable, Quadratus having been *consul ordinarius*; but there is nothing against 157/8 or even 158/9."

[3] Von Campenhausen, "Bearbeitungen und Interpolationen," 1–3.

[4] H. Grégoire and P. Orgels, "La véritable date du martyre de Polycarpe (23 févr. 177) et le *Corpus Polycarpianum*," AnBoll 69 (1951) 1–38.

[5] Musurillo, *Christian Martyrs*, xiii.

both works Eusebius was aware that he had no reliable account of Justin's martyrdom and had to rely on Tatian. Why the date? Eusebius knew that Justin addressed his *Apology* to Antoninus Pius (4.11.11). When he wrote the *Chronicle* he obviously did not suppose that he addressed another to Marcus Aurelius (Antoninus Verus's, 4.18.2). But there is a good deal of confusion in the *Chronicle*'s dating just at that point. Eusebius seems to have exchanged the true date of Justin's martyrdom for the true date of Polycarp's. In other words, Polycarp should have been set in 156/7, Justin a decade later.[6]

The arguments of Lightfoot, Barnes, Musurillo, and Grant are compelling for the acceptance of a date during the years 155–58 for the martyrdom of Polycarp.

The "Courtroom" of Polycarp's Trial

The setting that is given for Polycarp's trial should give us pause, for it is not a magistrate's tribunal or any other such municipal setting. Rather, the trial is described as a *pro forma* affair within the "stadium" (τὸ στάδιον).[7] This seems improbable for at least two reasons.

First, τὸ στάδιον[8] would most properly denote a race track and not a place of butchery such as was the amphitheater.[9] The stadium was normally a long and open-ended construction, often amounting to little more than race track between two hills upon which spectators sat. A stadium would not have had the high inner walls that an amphitheater possessed to keep wild animals and gladiators from killing spectators. Of course, it was not uncommon during the Empire for criminals to be executed in the amphitheater (τὸ ἀμφιθέατρον).[10] The martyrs of Lyons, who like Polycarp were victims of mob violence,[11] were tried both in the forum (ἀγορά)[12] and before the tribunal

[6] Grant, *Eusebius*, 115.
[7] Eusebius *Hist. eccl.* 4.15.16–17; Ps.-Pionius 8.3.
[8] Whence the measurement *stade* (= 606¾ feet).
[9] Note, however, that ἐν σταδίοις may mean "in the amphitheater" (LSJ, *s.v.* στάδιον).
[10] See Michael Grant, *Gladiators* (Harmondsworth: Penguin Books, 1967); Roland Auguet, *Cruelty and Civilization: The Roman Games* (London: Allen and Unwin); Ludwig Friedländer, *Roman Life and Manners under the Early Empire* (1909; reprinted New York: Barnes & Noble, 1968).
[11] On mob violence during the Empire, see P. A. Brunt, "The Roman Mob," in Finley, ed., *Studies in Ancient Society*, 74–102; and Ramsay MacMullen, *Roman Social Relations 50 B.C. to A.D. 284* (New Haven/London: Yale University, 1974).
[12] Eusebius *Hist. eccl.* 5.1.8.

(βῆμα)[13] before being tortured in prison and "executed" for the crowd's entertainment in the amphitheater.[14] The stadium, on the other hand, is an improbable place for games (*ludi*) that involved death and/or animals; its structure would not have well accommodated such activities.

Second, the stadium is also an improbable place for a trial. In the case of a mob uprising, a proconsul might well have held a mock trial in public to mollify the mob. The ancient mind (and often the modern) perceived disasters in terms of the wrath of the god or gods, who for some reason had taken offense at human actions. Those who were thought to cause divine wrath, the scapegoats and in this instance the Christians, were punished in an attempt to restore the *pax romanum* and *pax deorum*.[15] If there is a historical kernel to the account of Polycarp's execution in public, perhaps it is best to simply understand "amphitheater" for "stadium." As for the trial itself, it seems most probable that the proconsul actually did try Polycarp *pro tribunalis* but afterward held the perfunctory public affair that is described in the *Martyrdom of Polycarp*, which was designed to appease the angry crowd and thereby save his own neck. If this was the case, there would have been a *commentarius* of the trial.

Accuracy of Eusebian Quotations

Many scholars believe that Ps.-Pionius's version of *Martyrdom of Polycarp* preserves the text of the letter thought to have been written shortly after the martyrdom itself. Barnes believes that

> no compelling argument has yet been advanced to demonstrate that chaps. 1–20[16] cannot be what they purport to be—a contemporary letter from the Christians of Smyrna to the church of Philomelium. If genuine, therefore, the *Martyrdom* dates from no more than a few weeks after the death of Polycarp. For it was written in response to a request for a detailed account from the Christians of Philomelium, who seem to have heard vague rumours of what had happened in Smyrna (20.1). . . . H. von Campenhausen has attempted to show that the original letter has been considerably worked over and interpolated. Proof, he claims, is provided by the differences between the manuscript text of the *Martyrdom* [Ps.-Pionius] and the report of it by Eusebius. This is Campenhausen's

[13] Ibid., 5.1.10; 5.1.29.

[14] Ibid., 5.1.51.

[15] The search by historians for the precise legal charge(s) under which Christians were arraigned is futile. In the provinces, local magistrates, and in Rome the *prefectus urbi*, could, under a variety of charges, prosecute any person who threatened the *pax romanum*.

[16] I.e., chaps. 21–22, which are appendices to the letter.

central argument. But . . . it rests on a mistaken estimate of Eusebius, whose inaccuracy even in direct quotation can be abundantly documented.[17] In the present case, moreover, there appear to be wide divergences only where Eusebius is paraphrasing: where he is professedly quoting verbatim the differences are comparatively trivial.[18] Nor are Campenhausen's supporting arguments any stronger. If the truth has been distorted—e.g. by the "imitatio Christi" motif, which impels Campenhausen to the hypothesis of an "Evangelion-Redaktor"[19]—nothing so far adduced proves that the distortion cannot have been made by a contemporary.[20]

L. W. Barnard[21] and Musurillo[22] have also rejected von Campenhausen's redaction criticism,[23] ostensibly because "it is dangerous to place too much weight on the divergence of the manuscript tradition from the quotations offered by Eusebius."[24] Von Campenhausen's study has received endorsement by W. H. C. Frend,[25] Hans Conzelmann,[26] and Helmut Koester,[27] and I too find the basic conclusions of his study convincing. I shall return to von Campenhausen's study of the *Martyrdom of Polycarp* below, but first the question of the accuracy of Eusebius's quotations must be discussed.

Eusebius includes some 250 direct and 90 or so indirect quotations[28] from

[17] Barnes here cites Hugh Jackson Lawlor and John Ernest Leonard Oulton, *Eusebius: The Ecclesiastical History and the Martyrs of Palestine* (2 vols.; London: SPCK, 1927) 2. 19ff. A few of their conclusions are quoted below.

[18] Barnes here cites Henri-Irénée Marrou, Review of von Campenhausen, "Bearbeitungen und Interpolationen," *ThLz* 84 (1959) col. 362.

[19] Barnes notes that the theory of an *Evangelion-Redaktor* did not originate with von Campenhausen but was already argued by M. Joel, *Blicke in die Religionsgeschichte* 2 (1883) 156ff.

[20] Barnes, "Pre-Decian *Acta Martyrum*," 510–11.

[21] "In Defence of Pseudo-Pionius' Account of Saint Polycarp's Martyrdom," in Patrick Granfield and Josef A. Jungmann, eds., *Kyriakon: Festschrift Johannes Quasten* (2 vols.; Munster Westf.: Aschendorff, 1970) 1. 192–204.

[22] *Christian Martyrs*, xiv.

[23] Von Campenhausen, "Bearbeitungen und Interpolationen," 1–48.

[24] Ibid.

[25] Review of von Campenhausen, "Bearbeitungen und Interpolationen," *JTS* n.s. 9 (1958) 371; Frend, *Martyrdom and Persecution in the Early Church: A Study of a Conflict from the Maccabees to Donatus* (Garden City: Anchor Books, 1967) 216.

[26] "Bemerkungen zum Martyrium Polykarps," *NAkG* (1978) 40–58.

[27] *Introduction to the New Testament*, 2. 345–47.

[28] Lawlor and Oulton include the following passages in the category "indirect quotations": 1.6.10; 1.9.1; 1.8.15; 2.5.7; 3.36.10; 4.11.7; 4.14.1; 4.18.6; 5.17.1; 1.6.2, 3, 9; 2.20.4–6; 3.7.2; 3.10.7; 3.32.7–8; 1.11.1, 3; 2.19.1; 3.32.7; 3.36.10. "In none of these passages," they say, "can we believe that he was paraphrasing a text recently read. . . . The reasonable conclusion seems to be that when Eusebius made indirect quotations he trusted overmuch to a remarkably retentive memory, which on occasion played him tricks" (Lawlor and Oulton, *Eusebius*, 2. 20).

various sources in his *Historia ecclesiastica.*[29] The most thorough study of
Eusebius's quotations known to me is that of Lawlor and Oulton,[30] Regarding the direct quotations produced by Eusebius, they conclude that "in many
instances he presents them to his readers in an unsatisfactory form."[31] Their
findings on the direct quotations may be distilled and best seen in the following table:

"Unsatisfactory" Direct Quotations of
Eusebius *Historia ecclesiastica*

1) Quotations that begin or end in the middle of a sentence: 2.17.11; 1.10.2–4;
2) Quotations where a middle portion of the text has been omitted but the reader
   has not been warned of ellipsis: 1.13.21; 2.23.21; 3.8.4; 3.9.1; 3.39.4; 4.11.5;
   4.22; 5.11.4; 7.10.7; 8.17.3–5;
3) Extracts where a relative pronoun is given without the antecedent which is
   necessary to make the sense clear: 3.1.1; 4.8.2; 5.2.2; 5.24.14;
4) Principal verb omitted: 4.11.9; 5.17.2; 6.25.4, 14; 7.25.9;
5) Quotation is a fragment and sense is obscure: 2.17.17, 19; 3.23.3; 3.28.4;
   4.8.2ff.; 4.11.2; 4.16.6; 4.29.2, 3; 5.7.2; 5.8.5; 5.8.6; 5.7.6; 6.43.17; 7.24.9;
6) Quotations given without reference to the context: 1.5.6; 1.8.14; 3.6.1–16;
   3.8.1–9;
7) Mutilated quotations from the Bible: 1.2.3, 14, 15, 25; 1.3.13; 3.7.4, 5;
   3.39.10; 10.4.9, 32, 49–51.

B. Gustafsson discovered a Eusebian fault that is, to my mind, more
dangerous than those delineated by Lawlor and Oulton, namely, that "we
cannot always be sure whether Eusebius is using direct or indirect speech in
his quotations."[32] Gustafsson discusses 6.19.17–18, where Eusebius has
used *oratio recta* where he should have used *oratio obliqua.* Chadwick
discovered an instance where Eusebius quoted in *oratio recta* when *oratio
obliqua* was required.[33] Apart from the Eusebian mistakes pointed to by

[29] For good treatments of Eusebius's sources see Kirsopp Lake's Introduction to *Eusebius:
The Ecclesiastical History* (2 vols.; LCL; Cambridge: Harvard University Press; London:
Heinemann, 1975); and Grant, *Eusebius.*

[30] Lawlor and Oulton, *Eusebius*, 2. 19–27.

[31] Ibid., 2. 20.

[32] Gustafsson, "Eusebius' Principles in handling his Sources as found in his Church History,"
TU 79 (1961) 433.

[33] Henry Chadwick, *Origen: Contra Celsum: Translated with an Introduction and Notes*
(Cambridge: Cambridge University Press, 1980) 43. In *Hist. eccl.* 2.23.20 Eusebius purports to
quote the Jewish historian Josephus:

Ἀμέλει γέ τοι ὁ Ἰώσηπος οὐκ ἀπώκνησεν καὶ τοῦτ' ἐγγράφως ἐπιμαρτύρασθαι δι' ὧν
φησιν λέξεων ταῦτα δὲ συμβέβηκεν Ἰουδαίοις κατ' ἐκδίκησιν Ἰακώβου τοῦ δικαίου,

Gustafsson and Chadwick, it would appear that Eusebius's major "fault" was that of omission, of obscuring the sense of quoted materials by omitting portions of the quoted text. It is important to observe, however, that where Eusebius purports to produce the ipsissima verba, the portions of the text that he quotes in nearly all cases seem to be faithfully reproduced. The contention of Barnes, Barnard, Lawlor and Oulton, and others that Eusebius has omitted a portion of a text presupposes that our extant version of that source is the same text that was used by Eusebius himself. Where

---

ὃς ἦν ἀδελφὸς Ἰησοῦ τοῦ λεγομένου Χριστοῦ, ἐπειδήπερ δικαιότατον αὐτὸν ὄντα οἱ Ἰουδαῖοι ἀπέκτειναν.

The *oratio recta* is not in the traditional text of Josephus, and it is doubtful that Josephus described Jesus as "the so-called Christ." Eusebius has probably used and misread a secondary source here, namely, Origen's *Contra Celsum* 1.47:

Although he [Josephus] did not believe in Jesus as Christ, he sought for the cause of the fall of Jerusalem and the destruction of the temple. He ought to have said that the plot against Jesus was the reason why these catastrophes came upon the people, because they had killed the prophesied Christ; however, although unconscious of it, he is not far from the truth when he says that these disasters befell the Jews to avenge James the Just, who was a brother of "Jesus the so-called Christ", since they had killed him who was a very righteous man. . . . If therefore he says that the destruction of Jerusalem happened because of James, would it not be more reasonable to say that this happened on account of Jesus the Christ?

In his translation of this work, Chadwick notes,

Origen also quotes this as from Josephus in *Comm. in Matt.* x, 17. but it does not occur in any extant MS. of the *Antiquities* at the relevant place (*Antiq.* xx, 9, 1 [200–1]) or elsewhere. Eusebius, *Hist. eccl.* 2.23.20, quotes the sentence in *oratio recta*; Lawlor–Oulton (*ad loc.*) think Eusebius is independent of Origen, and suggest a common source, perhaps a collection of extracts. Eusebius's debt to Origen is vast enough to make this improbable, and his verbatim quotation corresponds exactly to Origen's words here with only such alterations as are necessary to turn it from *oratio obliqua*. The passage may be a Christian interpolation in the text of Josephus: cf. E. Schürer, *Geschichte des jüdischen Volkes im Zeitalter Jesu Christi* (4th ed. 1901), I, p. 581; C. Martin in *Revue Belge de philologie et d'histoire*, xx (1941), at p. 421, n. 1. H. st J. Thackeray (*Josephus the Man and the Historian* [1929], pp. 134f.) thinks Origen confused Josephus with Hegesippus who gives a Christian account of the death of James (*apud* Eusebius *Hist. eccl.* 2.23) which ends: "And immediately Vespasian besieged them." (Chadwick, *Origen: Contra Celsum*, 43 n. 2)

From my reading of Chadwick's translation, it is not necessarily true that Origen read the words "Jesus the so-called Christ" in his text of Josephus. Is not Origen being rhetorical when he says that Josephus *ought to have said* the catastrophes happened because the people killed the prophesied Christ? The appositive "Jesus the so-called Christ" may have been written by Origen himself to make clear his argument that Josephus's cause-and-effect argument would have been stronger had he believed this. Or it may have been an interpolation, as Schürer suggests, present in Origen's text. In either case, Eusebius either misread or misrepresented his source.

Eusebius's text is compared to an extant source and is found to "omit" a portion of the text, need we necessarily presuppose omission? With regard to the *Martyrdom of Polycarp*, is it not possible that the text seen by Eusebius has been interpolated before or by Ps.-Pionius? The possibility is the probability.

Collation of Texts

Lawlor and Oulton include Eusebius's version of the *Martyrdom of Polycarp* in the category "indirect quotation":

> The longest [indirect quotation] which it [*Hist. eccl.*] includes is the "abridgement" of the first seven sections of the extant *Martyrdom of Polycarp* (4.15.4 – 14). It is fairly clear that the text lay before Eusebius as he wrote. He follows the order of the original document, and its phrases appear in almost every line. Nevertheless it is practically rewritten. He omits, expands and glosses at will; but only in one instance can he be accused of misstating the facts.[34] This passage stands by itself. All the other indirect quotations which we can compare with the original texts are much shorter. The question therefore arises whether in all of them he wrote with his eye on the text.[35]

Von Campenhausen, however, collated Eusebius *Hist. eccl.* 4.15.3 – 14 with Ps.-Pionius 1 – 7 and successfully showed that it is not Eusebius who has "practically rewritten" and who "omits, expands and glosses at will," to use Lawlor and Oulton's words, but rather that Ps.-Pionius preserves a text that has been successively edited at various stages of its transmission.

The trial of Polycarp in the *Martyrdom of Polycarp* does not occur until 9.2 – 11.2 (Eusebius *Hist. eccl.* 4.15.18 – 24). Preceding the account of the trial in the texts is a narration of the mob violence that lead to the pagan cry, "Let Polycarp be sent for!" Polycarp, while praying, has a vision concerning the manner of his impending death. Meanwhile, the pagans are scouring the city for the old man and torturing slaves, possibly Polycarp's own slaves, for information leading to his whereabouts. At this point, the text of Ps.-Pionius (but not that of Eusebius) begins to show what had been meant earlier in the text by "nearly everything that happened before took place in order that the Lord might show us from above a martyrdom in accordance with the gospel. For he [Polycarp] waited to be delivered, as the Lord did also, so that we also might become his imitators" (Ps.-Pionius 1.1 – 1.2):

---

[34] *Hist. eccl.* 4.15.10.
[35] Lawlor and Oulton, *Eusebius*, 2. 20.

And so it was impossible for him [Polycarp] to remain in hiding, since those who betrayed him [tortured slaves] were of his own household.

And the police magistrate, who had inherited the very name, being called Herod, was eager to bring him into the stadium, in order that he might fulfill his own inheritance, being made a partner with Christ, while his betrayers would suffer the punishment of Judas. So taking the young slave, on Friday about the dinner hour, the mounted police and cavalry went out with their customary arms as though moving swiftly against a robber. And at a late hour they attacked together and found him in the upper room of a certain cottage reclined at meal. (Ps.-Pionius 6.2–7.1)

At this point, traces of *imitatio Christi* are felt, but the author or editor have so far only analogies. Later in the texts, in both that of Eusebius (4.15.15) and of Ps.-Pionius (8.1), the *imitatio Christi* motif becomes a wooden imitation of events: "They seated him on an ass and led him [Polycarp] into the city, it being a high sabbath."

The trial portion of *Martyrdom of Polycarp*, which is the primary concern of the present study, is not collated by von Campenhausen. Below, I have collated Eusebius's and Ps.-Pionius's versions of the trial of Polycarp. The "sigla" are not nearly so elaborate as those used by von Campenhausen.[36] The underlined portions of the collation are intended to merely show textual differences, without predisposition to priority of readings.

Eusebius *Hist. eccl.* 4.15	*Martyrdom of Polycarp* (Ps.-Pionius)
18 προσαχθέντος οὖν αὐτοῦ,	καὶ λοιπὸν προσαχθέντος αὐτοῦ,
θόρυβος ἦν μέγας ἀκουσάντων ὅτι	θόρυβος ἦν μέγας ἀκουσάντων ὅτι
Πολύκαρπος συνείληπται.	Πολύκαρπος συνείληπται.
λοιπὸν οὖν προσελθόντα ἀνηρώτα	9.2 προσαχθέντα οὖν αὐτὸν ἀνηρώτα
ὁ ἀνθύπατος εἰ αὐτὸς εἴη	ὁ ἀνθύπατός εἰ αὐτὸς εἴη
Πολύκαρπος. καὶ ὁμολογήσαντος	Πολύκαρπος. τοῦ δὲ ὁμολογοῦντος
ἔπειθεν ἀρνεῖσθαι λέγων·	ἔπειθεν ἀρνεῖσθαι λέγων·
Αἰδέσθητί σου τὴν ἡλικίαν	Αἰδέσθητί σου τὴν ἡλικίαν
(καὶ ἕτερα τούτοις ἀκόλουθα,	(καὶ ἕτερα τούτοις ἀκόλουθα,
ἃ σύνηθες αὐτοῖς ἐστι λέγειν)·	ὧν ἔθον αὐτοῖς λέγειν)·
Ὄμοσον τὴν Καίσαρος τύχην, μετα-	Ὄμοσον τὴν Καίσαρος τύχην, μετα-
νόησον, εἶπον· Αἶρε τοὺς ἀθέους.	νόησον, εἶπον· Αἶρε τοὺς ἀθέους.
19 ὁ δὲ Πολύκαρπος ἐμβριθεῖ τῷ	ὁ δὲ Πολύκαρπος ἐμβριθεῖ τῷ
προσώπῳ εἰς πάντα τὸν ὄχλον τὸν ἐν	προσώπῳ εἰς πάντα τὸν ὄχλον τὸν ἐν

---

[36] Von Campenhausen ("Bearbeitungen und Interpolationen," passim) isolates the following strata in the texts of Eusebius and Ps.-Pionius: *Überschüsse des eusebianischen Textes; Euangelion-Redaktion; nacheusebianische Interpolationen und Anhänge; voreusebianische Interpolationen; die Abgrenzung ist im einzelnen fraglich* and indicates these strata by various types of text and underlinings.

τῷ σταδίῳ
ἐμβλέψας ἐπισείσας
αὐτοῖς τὴν χεῖρα, στενάξας τε καὶ
ἀναβλέψας εἰς τὸν οὐρανὸν
εἶπεν· Αἶρε τοὺς ἀθέους.
20 ἐγκειμένου δὲ τοῦ ἡγουμένου καὶ
λέγοντος· Ὄμοσον, καὶ ἀπολύσω σε,
λοιδόρησον τὸν Χριστόν,
ἔφη ὁ Πολύκαρπος· Ὀγδοήκοντα καὶ
ἓξ ἔτη δουλεύω αὐτῷ καὶ οὐδέν
με ἠδίκησεν. καὶ πῶς δύναμαι
βλασφημῆσαι τὸν βασιλέα μου τὸν
σώσαντά με
21 ἐπιμένοντος δὲ πάλιν αὐτοῦ καὶ
λέγοντος· Ὄμοσον τὴν Καίσαρος
τύχην, ὁ Πολύκαρπος,
Εἰ κενοδοξεῖς, φησίν, ἵνα ὀμόσω
τὴν Καίσαρος τύχην, ὡς λέγεις προσ-
ποιούμενος ἀγνοεῖν ὅστις εἰμί, μετὰ
παρρησίας ἄκουε· Χριστιανός εἰμι.
εἰ δὲ θέλεις τὸν τοῦ
Χριστιανισμοῦ μαθεῖν λόγον, δὸς
ἡμέραν καὶ ἄκουσον.
22 ἔφη ὁ ἀνθύπατος· Πεῖσον τὸν
δῆμον. Πολύκαρπος ἔφη·
Σὲ μὲν καὶ λόγου
ἠξίωκα· δεδιδάγμεθα γὰρ
ἀρχαῖς καὶ ἐξουσίαις ὑπὸ θεοῦ
τεταγμέναις τιμὴν κατὰ τὸ προσῆκον
τὴν μὴ βλάπτουσαν ἡμᾶς ἀπονέμειν.
ἐκείνους δὲ οὐκ ἀξίους ἡγοῦμαι τοῦ
ἀπολογεῖσθαι αὐτοῖς.
23 ὁ δ᾿ ἀνθύπατος εἶπεν· Θηρία
ἔχω· τούτοις σε παραβαλῶ ἐὰν μὴ
μετανοήσῃς.
ὁ δὲ εἶπεν· Κάλει. ἀμετάθετος γὰρ
ἡμῖν ἡ ἀπὸ τῶν κρειττόνων ἐπὶ τὰ
χείρω μετάνοια, καλὸν δὲ
μετατίθεσθαι ἀπὸ τῶν χαλεπῶν ἐπὶ
τὰ δίκαια.
24 ὁ δὲ πάλιν
πρὸς αὐτόν· Πυρί σε
ποιήσω δαμασθῆναι ἐὰν τῶν θηρίων
καταφρονῇς, ἐὰν μὴ μετανοήσῃς.
Πολύκαρπος εἶπεν· Πῦρ ἀπειλεῖς
πρὸς ὥραν καιόμενον καὶ μετ᾿

τῷ σταδίῳ ἀνόμων ἐθνῶν
ἐμβλέψας καὶ ἐπισείσας
αὐτοῖς τὴν χεῖρα, στενάξας τε καὶ
ἀναβλέψας εἰς τὸν οὐρανὸν
εἶπεν· Αἶρε τοὺς ἀθέους.
9.3 ἐγκειμένου δὲ τοῦ ἀνθυπάτου καὶ
λέγοντος· Ὄμοσον, καὶ ἀπολύω σε,
λοιδόρησον τὸν Χριστόν,
ἔφη ὁ Πολύκαρπος· Ὀγδοήκοντα καὶ
ἓξ ἔτη δουλεύω αὐτῷ καὶ οὐδέν
με ἠδίκησεν. καὶ πῶς δύναμαι
βλασφημῆσαι τὸν βασιλέα μου τὸν
σώσαντά με
10.1 ἐπιμένοντος δὲ πάλιν αὐτοῦ καὶ
λέγοντος· Ὄμοσον τὴν Καίσαρος
τύχην, ἀπεκρίνατο·
Εἰ κενοδοξεῖς ἵνα ὀμόσω
τὴν Καίσαρος τύχην, ὡς σὺ λέγεις, προσ-
ποιεῖ δὲ ἀγνοεῖν με τίς εἰμι, μετὰ
παρρησίας ἄκουε· Χριστιανός εἰμι.
εἰ δὲ θέλεις τὸν τοῦ
Χριστιανισμοῦ μαθεῖν λόγον, δὸς
ἡμέραν καὶ ἄκουσον.
10.2 ἔφη ὁ ἀνθύπατος· Πεῖσον τὸν
δῆμον. ὁ δὲ Πολύκαρπος εἶπεν·
Σὲ μὲν καὶ λόγου
ἠξίωκα· δεδιδάγμεθα γὰρ
ἀρχαῖς καὶ ἐξουσίαις ὑπὸ τοῦ θεοῦ
τεταγμέναις τιμὴν κατὰ τὸ προσῆκον
τὴν μὴ βλάπτουσαν ἡμᾶς ἀπονέμειν.
ἐκείνους δὲ οὐχ ἡγοῦμαι ἀξίους τοῦ
ἀπολογεῖσθαι αὐτοῖς.
11.1 ὁ δὲ ἀνθύπατος εἶπεν· Θηρία
ἔχω· τούτοις σε παραβαλῶ ἐὰν μὴ
μετανοήσῃς.
ὁ δὲ εἶπεν· Κάλει. ἀμετάθετος γὰρ
ἡμῖν ἡ ἀπὸ τῶν κρειττόνων ἐπὶ τὰ
χείρω μετάνοια, καλὸν δὲ
μετατίθεσθαι ἀπὸ τῶν χαλεπῶν ἐπὶ
τὰ δίκαια.
11.2 ὁ δὲ πάλιν
πρὸς αὐτόν· Πυρί σε
ποιήσω δαπανηθῆναι εἰ τῶν θηρίων
καταφρονεῖς, ἐὰν μὴ μετανοήσῃς.
ὁ δὲ Πολύκαρπος εἶπεν· Πῦρ ἀπειλεῖς
τὸ πρὸς ὥραν καιόμενον καὶ μετ᾿

ὀλίγον σβεννύμενον· ἀγνοεῖς γὰρ τὸ
τῆς μελλούσης κρίσεως καὶ αἰωνίου
κολάσεως τοῖς ἀσεβέσι τηρούμενον
πῦρ. ἀλλὰ τί βραδύνεις
φέρε ὃ βούλει.

ὀλίγον σβεννύμενον. ἀγνοεῖς γὰρ τὸ
τῆς μελλούσης κρίσεως καὶ αἰωνίου
κολάσεως τοῖς ἀσεβέσι τηρούμενον
πῦρ. ἀλλὰ τί βραδύνεις
φέρε ὃ βούλει.

Translation

Eusebius *Hist. eccl.* 4.15	*Martyrdom of Polycarp* (Ps.-Pionius)
18 Therefore, as he was led in, there was a great uproar when they [the crowd] heard that Polycarp had been arrested. Finally, then, when he was led up, the proconsul asked him whether he was Polycarp. And admitting it, he tried to persuade him to deny, saying, "Have respect for your age," (and other such things that are customary for them to say); "swear by the genius of the emperor; recant and say, 'Away with the atheists!'" 19 And Polycarp, with a solemn expression, looked up at all the crowd in	(9.1) And at last, as he was led in, there was a great uproar when they [the crowd] heard that Polycarp had been arrested. 9.2 Then, when he was brought before him, the proconsul asked him whether he was Polycarp. And admitting it, he tried to persuade him to deny, saying, "Have respect for your age," (and other such things that are customary for them to say); "swear by the genius of the emperor; recant and say, 'Away with the atheists!'" And Polycarp, with a solemn expression, looked up at all the crowd of lawless pagans in
the stadium and shook his hand at them, groaned, looked up to heaven, and said, "Away with the atheists!" 20 But when the magistrate persisted, saying, "Swear and I will release you; curse (the) Christ," Polycarp said, "For eighty-six years I have served him and he has done me no wrong. How can I blaspheme my king who saved me?" 21 But when he persisted again, saying, "Swear by the genius of the emperor," Polycarp said, "If you imagine in vain that I will swear by the genius of the emperor, as you say, pretending to be ignorant of who I am, listen clearly: I am a Christian. But if you wish to learn the doctrine of Christianity, assign a day and listen."	the stadium and shook his hand at them, groaned, looked up to heaven, and said, "Away with the atheists!" 9.3 But when the proconsul persisted, saying, "Swear and I will release you; curse (the) Christ," Polycarp said, "For eighty-six years I have served him and he has done me no wrong. How can I blaspheme my king who saved me?" 10.1 But when he persisted again, saying, "Swear by the genius of the emperor," he answered, "If you imagine in vain that I will swear by the genius of the emperor, as you say, and pretend to be ignorant of who I am, listen clearly: I am a Christian. But if you wish to learn the doctrine of Christianity, assign a day and listen."

22 The proconsul said, "Persuade the people." Polycarp said, "I should have thought you worthy of discourse; for we have been taught to render such respect to the magistrates and powers appointed by God as will do us no harm. But those [the mob] I do not consider worthy that I should give a defense before them.
23 And the proconsul said, "I have beasts; I will expose you to them unless you change your mind." But he said, "Call [them]. For it is not possible for us to convert from better to worse, but it is good to convert from evil to righteousness.
24 But again he [said] to him, "I will have you killed by fire if you are not afraid of the beasts, unless you change your mind." Polycarp said, "You threaten with fire which burns for a while and soon is extinguished. For you are ignorant of the fire of the coming judgment and eternal punishment, which is kept for the impious. But why do you delay? Come, do what you want.

10.2 The proconsul said, "Persuade the people." Polycarp said, "I should have thought you worthy of discourse; for we have been taught to render such respect to the magistrates and powers appointed by God as will do us no harm. But those [the mob] I do not consider worthy that I should give a defense before them.
11.1 And the proconsul said, "I have beasts; I will expose you to them unless you change your mind." But he said, "Call [them]. For it is not possible for us to convert from better to worse, but it is good to convert from evil to righteousness.
11.2 But again he [said] to him, "I will have you consumed by fire if you are not afraid of the beasts, unless you change your mind." But Polycarp said, "You threaten with fire which burns for a while and soon is extinguished. For you are ignorant of the fire of the coming judgment and eternal punishment, which is kept for the impious. But why do you delay? Come, do what you want.

Conclusions

The form in which the trial is recounted is manifestly not *commentarius*-form. The author reveals not the slightest inclination to mimic the form. To argue for an ultimate derivation from a *commentarius* would be difficult. The prologues to the trial (Eusebius *Hist. eccl.* 4.15.3 – 17; Ps.-Pionius 1.1 – 9.1) are so extensive that they cannot be compared either to the *caput* of a *commentarius* or to the prologues of the *Acts of Justin* or other *acta Christianorum* that are arguably derived from *commentarii*. The *oratio recta* between Polycarp and the magistrate that is given is not *commentarius*-form. And, surprisingly, there is no κρίσις by the magistrate—he threatens Polycarp and Polycarp says, "Do what you will." The magistrate pronounces nothing further during the trial section—Polycarp, in effect, pronounces the κρίσις himself. The only similarity between the "form" of Polycarp's trial and *commentarius*-form is that both contain a section of *oratio recta*, and here the similarity ends, for even the *oratio recta* section is given in non-*commentarius*-form.

Like the introductions to *oratio recta* in Jesus' trial in the Gospels, the introductory clauses in the *Martyrdom of Polycarp* show no definite form. A wide variety of verbs of saying (e.g., εἶπεν, λέγοντος, ἔφη, φησίν), in addition to the direct introduction, is used. In *commentarii* from this period (ca. 156), *oratio recta* would be introduced by the speaker's name or, in the case of the magistrate, sometimes by name and title plus εἶπεν or ἀπεκρίνατο. Even when the εἶπεν introduction is used in the *Martyrdom of Polycarp* it is used with the copula ὁ δέ, which is not *commentarius*-form.

Most of the differences between the texts of the trial as given by Eusebius and Ps.-Pionius can be explained as simple scribal errors, such as haplographies and dittographies, or as editorial interpolations. But how are differences such as the following to be explained?

Eusebius *Hist. eccl.* 4.15.20	Ps.-Pionius 9.3
ἐγκειμένου δὲ τοῦ ἡγουμένου καὶ λέγοντος·...	ἐγκειμένου δὲ τοῦ ἀνθυπάτου καὶ λέγοντος·...

Eusebius *Hist. eccl.* 4.15.21	Ps.-Pionius 10.1
ὁ Πολύκαρπος, Εἰ κενοδοξεῖς, φησίν, ἵνα ὀμόσω...	ἀπεκρίνατο· Εἰ κενοδοξεῖς ἵνα ὀμόσω...

Eusebius *Hist. eccl.* 4.15.22	Ps.-Pionius 10.2
Πολύκαρπος ἔφη·	ὁ δὲ Πολύκαρπος εἶπεν·

The theory that a scribe worked from memory here seems improbable, since the texts of Eusebius and Ps.-Pionius are for the most part identical through the trial section. A scribe writing from dictation, however, is a plausible explanation. If derivation from a *commentarius* were to be argued here, a bilingual *commentarius* would be the natural argument. In bilingual *commentarii*, a scribe whose first language was Latin might record introductory clauses to *oratio recta* in Latin but the speeches, presumably spoken in Greek, he would record in Greek.[37] The textual differences between Eusebius and Ps.-Pionius in introductory clauses, according to such a theory, would be merely due to differences of translation. It seems more plausible, however, to posit the theory that copyists regarded *oratio recta*, and especially that of a martyr, as more sacrosanct than introductory clauses and therefore felt freer to edit introductions.

---

[37] See Appendix 3 at the back of this study.

It is intriguing that both texts have the following parenthetical remark:

Eusebius *Hist. eccl.* 4.15.18

(καὶ ἕτερα τούτοις ἀκόλουθα,
ἃ σύνηθες αὐτοῖς ἐστι λέγειν)·

Ps.-Pionius 9.2

(καὶ ἕτερα τούτοις ἀκόλουθα,
ὧν ἔθον αὐτοῖς λέγειν)·

Was this parenthetical remark in the original text of the letter? This is possible, but it seems equally possible that a later editor used the remark to abridge the text of the original. It is the sort of device that Eusebius used frequently. If the remark is Eusebian, it is certain evidence that Ps.-Pionius used the text of Eusebius. If we were to argue for derivation from a *commentarius* here, the parenthetical remark could be explained as an editorial expansion of an ellipsis phrase (μεθ᾽ ἕτερα).

In the *Acts of Justin* the mood is almost tranquil. The pattern of εἶπεν ... εἶπεν ... εἶπεν is soothing, and the lack of connectives such as καί and ὁ δέ gives the impression of leisurely pace. When the death sentence comes at the end, it comes as a surprise. In the *Martyrdom of Polycarp*, on the other hand, the use of copulas such as ὁ δέ, the use of participles, and phrases such as ἐπιμένοντος δὲ πάλιν αὐτοῦ καὶ λέγοντος create the impression of rapid movement. To this rapid movement is added the cacophany of verbs of saying, which heightens the atmosphere of tension and chaos. The mood created is much like the mood given to Jesus' trial in the Gospels—chaos, tension, mob violence. If the author of the *Martyrdom of Polycarp* did possess a *commentarius* of Polycarp's trial, which is doubtful, the *commentarius*-form would have been inimical to the intent of the writer.

7

The Acts of Ignatius

At least since Lightfoot's study of the *Acts of Ignatius*,[1] scholars have rejected or ignored these acts.[2] Not even René Aigrain,[3] Othmar Perler,[4] or Hippolyte Delehaye[5] felt the *Acts of Ignatius* worthy of treatment. Delehaye says, "Vain efforts have been made to rehabilitate the Ignatian Acts in their entirety."[6] Johannes Quasten included the *Acts of Ignatius* among the "legends of the martyrs which were composed for the purpose of edification long after the martyrdom took place."[7] Cyril Richardson's opinion of the acts is typical of scholars today:

> These Acts [the Antiochene version] date from the fifth century and rest on no historical foundation. Their textual history, however, is important, since the genuine text of Ignatius' Letter to the Romans is embedded in

---

[1] Lightfoot, *Apostolic Fathers*, 2. 363–584.

[2] All of the scholars who were listed as "pruners" in the opening of Chapter Four regard the *Acts of Ignatius* as inauthentic.

[3] *L'hagiographie*.

[4] "Das vierte Makkabäerbuch, Ignatius von Antiochien und die ältesten Martyrerberichte," *Rivista di archeologia cristiana* 25 (1949) 47–72. Perler compares the thought and language of 4 Maccabees with the epistles of Ignatius, *1 Clement*, the *Martyrdom of Polycarp*, and the *Martyrs of Lyons*.

[5] *Les passions des martyrs*.

[6] Delehaye, *The Legends of the Saints: An Introduction to Hagiography* (Notre Dame: University of Notre Dame Press, 1961) 119 n. 1.

[7] Quasten, *Patrology* (3 vols.; Utrecht-Antwerp: Spectrum, 1975) 1. 176.

them. They are current in Latin, Greek, and Syriac. Even more crudely
legendary are the Roman Acts, which belong to the sixth century.[8]

Few scholars today question the authenticity of the "middle version" of
Ignatius *Epistle to the Romans*.[9] However, the Greek text of this epistle exists
only as a part of the *Acts of Ignatius*. Regarding the close textual relationship
between the *Acts of Ignatius* and Ignatius *Epistle to the Romans*, Lightfoot
said:

> *Paris. Graec.* 1451 (formerly *Colbert.* 460), in the National Library at
> Paris. On fol 109a begins Μαρτύριον τοῦ ἁγίου (sic) ἱερομάρτυρος
> ἰγνατίου τοῦ θεοφόρου. Ἄρτι διαδεξαμένου κ.τ.λ. . . . They [the acts
> of martyrdom] incorporate the Epistle to the Romans, and were first pub-
> lished by Ruinart. . . . The Epistle to the Romans begins on fol. 111 a.
> The commencement of the epistle is not marked by any title, illumina-
> tion, or even capital letter, but the writing is continuous . . . [ellipsis
> Lightfoot] ὑποτέτακται. ἰγνάτιος ὁ καὶ θεοφόρος κ.τ.λ. The epistle
> ends . . . [ellipsis Lightfoot] ιῦ χῦ αμῆ. καταρτίσας τοίνυν κ.τ.λ. This
> MS may be ascribed to the 10th century, the date assigned to it in the
> printed Catalogue.[10]

Despite this relationship, scholars have saved the epistle as authentic and
have discarded the acts as imaginative and spurious legend. However, it is
not the contention here that the epistle was part and parcel of the *Acts of
Ignatius* from the beginning. Nor do we contend that any of the extant versions of the *Acts of Ignatius* are the original, or even resemble the original's
probable form. The brief study of the *Acts of Ignatius* below shows that the
second section of the extant account is derived from a second-century *Acts of
Ignatius*, and that our extant account has incorporated an edited version of
this and Ignatius *Epistle to the Romans*. Moreover, arguments will be given,
although not conclusively, that our extant Greek text of the *Acts of Ignatius* is
derived from a Latin translation of a no longer extant Greek text. The basic
contention here is that either the *Acts of Ignatius* must be taken more seriously or the *Epistle to the Romans* less seriously.

[8] Richardson, *Early Christian Fathers* (New York: Macmillan, 1970) 83.
[9] The epistles of Ignatius exist in three versions, which are today known as the "short,"
"middle," and "long." The modern consensus regarding the authenticity of the middle version
was first established by the studies of Theodor Zahn (*Ignatius von Antiochien* [Gotha: Perthes,
1873]) and Lightfoot (*Apostolic Fathers*.) On challengers of the middle version, see William R.
Schoedel, *Ignatius of Antioch: A Commentary on the Letters of Ignatius of Antioch* (Hermeneia;
Philadelphia: Fortress, 1985) 5–7.
[10] Lightfoot, *Apostolic Fathers*, 1. 75.

There are at least five versions of the *Acts of Ignatius*, which are today known by the labels attached to each by Lightfoot. The manuscripts of each version are as follows:

Acts of Ignatius

Version	Extant MSS
Antiochene	Greek: *Cod. Parisiensis-Colbertinus* 1451 (formerly *Colbertinus* 460); 10th/11th century Latin: published by Ussher in 1644 edition from two MSS (*Caiensis* 395 and *Montacutianus* [a parchment MS from the library of Richard Mountague or Montacute, Bp. of Norwich]) of the Anglo-Latin version of the Ignatian epistles; Syriac: published by Cureton, *Corp. Ign.* (London, 1849) 222 (three MSS).
Roman	Greek: *Cod. Vaticanus* 866; *Bodl. Laud. Graec.* 69 fol. 245b–255a; *Paris. Bibl. Nat. Graec.* 1491 (formerly *Colbert.* 450) fol. 86a col. 2–fol. 93b, col. 2.; 11th century. Coptic: *Vatic. Copt.* lxvi; *Taurin. Papyrus* 1.
Bollandist	Latin: published by Ussher, *Appendix Ignatiana* (1647).
Armenian	published by J. B. Aucher, *Armenian Lives of all the Saints of the Armenian Calendar* (Venice, 1810–14).
Metaphrast	Symeon the Metaphrast

Collation of Texts

Below I have collated the Greek text with the Latin of the Antiochene version, which contains the "middle version" of Ignatius *Epistle to the Romans*. Lightfoot's Greek text of this version incorporates readings from the Latin and Syriac manuscripts, that is, Latin or Syriac words to which he apparently gave Greek equivalencies.[11] This practice is objectionable. The Greek text below is based upon my comparison of T. Ruinart's[12] reading of *Cod. Parisiensis-Colbertinus* 1451 (the sole Greek manuscript) with J. Migne's[13] and Lightfoot's readings of that codex. The Latin text is from Lightfoot's printing of the Anglo-Latin version (*Caiensis* 395 and *Montacutianus*), which was originally printed by Ussher in 1644.[14] The numbers that are printed between the Greek and Latin texts are for the purposes of the discussion

---

[11] Lightfoot, *Apostolic Fathers*, 2. 473–91.

[12] *Acta primorum martyrum sincera et selecta* (1689; reprinted Ratisbon: Manz, 1859) 30–56.

[13] PG, 5. 979–88.

[14] Lightfoot, *Apostolic Fathers*, 2. 643–52.

which follows the collation and do not correspond, so far as I know, to any previous editions of these texts.

μαρτύριον τοῦ ἁγίου ἱερομάρτυρος
ἰγνατίου τοῦ θεοφόρου

MARTYRIUM SANCTI IGNATII
(Anglo-Latin version)

1 Ἄρτι διαδεξαμένου τὴν Ῥωμαίων   1
ἀρχὴν Τραιανοῦ, Ἰγνάτιος ὁ τοῦ
ἀποστόλου Ἰωάννου μαθητής, ἀνὴρ
ἦν τοῖς πᾶσιν ἀποστολικός, καὶ
ἐκυβέρνα τὴν ἐκκλησίαν Ἀντιοχέων·   5
ἐπιμελῶς, τοὺς πάλαι χειμῶνας μόλις
παραγαγὼν τῶν πολλῶν ἐπὶ
Δομετιανοῦ διωγμός, καθάπερ
κυβερνήτης ἀγαθός, τῷ οἴακι τῆς
προσευχῆς καὶ τῆς νηστείας, καὶ τῇ   10
συνεχείᾳ τῆς διδασκαλίας, τῷ τόνῳ
τῷ πνευματικῷ, πρὸς τὴν ζάλην τὴν
ἀντικειμένην ἀντεῖχεν· δεδοικὼς μή
τινα τῶν ὀλιγοψύχων ἢ ἀκεραιοτέρων
ἀποβάλῃ. τοιγαροῦν ηὐφραίνετο μὲν   15
ἐπὶ τῷ τῆς ἐκκλησίας ἀσαλεύτῳ,
λωφήσαντος πρὸς ὀλίγον τοῦ διωγμοῦ·
ἤσχαλλεν δὲ καθ᾽ ἑαυτόν,
ὡς μήπω τῆς ὄντως εἰς Χριστὸν
ἀγάπης ἐφαψάμενος μηδὲ τῆς τελείας   20
τοῦ μαθητοῦ τάξεως. ἐννόει γὰρ τὴν
διὰ μαρτυρίου γινομένην ὁμολογίαν
πλέον[15] αὐτὸν προσοικειοῦσαν τῷ
κυρίῳ. ὅθεν ἔτεσιν ὀλίγοις ἔτι
παραμένων τῇ ἐκκλησίᾳ, καὶ λύχνου   25
δίκην θεικοῦ τὴν ἑκάστου φωτίζων
διάνοιαν διὰ τῆς τῶν θείων γραφῶν
ἐξηγήσεως, ἐπετύγχανεν τῶν κατ᾽
εὐχήν.
2 Τραιανοῦ γὰρ μετὰ ταῦτα   30
ἐννάτῳ ἔτει τῆς αὐτοῦ βασιλείας
ἐπαρθέντος ἐπὶ τῇ νίκῃ τῇ κατὰ
Σκυθῶν καὶ Δακῶν καὶ ἑτέρων
πολλῶν ἐθνῶν καὶ νομίσαντος ἔτι
λείπειν αὐτῷ πρὸς πᾶσαν ὑποταγὴν   35
τὸ τῶν Χριστιανῶν θεοσεβὲς σύστημα,
καὶ εἰ μὴ τὴν τῶν δαιμόνων ἕλοιντο
λατρείαν μετὰ πάντων ὑπεισιέναι
τῶν ἐθνῶν, διωγμὸν ὑπομένειν
ἀπειλήσαντος,[16] πάντας τοὺς εὐσεβῶς   40

1 Nuper recipiente principatum
Romanorum Trajano, apostoli et
evangelistae Johannis discipulus Ignatius,
vir in omnibus apostolicus,
gubernabat ecclesiam Antiochenorum.
Qui quondam procellas vix
mitigans multarum sub
Domitiano persecutionum, quemadmodum
gubernator bonus, gubernaculo
orationis et jejunii, continuitate
doctrinae, robore
spirituali, fluctuationi adversantis
se opposuit potentiae, timens ne
aliquem eorum qui pusillanimes et magis
prosterneret. Igitur laetabatur quidem
de ecclesiae inconcussione,
quiescente ad paucum persecutione;
dubitavit autem secundum seipsum,
quod nondum vere in Christum
caritatem attigerat neque perfectam
discipuli ordinem. Cogitabat enim
eam quae per martyrium confessionem
plus ipsum adducere ad familiaritatem
Domini. Unde annis paucis adhuc
permanens ecclesiae, et ad lucernae
modum divinae cujusque illuminans cor
per scripturarum enarrationem,
sortitus est iis quae secundum
votum.
2 Trajano enim post,
quarto anno imperii sui,
elato de victoria illa
Scythas et Thraces et alteras
multas et diversas gentes, et existimante
adhuc deficere ipsi ad omnem subjectionem
Christianorum Deum venerantem congrega-
tionem, nisi daemoniacam cogeret culturam
cum omnibus subintrare
gentibus; persecutionem comminans,
omnes ipsos Dei cultores

---

[15] πλέον Lightfoot; πλεῖον Ruinart, Migne.

ζῶντας ἢ θύειν ἢ τελευτᾶν
κατηνάγκαζεν. τότε τοίνυν φοβηθεὶς
ὑπὲρ τῆς Ἀντιοχέων ἐκκλησίας ὁ
γενναῖος τοῦ Χριστοῦ στρατιώτης,
ἑκουσίως ἤγετο πρὸς Τραιανόν,   45
διάγοντα μέν κατ' ἐκεῖνον τὸν καιρὸν
κατὰ τὴν Ἀντιόχειαν, σπουδάζοντα
δὲ ἐπὶ Ἀρμενίαν καὶ Πάρθους. ὡς δὲ
κατὰ πρόσωπον ἔστη Τραιανοῦ τοῦ
βασιλέως·[17] Τίς εἶ, κακόδαιμον, τὰς   50
ἡμετέρας σπουδάζων διατάξεις[18]
ὑπερβαίνειν μετὰ τὸ καὶ ἑτέρους
ἀναπείθειν ἵνα κακῶς ἀπολοῦνται [19]
Ἰγνάτιος εἶπεν· Οὐδεὶς θεοφόρον
ἀποκαλεῖ κακοδαίμονα· ἀφεστήκασι   55
γὰρ ἀπὸ τῶν δούλων τοῦ θεοῦ τὰ
δαιμόνια. εἰ δέ, ὅτι τούτοις ἐπαχθής
εἰμι, καὶ κακόν με πρὸς τοὺς
δαίμονας ἀποκαλεῖς, συνομολογῶ·
Χριστὸν γὰρ ἔχων ἐπουράνιον   60
βασιλέα τὰς τούτων καταλύω
ἐπιβουλάς.
Τραιανὸς εἶπεν· Καὶ τίς ἐστιν
θεοφόρος
Ἰγνάτιος ἀπεκρίνατο· Ὁ Χριστὸν   65
ἔχων ἐν στέρνοις.
Τραιανὸς εἶπεν· Ἡμεῖς οὖν σοι δο-
κοῦμεν κατὰ νοῦν μὴ ἔχειν θεούς,
οἷς καὶ χρώμεθα συμμάχοις πρὸς
τοὺς πολεμίους   70
Ἰγνάτιος εἶπεν· Τὰ δαιμόνια τῶν
ἐθνῶν θεοὺς προσαγορεύεις
πλανώμενος· εἷς γάρ ἐστιν θεὸς ὁ
ποιήσας τὸν οὐρανὸν καὶ τὴν γῆν[20]
καὶ τὴν θάλασσαν καὶ πάντα τὰ ἐν   75
αὐτοῖς, καὶ εἷς Χριστὸς Ἰησοῦς ὁ υἱὸς
τοῦ θεοῦ ὁ μονογενής, οὗ τῆς
βασιλείας ὀναίμην.
Τραιανὸς εἶπεν· Τὸν σταυρωθέντα
λέγεις ἐπὶ Ποντίου Πιλάτου   80
Ἰγνάτιος εἶπεν· Τὸν
ἀνασταυρώσαντα τὴν ἐμὴν ἁμαρτίαν
μετὰ τοῦ ταύτης εὑρετοῦ καὶ πᾶσαν
καταδικάσαντα δαιμονικὴν πλάνην

existentes vel sacrificare vel mori
cogebat. Tunc igitur timens
pro Antiochenorum ecclesia
virilis Christi miles
voluntarie ductus est ad Trajanum,
agentem quidem secundum illud tempus
apud Antiochiam, festinantem autem
ad Armeniam et Parthos. Ut autem
coram facie stetit imperatoris Trajani,
Trajanus dixit: Quis es, cacodaemon,
nostras festinans praeceptiones
transcendere, cum et alteros
persuadere, ut perdantur male?
Ignatius dixit: Nullus theophorum
vocat cacodaemonem; recesserunt
enim longe a servis Dei
daemonia. Si autem, quoniam his gravis
sum, malum me adversus
daemones vocas, confiteor:
Christum enim habens supercaelestem
regem dissolvo horum
insidias.
Trajanus dixit: Et quis est
theophorus?
Ignatius respondit: Qui Christum
habet in pectore.
Trajanus dixit: Nos igitur tibi videmur
non habere secundum intellectum deos,
quibus utimur compugnatoribus adversus
adversarios?
Ignatius dixit: Daemonia
gentium deos appellas
errans. Unus enim est Deus,
qui fecit caelum et terram
et mare et omnia quae in
ipsis; et unus Christus Jesus, Filius
ipsius unigenitus, cujus
amicitia fruar.
Trajanus dixit: Crucifixum
dicis sub Pontio Pilato?''
Ignatius dixit:
Crucifigentem peccatum cum
hujus inventore, et omnem
condemnantem daemoniacam

---

[16] ἀπειλήσαντος Migne, Lightfoot; ἀπειλήσαντος ὁ φόβος Ruinart.
[17] βασιλέως Migne, Lightfoot; βασιλέος Ruinart.
[18] διατάξεις Migne, Lightfoot; lacking Ruinart.
[19] ἀπολοῦνται Ruinart, Lightfoot; ἀπολῶνται Migne.
[20] τὴν γῆν Migne, Lightfoot; γῆν Ruinart.

καὶ κακίαν ὑπὸ τοὺς πόδας τῶν   85
αὐτὸν ἐν καρδίᾳ φορούντων.
Τραιανὸς εἶπεν· Σὺ οὖν ἐν ἑαυτῷ
φέρεις τὸν σταυρωθέντα
Ἰγνάτιος εἶπεν· Ναί· γέγραπται γάρ
Ἐνοικήσω ἐν αὐτοῖς καὶ   90
ἐμπεριπατήσω.
Τραιανὸς ἀπεφήνατο· Ἰγνάτιον
προσετάξαμεν, τὸν ἐν ἑαυτῷ λέγοντα
περιφέρειν τὸν ἐσταυρωμένον,
δέσμιον ὑπὸ στρατιωτῶν γενόμενον   95
ἄγεσθαι παρὰ τὴν μεγάλην Ῥώμην,
βρῶμα γενησόμενον θηρίων εἰς
τέρψιν τοῦ δήμου. ταύτης ὁ ἅγιος
μάρτυς ἐπακούσας τῆς ἀποφάσεως
μετὰ χαρᾶς ἐβόησεν· Εὐχαριστῶ σοι,   100
δέσποτα, ὅτι με τελείᾳ τῇ πρός σε
ἀγάπῃ τιμῆσαι κατηξίωσας, τῷ
ἀποστόλῳ σου Παύλῳ δεσμοῖς
συνδήσας σιδηροῖς. ταῦτα εἰπὼν καὶ
μετ᾽ εὐφροσύνης περιθέμενος τὰ   105
δεσμά, ἐπευξάμενος πρότερον τῇ
ἐκκλησίᾳ καὶ ταύτην παραθέμενος
μετὰ δακρύων τῷ κυρίῳ, ὥσπερ κριὸς
ἐπίσημος ἀγέλης καλῆς ἡγούμενος,
ὑπὸ θηριώδους στρατιωτικῆς   110
δεινότητος συνηρπάζετο, θηρίοις
αἱμοβόροις ἐπὶ τὴν Ῥώμην
ἀπαχθησόμενος πρὸς βοράν.
3 Μετὰ πολλῆς τοίνυν
προθυμίας καὶ χαρᾶς, ἐπιθυμίᾳ τοῦ   115
πάθους, κατελθὼν ἀπὸ Ἀντιοχείας
εἰς τὴν Σελεύκειαν ἐκεῖθεν εἴχετο τοῦ
πλοός· καὶ προσχὼν μετὰ πολὺν²¹
κάματον τῇ Σμυρναίων²² πόλει, σὺν
πολλῇ χαρᾷ καταβὰς τῆς νηὸς   120
ἔσπευδε τὸν ἅγιον Πολύκαρπον τὸν
Σμυρναίων²³ ἐπίσκοπον τὸν
συνακροατὴν θεάσασθαι· ἐγεγόνεισαν
γὰρ πάλαι μαθηταὶ τοῦ ἁγίου
ἀποστόλου Ἰωάννου.²⁴ παρ᾽ ᾧ   125
καταχθεὶς καὶ πνευματικῶν αὐτῷ
κοινωνήσας χαρισμάτων καὶ τοῖς
δεσμοῖς ἐγκαυχώμενος, παρεκάλει
συναθλεῖν τῇ αὐτοῦ προθέσει,

malitiam sub pedibus eorum
qui ipsum in corde ferunt.
Trajanus dixit: Tu igitur in
teipso Christum circumfers?
Ignatius dixit: Etiam: scriptum est
enim: *Inhabitabo in ipsis et
inambulabo.*
Trajanus sententiavit: Ignatium
praecipimus, in seipso dicentem
circumferre crucifixum,
vinctum a militibus duci
in magnam Romam cibum
bestiarum in spectaculum
futurum plebis. Hanc audiens sanctus
martyr sententiam cum gaudio
exclamavit: Gratias ago tibi,
Domine, quoniam me perfecta ad te
caritate honorare dignatus es, cum
apostolo tuo Paulo vinculis
colligari ferreis. Haec dicens et
cum gaudio circumponens
vincula oransque prius pro
ecclesia et hanc
cum lacrimis commendans Domino, velut
aries insignis boni gregis dux,
a bestiali militari
duritia raptus est, bestiis
crudivorantibus ad Romam
ad cibum adducendus.
3 Cum multa igitur
promptitudine et gaudio, ex desiderio
passionis, descendens ab Antiochia
in Seleuciam illinc habebat
navigationem: et applicans post multum
laborem Smyrnaeorum civitati, cum
multo gaudio descendens de navi
festinabat sanctum Polycarpum
episcopum Smyrnaeorum
coauditorem videre; fuerant
enim quondam discipuli
Johannis. Apud quem adductus
et spiritualibus cum ipso
communicans charismatibus et
vinculis glorians, deprecabatur
concertare ipsius proposito

²¹ πολύν Migne, Lightfoot; πολήν Ruinart.
²² Σμυρναίων Migne, Lightfoot; Σμυρνέων Ruinart.
²³ Σμυρναίων Migne, Lightfoot; Σμυρνέων Ruinart.
²⁴ Ἰωάννου Migne, Lightfoot; Ἰοάννου Ruinart.

μάλιστα μὲν κοινῇ πᾶσαν ἐκκλησίαν 130
(ἐδεξιοῦντο γὰρ τὸν ἅγιον διὰ τῶν
ἐπισκόπων καὶ πρεσβυτέρων καὶ
διακόνων αἱ τῆς Ἀσίας πόλεις καὶ
ἐκκλησίαι, πάντων ἐπειγομένων πρὸς
αὐτόν, εἴ πως μέρος χαρίσματος 135
λάβωσι πνευματικοῦ), ἐξαιρέτως δὲ
τὸν ἅγιον Πολύκαρπον, ἵνα διὰ τῶν
θηρίων θᾶττον ἀφανὴς τῷ κόσμῳ
γενόμενος ἐμφανισθῇ τῷ προσώπῳ
τοῦ Χριστοῦ. 4 Καὶ ταῦτα οὕτως 140
ἔλεγεν, καὶ οὕτως διεμαρτύρατο,
τοσοῦτον ἐπεκτείνων τὴν πρὸς
Χριστὸν ἀγάπην, ὡς οὐρανοῦ μέλλειν²⁵
ἐπιλαμβάνεσθαι διὰ τῆς καλῆς
ὁμολογίας καὶ τῆς τῶν συνευχομένων 145
ὑπὲρ τῆς ἀθλήσεως σπουδῆς,
ἀποδοῦναι δὲ τὸν μισθὸν ταῖς
ἐκκλησίαις ταῖς ὑπαντησάσαις αὐτῷ
διὰ τῶν ἡγουμένων, γραμμάτων
εὐχαρίστων ἐκπεμφθέντων πρὸς 150
αὐτάς, πνευματικὴν μετ᾽ εὐχῆς καὶ
παραινέσεως ἀποσταζόντων χάριν.
τοιγαροῦν τοὺς πάντας ὁρῶν
εὐνοικῶς διακειμένους περὶ αὐτόν,
φοβηθεὶς μή ποτε ἡ τῆς ἀδελφότητος 155
στοργὴ τὴν πρὸς κύριον αὐτοῦ σουδὴν
ἐκκόψῃ, καλῆς ἀνεῳχθείσης αὐτῷ
θύρας τοῦ μαρτυρίου, οἷα πρὸς τὴν
ἐκκλησίαν ἐπιστέλλει Ῥωμαίων,
ὑποτέτακται. 160

maxime quidem communiter omnem ecclesiam
(honorabant enim sanctum per
episcopos, presbyteros, et
diaconos, Asiae civitates et
ecclesiae, omnibus festinantibus ad
ipsum, si quo aliquam partem charismatis
accipiant spiritualis), praecipue autem
sanctum Polycarpum; ut velocius per
bestias disparens mundo
factus appareat faciei
Christi. 4 Et hoc sic
dixit, sic testificatus est;
tantum extendens eam quae circa
Christum caritatem, ut caelum quidem
apprehendere per bonam
confessionem et per coorantium
pro certamine studium,
reddi autem mercedem
ecclesiis obivantibus ipsi
per praecedentes litteras
gratias agens appositas ad
ipsas, spiritualem cum oratione et
admonitionibus amplexantes gratiam.
Igitur omnes videns
amicabiliter dispositos ad ipsum,
timens ne forte fraternitatis
dilectio ad Dominum ipsius festinationem
abscindat, bona aperta ipsi
porta martyrii, talia ad
ecclesiam mittit Romanorum,
ut subordinata sunt.

Here Ignatius *Epistle to the Romans* is quoted

5 Καταρτίσας τοίνυν, ὡς
ἠβούλετο, τοὺς ἐν Ῥώμῃ τῶν
ἀδελφῶν ἄκοντας διὰ τῆς ἐπιστολῆς,
οὕτως ἀναχθεὶς ἀπὸ τῆς Σμύρνης
(κατεπείγετο γὰρ ὑπὸ τῶν στρατιωτῶν 165
ὁ Χριστοφόρος φθάσαι τὰς φιλοτιμίας
ἐν τῇ μεγάλῃ Ῥώμῃ, ἵνα ἐπ᾽ ὄψεσι
τοῦ δήμου Ῥωμαίων θηρσὶν ἀγρίοις
παραδοθεὶς τοῦ στεφάνου²⁶ τῆς
ἀθλήσεως ἐπιτύχῃ) προσέσχε τῇ 170

5 Perficiens igitur, ut
volebat, eos qui in Roma
fratrum absentes per epistolam,
sic ductus a Smyrna
(urgebatur enim a militibus
Christophorus occupare honores
in magna civitate, ut in conspectu
plebis Romanorum bestiis feris
projectus corona justitiae
per tale certamen potiatur) attigit ad

²⁵ μέλλειν Ruinart, Lightfoot; μέλλων Migne.
²⁶ στεφάνου Migne, Lightfoot; στεψάνου Ruinart.

Τρωάδι.²⁷ εἶτα ἐκεῖθεν καταχθεὶς ἐπὶ
τὴν Νεάπολιν, διὰ Φιλίππων
παρώδευεν Μακεδονίαν πεζὶ καὶ²⁸
τὴν Ἤπειρον τὴν πρὸς Ἐπίδαμνον, ἐν
τοῖς παραθαλαττίοις νηὸς ἐπιτυχὼν   175
ἔπλει τὸ Ἀδριατικὸν πέλαγος,
κἀκεῖθεν ἐπιβὰς τοῦ Τυρρηνικοῦ, καὶ
παραμείβων νήσους τε καὶ πόλεις,
ὑποδειχθέντων τῷ ἁγίῳ Ποτιόλων,
αὐτὸς μὲν ἐξελθεῖν ἔσπευδεν, κατ᾽   180
ἴχνος βαδίζειν ἐθέλων²⁹ τοῦ
ἀποστόλου Παύλου. ὡς δὲ ἐπιπεσόν
βίαιον πνεῦμα³⁰ οὐ συνεχώρει, τῆς
νηὸς ἐκ πρύμνης ἐπειγομένης,
μακαρίσας τὴν ἐν ἐκείνῳ τῷ τόπῳ   185
τῶν ἀδελφῶν ἀγάπην οὕτω παρέπλει.
τοιγαροῦν ἐν μιᾷ ἡμέρᾳ καὶ νυκτὶ τῇ
αὐτῇ, οὐρίοις ἀνέμοις
προσχρησάμενοι, ἡμεῖς μὲν ἄκοντες
ἀπηγόμεθα στένοντες ἐπὶ τῷ ἀφ᾽   190
ἡμῶν μέλλοντι χωρισμῷ τοῦ δικαίου
γίνεσθαι, τῷ δὲ κατ᾽ εὐχὴν ἀπέβαινεν
σπεύδοντι θᾶττον³¹ ἀναχωρῆσαι τοῦ
κόσμου, ἵνα φθάσῃ πρὸς ὃν ἠγάπησεν
κύριον. καταπλεύσας γοῦν εἰς τοὺς   195
λιμένας Ῥωμαίων, μελλούσης λήγειν
τῆς ἀκαθάρτου φιλοτιμίας, οἱ μὲν
στρατιῶται ὑπὲρ τῆς βραδύτητος
ἤσχαλλον, ὁ δὲ ἐπίσκοπος χαίρων
κατεπείγουσιν ὑπήκουσεν.   200
6 Ἐκεῖθεν γοῦν³² ἐώσθησαν ἀπὸ
τοῦ καλουμένου Πόρτου
(διεπεφήμιστο γὰρ ἤδη τὰ κατὰ τὸν
ἅγιον μάρτυρα) συναντῶμεν³³ τοῖς
ἀδελφοῖς φόβῳ καὶ χαρᾷ   205
πεπληρωμένοις, χαίρουσιν μὲν ἐφ᾽
οἷς ἠξίωντο τῆς τοῦ Θεοφόρου
συντυχίας, φοβουμένοις δὲ διότι περ
ἐπὶ θάνατον ὁ τοιοῦτος ἤγετο. τισὶ δὲ
καὶ παρήγγελλεν ἡσυχάζειν,³⁴ ζέουσι   210

Troadem. Deinde illinc ductus ad
Neapolim, per Philippenses
transivit Macedoniam pedes,
et terram quae ad Epidamnum. Cujus in
juxta marinis nave potitus
navigavit Adriacum pelagus,
et illinc ascendens Tyrhenicum et
transiens insulas et civitates,
ostensis sancto Potiolis,
ipse quidem exire festinavit, secundum
vestigia ambulare volens
apostoli Pauli: ut autem incidens
violentus non concessit ventus,
nave a prora repulsa,
beatificans eam quae in illo loco
fratrum caritatem, sic transnavigavit.
Igitur in una die et nocte
eadem prosperis ventis
utentes, nos quidem nolentes
abducimur, gementes de ea quae a
nobis futura separatione justi
fieri; ipsi autem secundum votum accidit,
festinanti citius recedere de
mundo, ut attingat ad quem dilexit
Dominum. Navigantes igitur in
portus Romanorum, debente finem
habere immunda inani gloria,
milites quidem pro tarditate
offendebantur, episcopus autem gaudens
festinantibus obediebat.
6 Illinc igitur expulsi a
vocato Portu
(diffamabantur enim jam quae secundum
sanctum martyrem), obviamus
fratribus timore et gaudio
repletis, gaudentibus quidem in
quibus dignificabantur eo quod Theophori
consortio, timentibus autem quia quidem
ad mortem talis ducebatur. Quibusdam
autem et annunciavit silere, ferventibus

---

²⁷ Τρώαδι Migne, Lightfoot; Τρόαδι Ruinart.
²⁸ πεζὶ καὶ Lightfoot; περὶ καὶ Ruinart; καὶ περί Migne.
²⁹ ἐθέλων Migne, Lightfoot; ἐθέλον Ruinart.
³⁰ πνεῦμα Migne, Lightfoot; lacking Ruinart.
³¹ θᾶττον Migne, Lightfoot; lacking Ruinart.
³² γοῦν Ruinart, Lightfoot; οὖν Migne.
³³ συναντῶμεν Migne, Lightfoot; σὺν αὐτῷ μέν Ruinart.
³⁴ ἡσυχάζειν Migne, Lightfoot; ἡσυχάζουσιν Ruinart.

καὶ λέγουσι καταπαύειν τὸν δῆμον
πρὸς τὸ μὲ ἐπιζητεῖν ἀπολέσθαι τὸν
δίκαιον. ὅς εὐθὺς γνοὺς τῷ πνεύματι
καὶ πάντας ἀσπασάμενος, αἰτήσας τε
παρ' αὐτῶν τὴν ἀληθινὴν ἀγάπην,   215
πλείονά τε τῶν ἐν τῇ ἐπιστολῇ
διαλεχθεὶς καὶ πείσας μὴ φθονῆσαι τῷ
σπεύδοντι πρὸς τὸν κύριον, οὕτω μετὰ
γονυκλισίας πάντων τῶν ἀδελφῶν
παρακαλέσας τὸν υἱὸν τοῦ θεοῦ ὑπὲρ   220
τῶν ἐκκλησιῶν,³⁵ ὑπὲρ τῆς τοῦ
διωγμοῦ καταπαύσεως, ὑπὲρ τῆς τῶν
ἀδελφῶν εἰς ἀλλήλους ἀγάπης,
ἀπήχθη³⁶ μετὰ σπουδῆς εἰς τὸ
ἀμφιθέατρον. εἶτα εὐθὺς ἐμβληθεὶς   225
κατὰ τὸ πάλαι πρόσταγμα τοῦ
καίσαρος, μελλουσῶν καταπαύειν
τῶν φιλοτιμιῶν (ἦν γὰρ ἐπιφανής, ὡς
ἐδόκουν, ἡ λεγομένη τῇ Ῥωμαικῇ
φωνῇ τρισκαιδεκάτη, καθ' ἣν   230
σπουδαίως συνῄεσαν), οὕτως θηρσὶν
ὠμοῖς παρὰ τῷ ναῷ παρεβάλλετο, ὡς
παρ' αὐτὰ τοῦ ἁγίου μάρτυρος
Ἰγνατίου πληροῦσθαι τὴν ἐπιθυμίαν,
κατὰ τὸ γεγραμμένον · Ἐπιθυμία   235
δικαίου δεκτή · ἵνα μηδενὶ τῶν
ἀδελφῶν ἐπαχθὴς διὰ τῆς συλλογῆς
τοῦ λειψάνου γένηται, καθὼς φθάσας
ἐν τῇ ἐπιστολῇ τὴν ἰδίαν ἐπεθύμει
γενέσθαι τελείωσιν. μόνα γὰρ τὰ   240
τραχύτερα τῶν ἁγίων αὐτοῦ
λειψάνων περιελείφθη, ἅτινα εἰς τὴν
Ἀντιόχειαν ἀπεκομίσθη καὶ ἐν λίνῳ
κατετέθη, θησαυρὸς ἀτίμητος, ὑπὸ τῆς
ἐν τῷ μάρτυρι χάριτος τῇ ἁγίᾳ   245
ἐκκλησίᾳ καταλειφθέντα.
7 Ἐγένετο δὲ ταῦτα τῇ πρὸ
δεκατριῶν καλανδῶν Ἰαννουαρίων,
τουτέστιν δεκεμβρίῳ εἰκάδι,
ὑπατευόντων παρὰ Ῥωμαίοις Σύρα   250
καὶ Σεδεκίου³⁷ τὸ δεύτερον. τούτων
αὐτόπται γενόμενοι μετὰ δακρύων
κατ' οἶκόν τε παννυχίσαντες καὶ
πολλὰ μετὰ γονυκλισίας καὶ δεήσεως
παρακαλέσαντες τὸν κύριον   255

et dicentibus quietare plebem
ad non expetere perdere
justum. Quos confestim spiritu
cognoscens, et omnes salutans, petensque
ab ipsis veram caritatem,
pluraque iis quae in epistola
disputans, et suadens non invidere
festinanti ad dominum, sic cum
genuflexione omnium fratrum
deprecans Filium Dei pro
ecclesiis, pro
persecutionis quietatione, pro
fratrum adinvicem caritate,
subductus est cum festinatione in
amphitheatro. Deinde confestim
projectus secundum quondam praeceptum
Caesaris, debentibus quiescere
gloriationibus (erat enim solennis, ut
putabant, dicta Romana
voce tertiadecima, secundum quam
studiose convenerunt), sic bestiis
crudelibus ab impiis apponebatur, ut
confestim sancti martyris
Ignatii compleretur desiderium
secundum quod scriptum est, *Desiderium
justi acceptabile*, ut sit nulli
fratrum gravis per collectionem
reliquiarum; secundum quod praeoccupans
in epistola propriam concupiscit
fieri fruitionem. Sola enim
asperiora sanctorum
ossium derelicta sunt ipsius; quae in
Antiochiam reportata sunt, et in capsa
reposita sunt, thesaurus inappreciabilis ab
ea quae in martyre gratia sanctae
ecclesiae relicta.
7 Facta autem sunt haec die ante
tredecim Kalendas Januarias,

praesidentibus apud Romanos Sura
et Senecio secundo. Horum
ipsimet conspectores effecti cum lacrimis,
et domi per totam noctem vigilantes, et
multum cum genuflexione et oratione
deprecantes Dominum

---

³⁵ τῶν ἐκκλησιῶν Migne, Lightfoot; lacking Ruinart.
³⁶ ἀπήχθη Migne, Lightfoot; ἀπέχθη Ruinart.
³⁷ Σεδεκίου Ruinart, Lightfoot; Σενεκίου Migne.

142   Acts of Martyrs and Commentarii

πληροφορῆσαι τοὺς ἀσθενεῖς ἡμᾶς ἐπὶ
τοῖς προγεγονόσιν, μικρὸν
ἀφυπνώσαντες, οἱ μὲν ἐξαίφνης
ἐπιστάντα καὶ περιπτυσσόμενον ἡμᾶς
ἐβλέπομεν, οἱ δὲ πάλιν ἐπευχόμενον   260
ἡμῖν ἑωρῶμεν³⁸ τὸν μακάριον
Ἰγνάτιον, ἄλλοι δὲ σταζόμενον ὑφ᾽
ἱδρῶτος ὡς ἐκ καμάτου πολλοῦ
παραγενόμενον καὶ παρεστῶτα τῷ
κυρίῳ μετὰ πολλῆς τοίνυν χαρᾶς   265
ταῦτα ἰδόντες, καὶ συμβαλόντες τὰς
ὄψεις³⁹ τῶν ὀνειράτων, ὑμνήσαντες
τὸν θεὸν τὸν δοτῆρα τῶν ἀγαθῶν καὶ
μακαρίσαντες τὸν ἅγιον,
ἐφανερώσαμεν ὑμῖν καὶ τὴν ἡμέραν   270
καὶ τὸν χρόνον, ἵνα κατὰ τὸν καιρὸν
τοῦ μαρτυρίου συναγόμενοι
κοινωνῶμεν τῷ ἀθλητῇ καὶ γενναίῳ
μάρτυρι Χριστοῦ καταπατήσαντι τὸν
διάβολον καὶ τὸν τῆς φιλοχρίστου   275
αὐτοῦ ἐπιθυμίας τελειώσαντι δρόμον

ἐν Χριστῷ Ἰησοῦ τῷ κυρίῳ ἡμῶν, δι᾽
οὗ καὶ μεθ᾽ οὗ τῷ πατρὶ ἡ δόξα καὶ τὸ   280
κράτος σὺν τῷ ἁγίῳ πνεύματι εἰς
αἰῶνας. ἀμήν.

certificare infirmos nos de
prius factis, parum
obdormitantes, hi quidem repente
astantem et amplexantem nos
videbant, hi autem rursus superorantem
nobis videbant beatum
Ignatium, quemadmodum ex labore
multo advenientem, et astantem Domino
in multa confidentia et ineffabili gloria.
Impleti autem gaudio
haec videntes,
et glorificantes
Deum datorem bonorum, et
beatificantes sanctum,
manifestavimus vobis et diem
et tempus, ut secundum tempus
martyrii congregati
communicemus athletae et virili
Christi martyri, qui conculcavit
diabolum et hujus insidias
in finem prostravit;
glorificantes in ipsius venerabili
et sancta memoria
Dominum nostrum Jesum Christum, per
quem et cum quo Patri gloria et
potentia cum Spiritu Sancto in
sancta ecclesia in saecula
saeculorum. Amen.

Translation

1 Not long after Trajan had succeeded to the empire of the Romans, Ignatius, the disciple of John the apostle, a man in all respects of an apostolic character, and who governed the church of the Antiochians with great care, having with difficulty escaped the former storms of the many persecutions under Domitian, inasmuch as, like a good pilot, by the helm of prayer and fasting, by the perseverance of his teaching and by his spiritual labor, he resisted the surge of the enemy's power against him, fearful that he might lose some of those who were deficient in courage or who were simple-minded. Therefore he rejoiced at the tranquil state of the church, when the persecution ceased for a little time, but he was distressed that he had not yet attained true love of Christ nor reached the complete rank of a disciple. For he considered that the confession which is made by martyrdom would bring him into a yet closer relationship to the Lord. Therefore, remaining a few years longer with the church and, like a divine lamp, illuminating every person's mind by his exposition of the holy Scriptures, he attained the object of his prayer.

³⁸ ἑωρῶμεν Migne, Lightfoot; ἤρωμεν Ruinart.
³⁹ ὄψεις Migne, Lightfoot; ὄφεις Ruinart.

2 For Trajan, in the ninth year of his reign, being elated at his victory over the Scythians and Dacians and many other nations, and thinking that the pious organization of the Christians was still lacking complete subjugation to him, and threatening them with persecution unless they should agree to worship demons, as did all other nations, and would have forced all who were living pious lives either to sacrifice or die. Therefore the noble soldier of Christ, being fearful for the church of the Antiochians, was of his own volition brought before Trajan, who was then staying at Antioch, but was preparing to campaign against Armenia and the Parthians. And when he was face to face with Emperor Trajan,

[Trajan said]: "Who are you, poor wretch, that you are so ready to disobey our commands, and seduce others to do the same, so that they should miserably die?"

Ignatius said, "No one should call the God-bearer [*theophorus*] wretched; for all the demons have departed from the servants of God. But if, because I am troublesome to these [demons], you call me a wretch to them, I quite agree with you; for since I have Christ the king of heaven [within me], I destroy all the devices of these [demons]."

Trajan said, "And who is the one who bears God [*theophorus*]?"

Ignatius answered, "He who has Christ within his breast."

Trajan said, "We, then, do not seem to you to bear the gods in our mind, whose assistance we employ in fighting against our enemies?"

Ignatius said, "You are wrong when you call the demons of the nations gods. For there is one God, who made heaven, and earth, and the sea, and all that are in them; and one Jesus Christ, the only begotten Son of God, whose kingdom may I enjoy."

Trajan said, "Do you mean him who was crucified under Pontius Pilate?"

Ignatius said, "I mean him who crucified my sin along with him who was its inventor, and who has sentenced every deceit and malice of the devil to be trampled under the feet of those who carry him in their heart."

Trajan said, "You, then, bear within yourself him who was crucified?"

Ignatius said, "Yes, for it is written, 'I will dwell in them, and walk in them.'"

Trajan pronounced sentence: "We command that Ignatius, who affirms that he bears within him him that was crucified, be bound by soldiers and carried to the great [city] Rome, there to be made food for the beasts, for the people's enjoyment."

When the holy martyr heard this sentence, he cried out with joy, "I thank you, Lord, that you have considered me worthy enough to perfect my love towards you, and have made me to be bound with chains of iron, like your Apostle Paul."

When he had said these things, he clasped the chains about himself with delight; and when he had first prayed for the church, and commended it to the Lord with tears, he was hurried away by the savage cruelty of the soldiers, like a choice ram, the leader of a goodly flock, that he might be carried to Rome to served as food to the bloodthirsty beasts.

3 So with great eagerness and joy, through his desire to suffer, he came down

from Antioch to Seleucia, from which place he set sail. And after much struggle he came to the city of the Smyrnaeans, where he disembarked with much joy and hurried to see the holy Polycarp, bishop of Smyrna, and his fellow-disciple, for they had both, long ago, been disciples of the holy apostle John. Being then brought to him, and having communicated to him some spiritual gifts, and glorying in his bonds, he begged him to assist him in the fulfilment of his desire, indeed earnestly asking this of the whole church (for the cities and churches of Asia had welcomed the holy man through their bishops, and presbyters, and deacons, all hurrying to meet him, in the hope that they might receive from him some spiritual gift), but above all, the holy Polycarp, that, by means of the wild beasts he would be sooner disappearing from this world, he might appear before the face of Christ.

4 And these things he thus spoke and thus testified, extending his love toward Christ as one who was about to seize heaven through his good confession and the devotion of those who joined their prayers to his over his combat; and he recompensed the churches which came to meet him through their rulers by sending letters of thanks to them, showering spiritual grace upon them with prayer and exhortation. Therefore, when he saw that all were so kindly disposed towards him, and fearing that the love of the brotherhood might hinder his zeal towards the Lord, when a good door of martyrdom was opened to him, he wrote to the church of the Romans the epistle, which is here subjoined:

Here follows Ignatius *Epistle to the Romans*

5 By means of this epistle, therefore, having settled, as he wished, those brethren in Rome who were averse [to his martyrdom]; and setting sail from Smyrna (for Christophorus [or: the Christ-bearer] was hurried by the soldiers to the public spectacles in the mighty [city] Rome, that by being given to the wild beasts in the sight of the Roman people he might obtain the victor's crown), he [next] landed at Troas. Then from there, having landed at Neapolis, passing through Philippi he traveled on foot across Macedonia and that part of Epirus which is near Epidamnus, and finding a ship in one of the seaports, he sailed across the Adriatic Sea, and from there entering the Tyrrhene, and passing islands and cities until Puteoli came in sight, where he was eager to disembark, having a desire to walk in the footsteps of the Apostle Paul. But a violent wind which arose prevented him from doing so, the ship being driven rapidly forwards; and, simply expressing his delight over the love of the breathren in that place, he sailed by. Therefore, continuing to enjoy fair winds, we were reluctantly hurried on in one day and a night, mourning [as we did] over the coming departure from us of this righteous man. But to him this happened just as he wished, since he was anxious to leave this world as soon as possible that he might join the Lord whom he loved. Sailing then into the Roman harbor, and the unholy games being just about to close, the soldiers began to be annoyed at our slowness, but the bishop yielded to their urgency with joy.

6 They debarked therefore from the place which is called Portus; and, the things relating to the holy martyr being already spread abroad, we met the breathren full of fear and joy; rejoicing indeed because they were thought worthy to meet with Theophorus [or: the God-bearer], but fearful because so eminent a

man was being led to death. Now he enjoined some to keep silence who, in their fervent zeal, were boiling and saying that they would not demand the destruction of this just one. He being immediately aware of this through the Spirit, and having saluted them all, and begged of them to show a true affection towards him, and having dwelt [on this point] at greater length than in his epistle, and having persuaded them not to deny him hastening to the Lord, he then, after he had, with all the brethren kneeling [beside him], entreated the Son of God in behalf of the churches, that a stop might be put to the persecution, and that mutual love might continue among the brethren, was led with all haste into the amphitheater. Then, being immediately thrown in, according to the command of Caesar given some time ago, the public spectacles being just about to close (for it was then a solemn day, as they deemed it, being that which is called the thirteenth [Saturnalia celebrated] in the Roman tongue, on which the people were wont to assemble in more than ordinary numbers), he was thus cast to the wild beasts close beside the temple, that so by them the desire of the holy martyr Ignatius should be fulfilled, according to that which is written, "The desire of the righteous is acceptable [to God]" [Prov 10:24], to the effect that he might not be troublesome to any of the brethren by the gathering of his remains, even as he had in his epistle expressed a wish beforehand that so his end might be. For only the harder portions of his holy remains were left, which were conveyed to Antioch and wrapped in linen, as an inestimable treasure left to the holy church by the grace which was in the martyr.

7 Now these things took place on the thirteenth day before the kalends of January, that is, on the twentieth of December, Sura and Senecio being then the consuls of the Romans for the second time. Having ourselves been eye-witnesses of these things, and having spent the whole night in tears within the house, and having entreated the Lord, with bended knees and much prayer, that he would give us weak men full assurance with respect to the things which were done, it happened, when we feel deeply asleep, that some of us saw the blessed Ignatius suddenly standing among us and embracing us, while others saw him again praying for us, and still others saw him dripping with sweat, as if he had just come from his great labor, and standing by the Lord. When, therefore, we had with great joy witnessed these things, and had compared our several visions [lit. "the visions of the dreams"] together, we sang praise to God, the giver of all good things, and expressed our sense of the happiness of the holy [martyr]; and now we have made known to you both the day and the time, that, assembling ourselves together according to the time of his martyrdom, we may have fellowship with the champion and noble martyr of Christ, who trode under foot the devil, and perfected the course which, out of love to Christ, he had desired, in Christ Jesus our Lord; by whom, and with whom, be glory and power to the Father, with the Holy Spirit, for evermore! Amen.

Prior Analyses and Considerations

As the reader can see, the center of interest of this version is Antioch, which caused Lightfoot to name them the "Antiochene" version. Ignatius is tried before Trajan, who is said to be in Antioch preparing for his campaign against the Armenians and Parthians. Trajan condemns Ignatius to be thrown to the beasts at Rome, after which event Ignatius's bones are carried back to Antioch to be preserved as relics. In the Roman version, the center of interest is Rome (hence the name "Roman" version).[40] Ignatius is sent to Rome to be tried before Trajan, and after his condemnation and martyrdom, his bones are preserved in Rome.

Lightfoot's reasons for rejecting the historicity of the Antiochene version, which he considered worth more consideration than the Roman version,[41] are partially based upon the criticisms by Uhlhorn[42] and Zahn.[43] The internal and external evidence, Lightfoot argues, "is decidedly adverse to their claims to be regarded as an authentic document, either wholly or in great part."[44] The Antiochene acts purport to have been written by eye-witnesses to the events (see §§ 5–7), but the language employed and events described are unlikely to have been written by a contemporary. The areas of difficulty noted by Lightfoot and others may be grouped under the following headings: (1) the dramatic date and place; (2) the route described; (3) noncontemporary language and descriptions; and (4) witnesses. These topics will be briefly taken in order below before we turn to the trial portion, the focal point of our study.

The Dramatic Date and Place

According to Lightfoot, the year of Trajan's reign given by the Antiochene acts cannot be reconciled with the consuls for the year who are named. On this point, Lightfoot is mistaken. The Antiochene and Roman versions give the following:

> Antiochene version: ... Trajan in the ninth year of his reign (§ 2) ...
> Now these things happened on the 13th before the Kalends of January, when Sura and Senecio for the second time were consuls among the Romans (§ 7).
>
> Roman version: In the ninth year of the reign of Trajan Caesar, being the second year of the 223rd Olympiad, in the consulship of Atticus Surbanus and Marcellus ... (§ 1).

The "ninth year" of Trajan's reign would be 106/7 CE. The Antiochene acts

---

[40] Lightfoot (*Apostolic Fathers*, 2. 380–81), however, believes that the Roman version actually originated in Alexandria. His arguments are convincing.

[41] Ibid., 382.

[42] *Die Ignatianischen Briefe*, 248ff.

[43] *Ignatius von Antiochien* (Gotha: Perthes, 1873) 41ff.

[44] Lightfoot, *Apostolic Fathers*, 2. 383.

indicate that "Sura and Senecio were then the consuls of the Romans for the second time" (§ 7). Q. Sosius Senecio was consul for the first time (with A. Cornelius Palma Frontonianus) in 99. L. Licinius Sura's first consulship, as Lightfoot notes, cannot have been an ordinary consulship, as it does not appear in the fasti, and its year is therefore unknown."[45] Sura was consul for the second time—but ordinary consul for the first time—in 102 (with L. Iulius Ursus Servianus). For the year 107, the common lists give: L. Licinius Sura III. Q. Sosius Senecio II.[46] Lightfoot reads ὑπατευόντων παρὰ Ῥωμαίοις Σύρα καὶ Σενεκίωνος τὸ δεύτερον (§ 7) as meaning either the second time that Sura and Senecio were consuls together, adding that "in fact Sura and Senecio never were consuls together more than once,"[47] or as when Sura and Senecio were consuls together, Senecio for the second time. Their consulship together in 107 was for both their second ordinary consulship. The discrepancy Lightfoot sees between the year of Trajan's reign and consuls listed in the Antiochene acts, in my opinion, does not exist.

There is a definite discrepancy between the regnal year and the consuls given in the Roman version. The fasti give Sex. Attius Suburanus Aemilianus II. M. Asinius Marcellus as the consuls for 104.

That the Antiochene acts place Trajan in Antioch in the year 106/7 is problematical. His campaign against the Parthians and stay in Antioch, as Lightfoot notes, "took place several years later than the date assigned to the martyrdom in these Acts, whether the year of Trajan's reign (§ 2) or the names of the consuls (§ 7) be taken to determine the time."[48] From 101–6 Trajan was involved in the Dacian Wars, against their king Decebalus. Dio Cassius records that after the first successful campaign, in 103,

> Trajan celebrated a triumph and was given the title of Dacicus; in the theatre he held contests of gladiators, in whom he delighted. . . . He did not, however, as might have been expected of a warlike man, pay any less attention to the civil administration nor did he dispense justice any less; on the contrary, he conducted trials, now in the Forum of Augustus, now in the Portico of Livia, as it was called, and often elsewhere on a tribunal.[49]

The *Acts of Ignatius* give the date of Ignatius's martyrdom as 107. In this year Trajan was back in Rome celebrating the final victory over the Dacians.

[45] Lightfoot, *Apostolic Fathers*, 2. 489 n.
[46] See, e.g., E. J. Bickerman, *Chronology*, 156.
[47] Ibid.
[48] Lightfoot, *Apostolic Fathers*, 2. 384.
[49] Dio Cassius 68.10.2. Trans. Earnest Cary, *Dio's Roman History* (9 vols.; LCL; London: Heinemann; Cambridge: Harvard University Press, 1954).

According to Dio Cassius, in 107 Trajan "gave spectacles on one hundred and twenty-three days, in the course of which some eleven thousand animals, both wild and tame, were slain, and ten thousand gladiators fought."[50] So far as is known, Trajan did not concern himself with the Parthians and Armenians until about 110, when the Parthian king Osroes deposed the client king of Armenia. In 113 Trajan himself led a large invasion force into Armenia and succeeded in making it an imperial province. Trajan spent the winter of 113–14 in Antioch and from there proceeded against Mesopotamia, probably in the spring of 114. In 117 he was again in Antioch, when he fell ill and died in Cilicia on his return trip to Rome.

In any case, the regnal year and the consuls given, in either version, are possibly later interpolations, if we assume the possibility of an authentic residuum. It is perhaps worth noting that the years of the consuls given by the Antiochene and Roman versions, 107 and 104 respectively, very nearly coincide with the two years (103 and 107) in which Trajan is recorded as celebrating *ludi*. Perhaps this is only coincidence, but it may reflect different attempts by redactors to flesh out a tradition that Ignatius had been martyred in Rome during one of Trajan's *ludi*.

The route taken by Ignatius in the Antiochene acts is not easily reconcilable with the route scholars have reconstructed from Ignatius's epistles. Those portions of the acts that contain the narrative of Ignatius's route lie outside the perimeters of this study.

Noncontemporary Language and Descriptions

Three difficulties in particular have been noted in this category. (1) The descriptions of political events given in the opening chapters, Lightfoot says, are "conceived altogether in the manner of a historian writing long after the occurrences. A contemporary, addressing contemporaries, would not have introduced this elaborate statement [the opening chapters] which was superfluous alike for himself and for his readers."[51] (2) In Ignatius's epistles, the churches in Asia Minor do not appear to be persecuted; in the acts, persecution is pervasive. (3) In Ignatius *Epistle to Polycarp* 1, it appears that Ignatius has met Polycarp for the first time, whereas in the Antiochene acts (§ 3) they are represented as having been fellow disciples of John.

These points are damaging to any argument for the historicity of the Antiochene acts, but any case, either for or against, must not stand upon language that is subjectively thought to be noncontemporary. A very large part of ancient Christian literature contains "superfluous" descriptions of

[50] Ibid., 68.15.1.
[51] Lightfoot, *Apostolic Fathers*, 2. 384.

events, miraculous deeds, elaborate descriptions of martyrs' sufferings and deaths, etc. In any case, I am not arguing here that the Antiochene acts as a whole are historical. I am rather questioning the rejection of them as a whole.

Witnesses

According to Lightfoot, "not a single witness to the existence of [the Antiochene acts] has been adduced till the close of the sixth century."[52] Eusebius, Chrysostom, and Jerome do not make use of the Antiochene version. The first writer who clearly uses the Antiochene acts is Evagrius Scholasticus in his *Historia ecclesiastica* (1.16), which was written near the end of the sixth century. The epistles of Ignatius are early and well attested.[53] Witnesses to Ignatius *Epistle to the Romans* unfortunately do not necessarily attest to the *Acts of Ignatius*.[54] It has been argued that Lucian of Samosata had read at least one of the epistles of Ignatius and that he may have been familiar with the *Martyrdom of Polycarp*.[55] Lucian was born in Samosata, which was northeast of Antioch on the Euphrates in the Commagene, about the year 120 and died some time after 180. He occasionally called himself a Syrian. His geographical and chronological proximity to Ignatius and Polycarp add weight to any argument that he was familiar with writings of these Christians. Lucian was a satiric, even sarcastic, writer who loved to scoff at the objects of his writings.[56] In his *Passing of Peregrinus* he recounts the life

---

[52] Ibid., 2. 385.

[53] Ibid., 1. 127–221.

[54] The more important witnesses from the second century are: Polycarp *Epistle to the Philippians* 1 (cf. Antiochene *Acts of Ignatius* 5), 9 (cf. Ignatius *Epistle to the Romans* 6); *Martyrdom of Polycarp* 3 (cf. Ignatius *Epistle to the Romans* 5), 14 (cf. Antiochene *Acts of Ignatius* 2); Irenaeus *Adv. haer.* 5.28.4 (cf. Ignatius *Epistle to the Romans* 4); and *Martyrdom of Perpetua* 14 (cf. Ignatius *Epistle to the Romans* 5).

[55] E.g. Lightfoot, *Apostolic Fathers*, 2. 356, note to line 4; A. M. Harmon states:

"In the letters of Ignatius he recommends to the Church of Smyrna the election of a special messenger, styled 'ambassador of God' (θεοπρεσβευτής: *ad Smyrn.*, 11) or 'courier of God' (θροδρόμος: *ad Polyc.* 7), to be sent to Syria. The verbal coincidence [with νεκραγγέλους καὶ νερτεροδρόμους κτλ.; see below] is notable [cf. Lightfoot], and seems to indicate a knowledge of these letters, but on the part of Peregrinus, not Lucian" (*Lucian* [5vols.; LCL; Cambridge: Harvard University Press, 1972] 5. 47).

If there is a knowledge, it is on Lucian's part.

[56] Albin Lesky writes:

"Lucian read widely and learnt a great deal in the school of rhetoric, but he did not have the gift of making the fruits of his learning his own property. On the other hand the opinion of modern scholars who would deprive him almost completely of imagination goes a great deal too far" (*A History of Greek Literature* [New York: Crowell, 1957] 838).

of a charlatan Cynic philosopher, who is said to have cremated himself at the Olympic games of 165 CE. Although Proteus Peregrinus was a real person, Lucian's "Peregrinus" is a conglomeration of persons from classes of society against which Lucian wished to poke jest and berate, the Christians included. Many of the details recounted by Lucian strongly suggest to me that he was familiar with the epistles and *Acts of Ignatius* and the *Martyrdom of Polycarp*. Among the more suggestive passages are the following:

"Proteus, who was imprisoned in Syria" (*Peregrinus* 4).[57]

Proteus is said to be "also called Theagenes" (*Peregrinus* 5).[58]

"It was then that he learned the wondrous lore of the Christians, by associating with their priests and scribes in Palestine. ... he was prophet, cult-leader, head of the synagogue, and everything, all by himself. He interpreted and explained some of their books and even composed many, and they revered him as a god, made use of him as a lawgiver, and set him down as a protector, next after that other, to be sure, whom they still worship, the man who was crucified in Palestine because he introduced this new cult into the world. Then at length Proteus was apprehended for this and thrown into prison, which itself gave him no little reputation as an asset for his future career and the charlatanism and notoriety-seeking that he was enamoured of. Well, when he had been imprisoned, the Christians, regarding the incident as a calamity, left nothing undone in the effort to rescue him. Then, as this was impossible, every other form of attention was shown him, not in any casual way but with assiduity; and from the very break of day aged widows and orphan children could be seen waiting near the prison, while their officials even slept inside with him after bribing the guards. Then elaborate meals were brought in, and sacred books of theirs were read aloud, and excellent Peregrinus— for he still went by that name—was called by them 'the new Socrates.' Indeed, people came even from the cities in Asia, sent by the Christians at their common expense, to succour and defend and encourage the hero." (*Peregrinus* 11 – 13)[59]

"He set sail for Italy and immediately after disembarking he fell to abusing everyone, and in particular the Emperor." (*Peregrinus* 18)

The manner of Proteus's death, fire, is predicted. (*Peregrinus* 4, 5, 29)[60]

[57] This may be compared to Ignatius's arrest in Antioch.
[58] Ignatius is "also called Theophorus" (e.g., *Acts of Ignatius* 2 and the prologues to Ignatius's epistles, which he opens Ἰγνάτιος ὁ καὶ Θεοφόρος).
[59] Many comparisons can be drawn from this passage with the epistles of Ignatius, *Acts of Ignatius*, and *Martyrdom of Polycarp*.
[60] Compare *Martyrdom of Polycarp* 5, where Polycarp has a dream in which his death by fire is predicted.

".... when the pyre was kindled and Proteus flung himself bodily in, a great earthquake first took place, accompanied by a bellowing of the ground, and then a vulture, flying up out of the midst of the flames, went off to Heaven, saying, in human speech, with a loud voice: 'I am through with the earth. ....' " (*Peregrinus* 39)[61]

The story is that he despatched missives to almost all the famous cities—testamentary dispositions, so to speak, and exhortations and prescriptions—and he appointed a number of ambassadors for this purpose from among his comrades, styling them "messengers from the dead" and "underworld couriers" So ended that poor wretch Proteus. ... [O]n my return from Syria I recounted how I sailed from the Troad in his company, and about his self-indulgence on the voyage ... when we were disturbed during the night in mid-Aegean by a tempest that descended and raised an enormous sea. .... (*Peregrinus* 41)[62]

Form-critical Analysis of the *Acts of Ignatius*

Does the Antiochene Version Preserve a Residuum?

Previous attempts to answer this question have focused upon the passages which purport to be recounted by eyewitnesses, especially the "we" sections. Lightfoot concluded,

If the writers [of the Antiochene version] were Philo and Rhaius Agathopus, whom we learn from the letters to have been in the martyr's company at Troas (*Philad.* 11, *Smyrn.* 10, 13), as many critics suppose, the "we" might be expected to appear, while the martyr was still on the shores of the Aegean. ... As a matter of fact, its first occurrence is where we should least look for it—on the Tyrrhene Sea, as the ship is approaching the Italian shore. ... Still the objection is very far from being fatal; while on the other hand there is at least a naturalness in its introduction without any attempt to justify or explain it. Moreover I cannot help feeling impressed with the air of truthfulness, or at least of verisimilitude, in some incidents in the latter portion of the narrative which

---

[61] The manuscripts of the *Martrydom of Polycarp* 16 have "when these vicious men realized that his body could not be consumed by the fire they ordered a *confector* to go up and plunge a dagger into the body. When he did this there came out a dove and such a quantity of blood that the flames were extinguished." But "dove and" is not in Eusebius's text and is probably best understood as an interpolation.

[62] To this passage, compare: *Acts of Ignatius*, my collation line 50; cf. line 55; *Acts of Ignatius* 3–5; Ignatius *Epistle to the Smyrnaeans* 11; Ignatius *Epistle to Polycarp* 7; and Ignatius *Epistle to the Philadelphians* 10–11.

have excited the suspicions of others. Thus Hilgenfeld (*A.V.* p. 215)
argues that the desire of landing at Puteoli, attributed to Ignatius, is due
to the writer's wish "to make his journey to Rome as like as possible to
that of the Apostle." To my mind it suggests the very opposite inference. It is not easy to see how two journeys from the shores of the
Levant to Rome could differ more widely. S. Paul goes by sea to Melita;
Ignatius crosses over Macedonia and Epirus to Dyrrhachium. S. Paul
lands at Puteoli; Ignatius is prevented from landing there and disembarks
at Portus. The two journeys in short have nothing in common, except
the fact that both travellers were on the Adriatic and Tyrrhene seas. . . . I
should be disposed to believe, that the martyrologist had incorporated
into the latter portion of his narrative a contemporary letter of the
martyr's companions containing an account of the journey from Philippi
and the death, though freely interpolating and altering it, where he was
so disposed. But one consideration is so serious as to be almost fatal to
this hypothesis. It is extremely improbable that such a document should
turn up in the fifth or sixth century, though wholly unknown to previous
ages.[63]

Any attempt to answer the question of how traditional legends might have
been woven together to form our acts, must be avoided here, since the topic
lies outside the perimeters of this study. Lightfoot's principal reason for
rejecting the Antiochene acts, as can be seen in the quotation above, is its
lack of early witnesses. If we assume an authentic "residuum," is it certain
that it would be textually recognizable in the extant form of these acts? The
overall form of the Antiochene *Acts of Ignatius* is not really the genre we
have called *acta Christianorum*. It is rather of the genre "romance," which,
as Helmut Koester succinctly describes, was

  a popular type of literature in the Hellenistic and Roman periods . . .
  which reflected the new experience of life that Hellenism had made possible. The heros of the romance travel by land and by sea . . . to strange
  countries, see untold marvels, encounter numerous obstacles which they
  overcome miraculously, and speak of the ideals of love and morality to
  foreign kings and barbarian audiences. . . . A number of motifs from
  older Greek literature recur, but the chief concentration is upon the
  individual's fate, experiences, troubles, and ultimate success.[64]

In the *Acts of Ignatius*, the principal difference is that the theology of martyrdom that "death is victory" has reversed many of the motifs of the genre.

---

[63] Lightfoot, *Apostolic Fathers*, 2. 388–90.
[64] Koester, "Literature, early Christian," *IDBSup*, 555.

The Antiochene Acts of Ignatius and Commentarius-Form

As noted above, the overall form of the account is "romance," but the acts have been given this form by a later editor in order to meet new needs with a Christian community. The trial of Ignatius is contained in § 2 (collation lines 30–113)[65] of the *Acts of Ignatius*, and this section, although manifestly edited, still retains the *commentarius*-form. If γάρ μετὰ ταῦτα in line 30 is understood as an editorial copula, a splice between § 1 and an exemplar of Ignatius's trial, § 2 stands very naturally by itself. It appears to be the "residue" of an "authentic account."

A difficulty to this thesis might be thought to exist in the fact that ὁ γενναῖος τοῦ Χριστοῦ στρατιώτης (line 44) assumes a prior mention of the name Ἰγνάτιος, which does not appear in the preceding lines of § 2. However, notice the opening lines of the *Acts of Justin*:

Μαρτύριον τῶν Ἁγίων Ἰουστίνου, Χαρίτωνος,
Χαριτοῦς, Εὐελπίστου, Ἱέρακος, Παίονος, Λιβεριανοῦ,
καὶ τῆς Συνοδίας αὐτῶν
Ἐν τῷ καιρῷ τῶν ἀνόμων προσταγμάτων τῆς εἰδωλολατρείας
συλληφθέντες οἱ μνημονευθέντες ἅγιοι εἰσήχθησαν πρὸς τὸν τῆς
Ῥώμης ἔπαρχον Ῥούστικον. (Rec. A)

The martyrs' names in the title are necessary antecedents to the text. It is possible that a title such as Μαρτύριον τοῦ Ἰγνατίου τοῦ Θεοφόρου originally provided the antecedent to ὁ γενναῖος κτλ.

The form of § 2, understood as a unit, is very like the form of the "canonical" recensions A and B of the *Acts of Justin* and the *Martyrdom of Apollonius*. The form of these *acta* comprises four major divisions: (1) a *prologue* that briefly describes the church in the midst of persecution and the martyr arrested and about to face trial; (2) a middle section containing the *oratio recta* between the martyr and magistrate; (3) the magistrate's sentence of death; and (4) a brief epilogue in which the martyrs are shown glorifying God. The *oratio recta* is the definite focal point of these accounts. The prologue merely provides a setting, the magistrate's sentence is merely stated, and the epilogue is a sentence or two showing the martyr's joy at being condemned to death. One expects detailed descriptions of the martyr's suffering and death in *acta Christianorum*. Aigrain has noted that the redactors of the accounts were equally "insatiable in the description of the sufferings of the

[65] In the discussion below, "collation" refers to the collated Greek and Latin texts above; "line" refers to the line numbers given between the texts. Whenever reference is made to the *Acts of Ignatius* without the specification of version, the Antiochene version is meant.

martyrs.''[66] But in the *Acts of Justin* and *Martyrdom of Apollonius* no such descriptions are given—the magistrate passes sentence, the martyr praises God, and the document abruptly ends. Like these acts, *Acts of Ignatius* 2 is divided into four sections: (1) a prologue that places the church in the midst of persecution and presents Ignatius about to appear for trial; (2) an *oratio recta* section, which is the focal point; (3) Trajan's sentence; and (4) a brief epilogue showing Ignatius's extreme joy at the verdict. Like the *Acts of Justin* and the *Martyrdom of Apollonius*, the *Acts of Ignatius* 2 ends without a description of the martyr's death.

The overall form of the *commentarius*, as argued in Chapter Two, falls into four divisions: (1) *caput*, which usually contains the extract phrase, the name and title of the magistrate, the date formula, location, participants, and occasionally a sentence or two of *oratio obliqua* that summarizes details relevant to the case; (2) the body of the trial, the *oratio recta* portion; (3) the κρίσις; and (4) concluding matters, such as summaries of fines exacted or merely the word ἀνέγνων. The coincidence between the four major divisions of *commentarius*-form and the form of many *acta Christianorum* suggests that these *acta* may have originated from *commentarii*. I have argued elsewhere[67] that the *Acts of Justin* originated from a *commentarius* but the extant form is the result of a redactor modifying the *commentarius*-form to meet the needs of the Christian community. The *caput* of the *commentarius* was modified to a prologue, the body was edited but left largely intact, and a brief epilogue was added or substituted for the "concluding matters" of the *commentarius*. The *Acts of Ignatius* 2 fit this form well. However, a form-critical method that merely looks for the major divisions of a *commentarius* in the *acta Christianorum* is entirely inadequate. The methodology must penetrate to the smaller units, to the form of the individual elements, the fifteen elements presented in Chapter Two. If a form-critical approach gives us reason to believe that a *commentarius* lies at the base, or that *commentarius*-form has exerted a strong influence, but that the account has been edited, the employment of redaction criticism will show how the smaller units have been consciously reworked to meet the intended needs.

Thus, based upon an assumption that *Acts of Ignatius* 2 may be isolated as *acta Christianorum*, let us compare it to *commentarius*-form.

[66] Aigrain, *L'hagiographie*, 146.
[67] Bisbee, "Acts of Justin."

Caput

The prologue to the *Acts of Ignatius* is not given in the form of a *caput* to a *commentarius*. But traces of several *caput* elements are to be found. The magistrate's name is given in line 30, and although the full form of the name would be expected, that it is in the genitive is intriguing. One of the forms in which the extract phrase and magistrate's name were given in *commentarii* was to give the magistrate's name alone in the genitive. Moreover, ἐπαρθέντος κτλ. (line 32) is awkwardly separated from Τραϊανοῦ (line 30) by γὰρ μετὰ ταῦτα (the editorial splice) ἐννάτῳ ἔτει τῆς αὐτοῦ βασιλείας (the date). In forming the splice to § 1 and the interpolation ἐπαρθένος κτλ., we might argue, an editor has obscured the *commentarius*-form of the extract phrase, the magistrate's name, and the date. In line 45 there is a presence phrase (ἤγετο πρὸς Τραϊανόν), and the location is indicated in line 47. Even if these considerations are taken together, it cannot be proven that a *commentarius* lies at the base of the prologue to the *Acts of Ignatius*, but the coincidences are suggestive. In any case, the prologue compares favorably to the prologue of recension A of the *Acts of Justin* quoted above and to that of recension B quoted below:

Ἐν τῷ καιρῷ τῶν ἀνόμων ὑπερμάχων τῆς εἰδωλολατρείας προσ-τάγματα ἀσεβῆ κατὰ τῶν εὐσεβούντων Χριστιανῶν κατὰ πόλιν καὶ χώραν ἐξετίθετο, ὥστε αὐτοὺς ἀναγκάζεσθαι σπένδειν τοῖς ματαίοις εἰδώλοις. συλληφθέντες οὖν οἱ μνημονευθέντες ἅγιοι ἄνδρες εἰσήχθησαν πρὸς τὸν τῆς Ῥώμης ἔπαρχον ὀνόματι Ῥούστικον.

Body of the Trial

The first *oratio recta* of a *commentarius* is often introduced in a form unlike subsequent *orationes rectae*. The first *oratio recta* of the Greek *Acts of Ignatius* (lines 49–50) is introduced directly, without verb of saying, in the unliterary, terse style of a *commentarius*, whereas all the speeches, except the κρίσις, are introduced by εἶπεν. The Latin version introduces the first speech by *Trajanus dixit*, and this is yet another indication that Cod. Paris. 1451 is not a translation of the Anglo-Latin version. The absence of a leading verb in lines 49–50 of the Greek is remarkable, since a writer wishing merely to mimic *commentarius*-form is unlikely to have noticed this stylistic subtlety.

However, the consistent use of εἶπεν is problematical. On the surface, the body of the trial (lines 50–91) fits *commentarius*-form. The style is terse, with the pattern Τραϊανός εἶπεν … Ἰγνάτιος εἶπεν consistently introducing their speeches. Connective phrases such as ὁ δέ and καί are absent, as are intrusive descriptions of the speakers' reactions and other such narrative. In spurious accounts and in most accounts that have been edited at later dates, the terse style of speaker's name plus εἶπεν alone to introduce *oratio recta* is rare.[68] A variety of verbs normally not used in *commentarii*, such as ἔφη and φησίν are used,[69] and εἶπεν is often used in constructions such as εἶπεν πρὸς αὐτόν that are non-*commentarius*-form. Recension C of the *Acts of Justin* is a good example of how the *commentarius*-form of an "authentic" *acta Christianorum* could become obscured by redaction. The simple εἶπεν introductions of recensions A and B are completely lost, since they have been replaced by a wide variety of introductions of non-*commentarius*-form such as ἔφη ὁ ἅγιος, direct introductions of the form καὶ ὁ ἅγιος, literary forms of introduction (e.g., *oratio recta* → φησιν, → *oratio recta*), ὁ ἔπαρχος λέγει, and ὁ ἔπαρχος ἔφη.[70]

Moreover, we would expect Ἰγνάτιος to modified by ἅγιος or μακάριος if the document is indeed as late as the fifth or sixth century, but not too much can be made of the absence of the word "saint," since there are sufficient late examples where the word is not used. Arguments can be made from the presence of ἅγιος or μακάριος, but none should be made from their absence.

Our knowledge of *commentarius*-form reveals that the real problem is the consistent use of εἶπεν. First of all, the *orationes rectae* of the Roman version, which are a completely different set of questions and answers from the Antiochene version, are likewise introduced by εἶπεν (and without "saint" modifying "Ignatius"). Moreover, it was argued in Chapter Two, and confirmed in Appendix One below, that prior to about 129 CE scribes used the direct form of introduction to *oratio recta*. After 136, scribes consistently use εἶπεν, and about 234 they begin to use the abbreviated form εἶ(πεν). According to this evidence, the εἶπεν introductions to *oratio recta* in the *Acts of Ignatius* are anachronistic by at least twenty years.

However, the case for authenticity is still not damaged beyond repair, for there are several viable explanations of the εἶπεν problem. It must be remembered that the bulk of our evidence derives from Egypt and here we are treating an account from Antioch or Rome. The εἶπεν introductions could be original, although I am inclined to believe that the original *commentarius* of Ignatius's trial either introduced *oratio recta* directly or was recorded in Latin. This belief is partially based upon the relationship of the Greek and Latin texts of these acts. Lightfoot recognized that the value of

---

[68] So far as I know, this phenomenon is unique to the Antiochene and Roman versions of the *Acts of Ignatius*.

[69] ἔφη is occasionally used in *commentarii*, but as Coles has remarked, it "does not seem to belong properly to that group of indicative verbs that are on a par with εἶπεν" (Coles, *Reports of Proceedings*, 43 n.).

[70] The full text of recension C of the *Acts of Justin* may be found in Musurillo, *Christian Martyrs*, 54–60.

the Latin MSS of the middle version (*Caiensis* 395 and *Montacutianus*) consists in its extreme literalness. To this end the contruction of the Latin is consistently sacrificed . . . Moreover the MS which the translator used was evidently superior to the existing MSS of the Greek (*Laur.* lvii. 7 and *Paris. Graec.* 1451). Thus it is free from several interpolations in these MSS (mostly found also in the Long recension, and frequently quotations from the N.T.); e.g. *Ephes.* 1 τοῦ ὑπὲρ ἡμῶν ἑαυτὸν ἀνενεγκόντος Θεῷ προσφορὰν καὶ θυσίαν, *ib.* 2 κατηρτισμένοι τῷ αὐτῷ νοΐ κ.τ.λ., *ib.* 3 τὰ γὰρ βλεπόμενα πρόσκαιρα κ.τ.λ., *ib.* 4 κοσμικὸν ἢ μάταιον, *Rom.* 5 ἀνατομαὶ διαιρέσεις, *ib.* 6 τί γὰρ ὠφελεῖται ἄνθρωπος κ.τ.λ., *ib.* 10 τουτέστιν Αὐγούστου εἰκάδι τρίτῃ. Similarly it is free from the omission of λόγος after Θεοῦ and the substitution of τρέχων for φωνὴ in *Rom.* 2. Again, in several instances it gives words and clauses which have dropped out of these MSS through inadvertence; e.g. *Ephes.* 1 'videre festinastis,' *Trall.* 7 'qui vero extra altare est, non mundus est,' *Philad.* 7 'Dei voce,' *Rom.* 6 'neque per materiam seducatis,' *Mart.* 5 'justitiae per tale.' Again in many places, where the reading is changed or corrupted, it preserves a correct text; e.g. *Polyc.* 1 'consuetudinem' (ὁμοήθειαν for βοήθειαν), *Philad.* 5 'imperfectus' (ἀναπάρτιστος for ἀνάρπαστος), *Rom.* 3 'suasionis' (πεισμονῆς for σιωπῆς μόνον), *ib.* 6 'termini' (πέρατα for περπνά), *Mart.* 6 'ab impiis' (παρὰ τῶν ἀθέων for παρὰ τῷ ναῷ). Again, it is free from some glosses which disfigure the Greek text; e.g. *Magn.* 8 'secundum Judaismum' (for κατὰ νόμον Ἰουδαϊσμόν), *ib.* 9 'secundum dominicam' (for κατὰ κυριακὴν ζωήν), *Rom.* 6 'homo ero' (for ἄνθρωπος Θεοῦ ἔσομαι).

At the same time, though much superior, it belonged to the same family with these. This is clear from the arrangement of the epistles and the presence of the confessedly spurious letters. . . . This close relationship moreover is confirmed by the presence of the same corrupt readings in both. . . . At the same time the advantage is not always on the side of the Latin text, as compared with the Greek MSS. Thus in *Smyrn.* 6 ὁ χωρῶν χωρείτω· τόπος μηδένα φυσιούτω, the Latin rendering, 'qui capit capiat; qualiter nullis infletur,' arises obviously from a corruption χωρειτω[το]πως for χωρειτωτοπος. . . . So also in *Rom.* 7 the Latin 'ignis amans aliquam aquam, sed vivens' is certainly corrupt, while the Greek πῦρ φιλόϋλον, ὕδωρ δὲ ζῶν may perhaps give the original reading. But the passages where the text of the Greek MSS contrasts favourably with that of the Latin Version are very few in all.[71]

The Greek and Latin texts of the Antiochene acts obviously derive from the same textual tradition, and Lightfoot is right that the Latin is a translation from a Greek exemplar. In addition to the comparisons made by Lightfoot

[71] Lightfoot, *Apostolic Fathers*, 1. 78.

above, the Latin's reading *cacodaemon* (lines 50 and 55) would be a clear indication that in the exemplar was the Greek κακόδαιμον.[72] Moreover, as Lightfoot amply demonstrated, the exemplar was not *Cod. Paris.* 1451. Thus, so far it appears that the Greek and Latin texts given in the collation above are derived from a Greek exemplar. If that Greek exemplar were in turn a translation from a Latin, and this is only conjecture, the presence and consistent use of εἶπεν is easily explained. Latin nearly always introduces *oratio recta* by *dixit* or other forms of *dicere*. Latin simply does not have the wide variety of verbs of saying that Greek does. Thus when Greek verbs of saying were translated into Latin, a variety of Greek verb forms would all be translated *dixit*. Now the *orationes rectae* are consistently introduced in the same way. Then when such a Latin text was translated back into Greek, *dixit* was consistently translated εἶπεν. For example, notice the clauses introducing *oratio recta* in the two Greek translations of the Latin text of the *Acts of Andrew* (6th cen.?):[73]

Passio Andreae 2–4

Cui Aegeas dixit: . . .
Andreas respondit: . . .
Aegeas dixit: . . .
Andreas respondit: . . .
Aegeas dixit: . . .
Andreas respondit: . . .
Aegeas dixit: . . .
Andreas respondit: . . .
Aegeas dixit: . . .
Andreas respondit: . . .
Aegeas dixit: . . .
Andreas respondit: . . .
Aegeas dixit: . . .

ὁ ἅγιος Ἀνδρέας εἶπεν· . . .   ὁ μακάριος Ἀνδρέας εἶπεν· . . .
Αἰγέας εἶπεν· . . .   Ὧιτινι ὁ Αἰγεάτης εἶπεν· . . .
Ὁ ἅγιος Ἀνδρέας εἶπεν· . . .   Ὁ μακάριος Ἀνδρέας εἶπεν· . . .
Αἰγέας εἶπεν· . . .   Ὁ Αἰγεάτης εἶπεν· . . .
Ὁ ἅγιος Ἀνδρέας ἀπεκρίθη· . . .   Ὁ μακάριος Ἀνδρέας ἀπεκρίνατο· . . .

---

[72] Κακοδαίμον, "poor wretch" or "wretched devil" was frequently used in comedy, e.g., Aristophanes (5th/4th cen. BCE) *Plutus* 386; *Equites* 112; Pherecrates (5th cen. BCE) 117.

[73] Full text in Richard Albert Lipsius and Maximilian Bonnet, *Acta apostolorum apocrypha* (2 vols.; Leipzig: Mendelssohn, 1891–1903; reprint ed. Hildesheim: Georg Olms Verlagsbuchhandlung, 1959).

Αἰγέας εἶπεν·...	Ὁ Αἰγεάτης εἶπεν·...
Ὁ ἅγιος Ἀνδρέας ἀπεκρίθη·...	Ὁ ἅγιος Ἀνδρέας ἀπεκρίνατο·...
Αἰγέας εἶπεν·...	Ὁ Αἰγεάτης εἶπεν·...
Ὁ ἅγιος Ἀνδρέας ἀπεκρίθη·...	Ὁ μακάριος Ἀνδρέας ἀπεκρίνατο·...
Αἰγέας εἶπεν·...	Ὁ Αἰγεάτης εἶπεν·...
Ὁ ἅγιος Ἀνδρέας ἀπεκρίθη·...	Ὁ μακάριος Ἀνδρέας εἶπεν·...
Αἰγέας εἶπεν·...	Ὁ Αἰγεάτης εἶπεν·...
Ὁ ἅγιος Ἀνδρέας ἀπεκρίθη·...	Ὁ μακάριος Ἀνδρέας ἀπεκρίνατο·...
Αἰγέας εἶπεν·...	Ὁ Αἰγεάτης εἶπεν·...
Ὁ ἅγιος Ἀνδρέας ἀπεκρίθη·...	Ὁ ἅγιος Ἀνδρέας εἶπεν·...
Αἰγέας εἶπεν·...	Ὁ Αἰγεάτης εἶπεν·...

It seems evident that the Latin exemplar used by both Greek translators had already been edited, the word *sanctus* being consistently added to *Andreas*. Both Greek texts give εἶπεν as the translation of *dixit*, but one translator decided upon ἀπεκρίθη for *respondit* and ἅγιος for *sanctus*, whereas the other decided upon ἀπεκρίνατο and μακάριος.

Two other facets of the *oratio recta* section of the *Acts of Ignatius* should be briefly noted here. First, the line of questioning, which centers around the word "Theophorus," is innocuous and the death sentence comes almost as a surprise. The same phenomenon is found in several of the "canonical" *acta Christianorum*. Neither the *commentarii* nor a knowledge of Roman criminal law will provide conclusive evidence that the line of questioning in the *Acts of Ignatius* is not historical.[74]

In the majority of pre-Decian *acta Christianorum*, trials are opened with either (1) a demand to sacrifice/swear allegiance to the emperors and the gods, or (2) the question "Are you a Christian?" In many of the post-Decian *acta*, the magistrate's first question is "What is your name?" (e.g., *Martyrdom of Conon; Acts of Maximilian; Martyrdom of Julius the Veteran; Martyrdom of Dasius*) and not a command to perform sacrifice as might be expected. In most of the *acta* the line of questions and answers is a mixture of banter, rhetoric, and apology, with the martyr often taking control of the trial's flow. The *commentarii* reveal that the Roman magistrates remained in complete control and kept the proceedings simple and direct. The line of questions and answers in the Antiochene *Acts of Ignatius* (but certainly not in the Roman version) reveal nothing that should cause us to regard § 2 as spurious.

---

[74] As was shown in Chapter One, the *cognitio extra ordinem* of the empire was conducted before a single magistrate, and without a jury. The course of the trial, the questions asked, and the judgments or punishments delivered were normally determined solely by the presiding magistrate, although magistrates often did attempt to follow legal precedent.

Scholars have assumed that the *Acts of Ignatius* were written during the fourth or fifth century. By then the church had very definite theological stances. The Antiochene *Acts of Ignatius* 2 presents several difficulties to the arguments for lateness. First, we probably would not have expected the unabashed admission that Ignatius was a "volunteer martyr" in line 45 in a spurious writing of the fourth or fifth century.[75] Second, we would have expected the writer to have made more of a theological point by Ignatius's answer to Trajan's question "Who is theophorus?" (lines 63–64). Ignatius's answer, "He who has Christ within his breast," is not the type of theological statement of doctrine we would expect following the Apollinarian and Nestorian controversies. Third, in the *acta Christianorum* it is usual for the martyr to give an *apologia* or statement of the *regula fidei*,[76] and these theological statements were commonly "updated" by redactors to keep the martyr's theology orthodox. The brief theological statements of lines 71–78 and 81–86, although perhaps not the ipsissima verba of Ignatius, are more likely to be from the second century than from the fourth or fifth.

Κρίσις

Trajan's judgment is introduced in the *Acts of Ignatius* in *commentarius*-form: Τραϊανὸς ἀπεφήνατο [*oratio recta*]. No formal objection can be raised against the form, since ἀπεφήνατο is used only to introduce judgments in *commentarii* and is found as early as 115 CE in *P. Oxy.* 706 and 118 in *SB* 9252. Moreover, Trajan's sentence reveals that the entire line of questioning that centers on the word "Theophorus" is really the question, "Are you a

---

[75] Of the known pre-Decian martyrs, most must be categorized as "voluntary martyrs," that is, individuals who actually provoked their own martyrdom. This assertion, of course, runs counter to the stereotyped view that the early Christians were hunted down mercilessly, without provocation on their part, by Roman troops and pagan mobs. This is not to say, however, that such things were not experienced by pre-Constantinian Christians, for it is certain that they were. For a view similar to my own, see G. E. M. de Ste Croix, "Aspects of the 'Great' Persecution," *HTR* 47 (1954) 75–113. The attitude of the martyr was not one of resignation, as is commonly reported by prisoners, for example by those in Nazi death camps, Viet Cong tiger cages, and by the embassy hostages in Iran (1980), but an actual desire to experience death at the hands of the "enemy." The "orthodox" stance eventually came to be that voluntary martyrdom was not true martyrdom, that it was in fact heretical. For the second century, however, "orthodox/catholic" is an anachronism, and even during the third and fourth centuries the dividing line between voluntary and true martyrdom was a fine one. To flee or keep a low profile during persecution was deemed a betrayal of the Lord, but to provoke one's own martyrdom was heretical. One had to remain highly visible during persecution—but not "too" visible.

[76] See Adalbert Hamman, "La Confession de la foi dans les premiers actes des martyrs," in Jacques Fontaine and Charles Kannengiesser, eds., *Epektasis: Mélanges Patristiques offerts au Cardinal Jean Daniélou* (Paris: Beauchesne, 1972) 99–105.

Christian?'' This, as we know from the famous Pliny–Trajan correspondence,[77] was Trajan's preferred policy in questioning and convicting Christians.

Concluding Matters

As in other *acta Christianorum*, any remnants of concluding matters are lacking in the *Acts of Ignatius*. Instead we have the epilogue to the account that has Ignatius crying out in joy at being condemned to the beasts in Rome, where Paul had been martyred.

Conclusions

This study of the Antiochene version of the *Acts of Ignatius* was not intended to form the sorts of conclusions that were the object of my more thorough form-critical study of the *Acts of Justin*. It is hoped, however, that this study has shown that the *Acts of Ignatius*, especially § 2, warrant more consideration by the community of scholars. It was argued above that § 2 is a separate account of Ignatius's trial that has been incorporated into the extant form, as was Ignatius *Epistle to the Romans* incorporated into that form. An analysis of § 2 according to *commentarius*-form reveals that this section is of the same form as the canonical *Acts of Justin* and *Martyrdom of Apollonius*, which were originally derived from *commentarii* but redacted to suit the needs of the Christian community. The εἶπεν introductions to *oratio recta* in the *Acts of Ignatius* are not used until after about 130 in *commentarii*. Yet I am very much inclined to regard § 2 as a product of the second century, being either originally written or derived from the actual *commentarius* of Ignatius's trial and edited at roughly the same period as the *Acts of Justin* were first edited.[78]

---

[77] Pliny *Ep.* 10.96. On this correspondence, see esp. Robert M. Grant, ''Pliny and the Christians,'' *HTR* 41 (1948) 273–74; A. N. Sherwin-White, *The Letters of Pliny: A Historical and Social Commentary* (Oxford: Clarendon, 1966).

[78] See Bisbee, ''Acts of Justin,'' 157: ''Lazatti dated the editing of recension A 'before the conclusion of the persecutions' and recension B 'probably to the fourth century' [Lazzati, *Gli sviluppi della letteratura sui martiri*, 119]. Others, such as Freudenberger, would date the editing of both recensions to the fourth century, based principally upon the wording of the prologues. I have attempted to show that the prologues need not date so late as is commonly assumed and that there are difficulties with dating either recension as late as the fourth century. Especially relevant to this question are the absence of a dramatic date and the early form of the creedal statements. The reference to Rusticus in A's prologue may indicate quite an early date for one editing. The predominant use of Rusticus's title throughout both recensions perhaps indicates another editing ca. the mid-third century, but I would not date the final editing of either A or B beyond the late third century.''

If the *Acts of Ignatius* derived from the *commentarius*, we would have expected *oratio recta* to have been introduced directly, by the speaker's name alone and no verb of saying. One explanation given above for the εἶπεν introductions is that the original Greek *Acts of Ignatius* were translated into Latin, whereupon the direct introductions became *dixit*, and then back into Greek, whereupon *dixit* became εἶπεν. If this theory warrants further investigation, the Greek text of the "authentic" Ignatius *Epistle to the Romans* should be reexamined in order to see if it has also passed through the same stages.

Representative Texts

A Representative First-century *Commentarius*

P. Oxy. 37 (49 CE)

Column 1

1 Ἐξ ὑπομ[ν]ηματισμῶν Τι[βερίο]υ Κλαυδ[ίο]υ Πασίωνος στρατη(γοῦ).
(ἔτους) ἐνάτ[ο]υ Τιβερίου Κλαυδίου Καίσαρος Σεβαστοῦ Γερμανικοῦ
Αὐτοκ[ρά]τορος, Φαρμοῦθι ϛ̄. ἐπὶ τοῦ βήματος,
[Π]εσοῦρι[ς] πρὸς Σαραεῦν. Ἀριστοκλῆς ῥήτωρ
5 ὑπὲρ Πεσούριος, "Πεσοῦρις, ὑπὲρ οὗ λέγωι, ζ (ἔτους)
Τιβερίου Κλαυδίου Καίσαρος τοῦ Κυρίου ἀνεῖλεν
ἀπὸ κοπρίας ἀρρενικὸν σωμάτιο ὄνομα Ἡρα-
κ[λᾶν]. τοῦτο ἐνεχείρισεν τῆι ἀντιδίκωι· ἐγένετο ἐνθάδε ἡ τροφεῖτις εἰς υἱὸν τοῦ Πεσούριος.
10 τοῦ πρώτου ἐνιαυτοῦ ἀπέλαβεν τὰ τροφεῖα.
ἐνέστηι ἡ προθεσμία τοῦ δευτέρου ἐνιαυτοῦ,
κα[ὶ] πάλιν ἀπέλαβεν. ὅτι δὲ ταῦτα ἀληθῆι λέγωι,
ἔστιν γράμματα αὐτῆς δι᾽ ὧν ὁμολογεῖ εἰλη-
φέναι. λειμανχουμέν[ο]υ τοῦ σωματ[ί]ου ἀπέ-
15 σπασεν ὁ Πεσοῦρις. μετ[ὰ] ταῦτα καιρὸν εὑροῦσ[α
εἰσεπήδησεν εἰς τὴν τοῦ ἡμετέρου [ο]ἰκίαν
καὶ τὸ σωμάτιον ἀφήρπασεν, καὶ βούλεται ὀν[ό-
ματι ἐλευθέρου τὸ σωμάτιον ἀπενέγκασ-
θαι. ἔχω[ι] πρῶτον γράμμα τῆς τροφείτιδος,
20 ἔχωι δεύτερο[ν] τῶν τροφείων τὴν [ἀ]ποχή[ν.
ἀξιῶι ταῦ[τα] φυλαχθῆ[ν]αι." Σα[ρα]εῦς,
"ἀπεγαλάκ[τισά] μου τὸ [π]αιδίον, κα[ὶ] τούτων

σωμάτιόν μοι ἐνεχειρίσθηι. ἔλαβ[ον] παρ᾽ αὐτῶν τοὺ[ς] πάντας ὀκτὼι στατῆρας. μετὰ
25 ταῦτα [ἐτελεύ]τησεν τ[ὸ σ]ωμάτιο[ν στα-
τήρων π[ερ]ιόντων. νῦν βούλον[ται τὸ

Column 2

1 ἵ[δι]όν μου τέκνον ἀποσπάσαι." Θέων,
"γράμματα τοῦ σωματίου ἔχομεν."
ὁ στρατηγός, "ἐπεὶ ἐκ τῆς ὄψεως φαίνεται τῆς
Σαραεῦτος εἶναι τὸ παιδίον, ἐὰν χιρογραφήσηι
5 αὐτήι τε καὶ ὁ ἀνὴρ αὐτῆς ἐκεῖνο τὸ ἐνχει
ρισθὲν αὐτῆι σωμάτιον ὑπὸ τοῦ Πεσούριος
τετελευτηκέναι, φαίνεταί μοι κατὰ τὰ ὑπὸ
τοῦ κυρίου ἡγεμόνος κριθέντα ἀποδοῦσαν
αὐτὴν ὃ εἴληφεν ἀργύριον ἔχειν τὸ [ἴδιο]ν
10 τέκνον."

A Representative Second-century *Commentarius*

BGU 15 (= W.*Chr.* 393) (194 CE)

1 Ἐξ ὑπομνηματισμῶν Ἰουλίου Κουιντιανοῦ τοῦ κρατίστου
ἐπιστρατηγοῦ. ἔτους δευτέρου Λουκίου
Σεπτιμίου Σεουήρου Περτείνακος Σεβαστοῦ Μεσορὴ β. μεθ᾽ (ἕτερα)·
κληθέντος Πεκύσις Ἀπύγχεως καὶ ὑπακούσαντος Διάδελ-
5 φος ῥήτωρ εἶπεν· ἐάν σοι δοκῇ, κάλεσον τὸν τῆς Νείλου
πόλεως κωμογραμματέα, ᾧ ὁ ἡμέτερος ἐνκαλεῖ. κληθέντος καὶ μὴ ὑπακούσαντος Ἀρτεμίδωρος στρατηγὸς εἶπ[ε]ν·
κωμογραμματέα οὐκ ἔχι ἡ Νείλου πόλις, ἀλλὰ πρεσβυτέρους
διαδεχομένους. Διάδελφος ῥήτωρ εἶπεν· κεκέλευσται ὑπὸ
10 τῶν κατὰ καιρὸν ἡγεμόνων ἕκαστον ἰς τὴν ἑαυτοῦ κώ-
μην καὶ μὴ ἀπ᾽ ἄλλης κώμης εἰς ἄλλην μεταφαίρεσθαι.
ὅτι νῦν κωμογραμματεὺς ἐπηρεάζει τῷ συνηγορου-
μ[έ]νῳ, ἀνέδωκεν αὐτὸν πράκτορα ἀργυρικῶν τῆς ἰδίας
κώμης εἰς ἄλλην λειτουργείαν. ἀξιοῖ ἀναγεινώσκων τὰ κε-
15 κελευσμένα μὴ ἀφέλκεσθαι ἀπὸ τῆς ἰδίας εἰς ἀλλοτρίαν.
Κοιντιανὸς εἶπεν· στρατηγὸς διαλήμψεται, ὃ τῶν ἐμῶν
17 μερῶν καταλάβηται, ἐπ᾽ ἐμὲ ἀναπέμψιν.

An Anomalous Text

P. Fam.Teb. 24 (= P. Lug.Bat. 6) (up to 124 CE)

On this text, see the discussion in Chapter Two. This text exists in two
copies, British Museum 1888 (= B.M.) and Berlin 13992 (= B), which are

virtually identical except for a short passage near the end of B.M. The line numbers at the far left are of B and those in paretheses are B.M. The text given below is that of B.M.

Column 1

1 (1) Ἐξ ὑπομνηματισμῶν Ἀπολλωνίου γεναμένου στρατηγ]οῦ Θεμίστου μ[ε]ρίδος

2 (2) κ⌐ριτοῦ καὶ ἐπὶ τῆς ἀνακτήσεῳ⌐ Ι τῶν   ἀλλοτ]ριουμένῳν[

3 (3) Καταστῆναι ἐπ' ἐμου ∟ θ̄ Αὐτο⌐κράτορος Καίσαρος Τρα]ιανοῦ⌐ Ι Ἀδριαν[οῦ Σεβαστοῦ

4 (4) μηνὸς Παχὼν (date) Εὐάγγελον Πάτρωνος καὶ Ἡρακλείδη]ν‵ τὸν‵καὶ ⌐Οὐαλέριον καὶ

5 (4) Λυσίμαχον ἀμφοτ⌐ Ι ἕρους Ἡρακλείδου καὶ Ἁρποκρατίωνα καὶ] Ἀκουσίλαον ἀμφοτέροις

6 (5) Λεωνίδου Σα⌐ραπίωνι Ἡρακλείδου. Εὐαγγέλου⌐ Ι δι]ὰ τῶν συνηγορούντων

7   αὐτῷ (names) ῥητόρων εἴπαν⌐τος τὸν πατ]έρα αὐτοῦ Πάτρωνα⌐

8 (6) Ι κατασταθέντα δημοσίων λόγων βιβλιοφύλακ]α τῶι δεκάτῳ ἔτει

9 (7) ἐν μ⌐ηνὶ Ἐπὶφ καὶ μείναντα ἐν τῇ τάξει⌐ Ι τετελευτηκένα]ι̣ τῷ δωδεκάτῳ ἔτει

10   ἐν μηνὶ   παραλα]βόντα παρ⌐ὰ τῶν πρὸ

11 (8) αὐτοῦ βιβλιοφυλάκων⌐ Ι διὰ τοῦ γραματέως Λεωνίδου το]ῦ πατρὸς Ἁρποκρατίω νο(ς)‵

12 (9) καὶ Ἀκουσιλάου ⌐τεταγμένω.....δε κοινωνόν∙⌐ Ι]του Ἡρακλείδ( ) [τὸ]ν πατέρα

13   Σουλπικίῳ] Σιμ⌐ίλι τῶι ἡγεμονεύ-

14 (10) σαντι τῷ[ν]⌐Ι διὰ τῶν τοῦ ῑᾱ ⌐ διαλογι]σμοῦ ὑποδιγμ[ατισμ]ῶν

15 (11)]..[.κ]έναι κ[αὶ ἀξιοῦντα]⌐ Ι παραλα]μβάνειν αὐτ[ὸν τὰ βιβ]λία

16 (12)]ναι τῷ γραμα̣τ[εύσαντι Λ⌐εω]νί[δῃ]ρα̣.‵τιν αὐτὸν εἰς τὴν⌐ Ι β...

17   ].τινο. καὶ [..........] ...α[.]. Ἡρακλείδου κ[

18   Λ]εωνίδου τε‵ τοῦ⌐ Ι γραματεύσα[ντος τοῦ π]ατρὸ[ς αὐ]τοῦ καὶ τοῦ Ἡρ[ακλείδου

19   ἐπιζητοῦντος τίνος κι]νδύνου τὴν παράλ⌐η[μψιν] τῶν βι̣[βλ]ί̣ων δεῖ γε[νέσθαι,⌐

20 (13) Ι τὸν στρατηγήσαντα Λε]ωνίδην κεκρικέ[ν]α[ι ......] Λεωνί[δου] τοῦ γραματέω[ς

21   ].αρ.υ.θεν τὴν‵ α...‵παρα̣ [......].. τῷ[ν α]ὐθεντῶν πο[...

22   ]....οπ...ω..ιη...ο̣..εζητη[...].τῷ τοῦ ς̄∟ [θεοῦ

23   Τραιανοῦ δια]λογσμῷ περί τινων βιβλ[ί]ων παρα[λη]μφθέντων ὑ[πὸ τῶν πρὸ

24   αὐτῶν βιβλιοφυλά]κων καὶ ἀποκειμένων ἐν μέρ[ι] τιν[ὶ τ]ῆς βιβλιοθήκ̣η̣[ς......

25   ]ρώτα, τὸν κράτισ[τ]ον ἡ[γ]εμώνα [τὸν] στρατηγὸν [......

26   τα εἶναι ἄχρηστα καὶ δηλῶσε το[..] γὰρ σταθήσεται̣[....

27   γ]ε̣ναμ[έ]νῳ διαλογισμῷ τὸν στρα[τη]γήσαντα Πτο[..

28   ].κέναι καὶ δεδηλωκέναι τίνα ἐστ[ὶν τ]ὰ βιβλία καὶ [τὸν

Column 2

29 ἡγε]μώνα κεκρ⟨ι⟩κέναι τοὺς ἐνεχωμένους τῇ παραδώσει ὅσα δεῖ ἐκ τῶν
αλ.[...

30 ..].[.]...ζομένω[ν] ἐν ἐξαμήνῳ ἀναμεταιτῆσαι ἢ πραχθῆναι τά[λα]ντον
καὶ ποιήσα-

31 σθ]αι · πρὸς ταῦτα ὑ[...]βον[..δ]ʹ[αι]ʹ αὐτὸν καὶ ἀξιοῦντα μὴ [ἐ]νέχεσθαι
διὰ τὸ τὰ μὲν παρα-

32 λ]ημφθέντα ὑπὸ [τοῦ] πατρὸς αὐτο[ῦ] παραδεδόσθαι, τὸν δὲ ἀνεπιτήδιον
ὄντα μὴ

33 ἐ]νέχεσθαι, ἅμ[α] τε τὰ ζητούμενα βιβλία ὑπὸ τοῦ γραμ̣ατέως Λεωνίδου
παριλῆμ-

34 φ]θε, ἐσχηκέναι κριτὴν σὲ τὸν σήμερον ἀκούοντα · ὅθεν ἀξιοῦν μὴ
ἐνεχόμενον

35 α]ὐτὸν μὴ κρατῖσθαι. Ἡρακλείδο[υ] τοῦ καὶ Οὐαλερί[ο]υ καὶ
Λυσιμάχου δηὰ τῶν συν-

36 η]γορησάντων αὐτοῖς Ἀμωνίου καὶ Ἑρμίου ῥητόρων ἀποκριναμένων
τὸν

37 π]ατέρα αὐτῶν [Ἡ]ρακλείδην γενάμενον βιβλιοφ[ύλ]ακα δημωσίων
λόγων σὺν

38 τ]ῷ τοῦ Εὐαγγέλ[ου] πατρὶ Πάτρωνι [ἐ]ν τῷ αὐτῷ χρό[ν]ῳ
κατασταθέντας, ἀλλὰ προτέ[ρο]υ

A *Commentarius* in an Inscription

IG 14.830 (174 CE; from Puteoli)

(lines 1 – 19 of the inscription are
an Ἐπιστολὴ γραφεῖσα τῇ πόλει Τυρίων)

20 Ἀπὸ ἄκτων βουλῆς ἀχθείσης κα′ Δίου τοῦ ἔτους τ′, ἐφημεροῦντος
[ἐφημερεύοντος] Γ. Οὐαλερίου
Καλλικράτους Παυσανίου προέδρου.
Ἀνεγνώσθη ἐπιστολὴ Τυρίων στατιωναρίων ἀναδοθεῖσα ὑπὸ Λάχητος
ἑνὸς αὐτῶν, ἐν ᾗ ἠξίο[υ]ν πρόνοιαν ποιήσασθαι αὐτοῖς (δηναρίων) σν′ ·
[ἀναλίσκειν γὰρ] εἴς τε θυσίας
καὶ θρησκείας τῶν πατρίων ἡμῶν θεῶν ἐκεῖ ἀφωσιωμένων ἐν ναοῖς

25 καὶ μὴ εὐτονεῖν τὸν μισθὸν τῆς στατίωνος παρέχειν κατ᾽ ἔτος (δηναρίων)
[σν′,
καὶ τὰ ἀναλώματα εἰς τὸν ἀγῶνα τὸν ἐν Ποτιώλοις τῆς βουθουσίας αὐτοῖς προστεθῆναι · τῶν γὰρ ἑτέρων ἀναλωμάτων [καὶ τῶν] γεινομένων εἰς
ἐπι-
σκευὴν τῆς στατίωνος εἰς τὰς ἱερὰς ἡμέρας τοῦ κυρίου αὐτοκράτορος σ[υν-
πεσούσης αὐτοῖς ἐλογίσαντο, ἵνα μὴ τὴν πόλιν βαρῶσιν· καὶ ὑπεμίμνη-

30 σκον ὅτι οὐδεμία πρόσοδος γείνεται αὐτοῖς οὔτε παρὰ ναυκλήρων οὔτε
παρὰ ἐμπόρων ὡς ἐν τῇ βασιλίδι Ῥώμῃ. Μεθ᾽ ἣν ἀνάγνωσιν Φιλοκλῆς Διο-
δώρου εἶπεν · οἱ ἐν Ῥώμῃ στατιωνάριοι ἔθος εἶχον ἀεί ποτε ἐξ ὧν αὐτοὶ λαμ-

βάνουσιν παρέχειν τοῖς ἐν Ποτιόλοις (δηναρίους) σν'· ἀξιοῦσι καὶ νῦν οἱ ἐν
Ποτιόλοις
στατιωνάριοι αὐτὰ ταῦτα αὐτοῖς τηρεῖσθαι ἢ εἰ μὴ βούλονται οἱ ἐν Ῥώμῃ
αὐ-
35 τοῖς παρέχειν, αὐτοὶ ἀναδέχονται τὰς δύο στατίωνας ἐπὶ τῇ αὐτῇ αἱρέσι.
Ἐ-
πεφώνησαν· καλῶς εἶπεν Φιλοκλῆς· δίκαια ἀξιῶσι [ἀξιοῦσι] οἱ ἐν
Ποτιόλοις· ἀεὶ
οὕτως ἐγείνετο καὶ νῦν οὕτως γεινεσθω· τοῦτο τῇ πόλει συμφέρει· φυλαχθή-
τω ἡ συνήθεια. Ἀνεγνώσθη πιττάκιον δοθὲν τὸ [τὸ δοθὲν?] ὑπὸ Λάχητος..
..
..... καὶ Ἀγαθόποδος υἱοῦ αὐτοῦ Τυρίων στατιωναρίων στατίωνος Τυρια-
40 κῆς τῆς ἐν κολωνίᾳ Σεβαστῇ Ποτιόλοις, ἐν ᾧ ἐδήλουν παρέχειν τὴν
ἡμετέραν
πατρίδα στατίωνας δύο, τὴν μὲν ἐν τῇ βασιλίδι Ῥώμῃ, [τὴν δὲ..........

An Anomalous Text

P. Paris 69 (232 CE)

Column 1

(1st hand)   [Ὑπομνημα]τισμοὶ Αὐρηλίου Λεοντᾶ [στρατηγοῦ]
        [Ὀμβίτου]   Ἐλεφαν[τίνης]
        [(Ἔτους) ια Αὐτοκρ]άτορος Καίσαρος Μάρ[κου Αὐρηλίου]
        [Σεο]υήρου Ἀλεξάνδρου Εὐσεβοῦ[ς Εὐτυχοῦς]
    5   [Σεβαστοῦ]
        [Παχ]ὼν α̅ ὁ στρατηγὸς ἔωθεν [ἐπιδη]-
        [μ]ήσας πρὸς τῷ λογιστηρίῳ το[ῖς]
        [δια]φέρουσι ἐσχόλασεν. (2d hand) Ἀνέγνω[ν].
(1st hand)   [β̅ ὁ στρατηγ]ὸς πρὸς τῷ λογιστηρίῳ τοῖ[ς]
    10   [διαφ]έρουσι ἐσχόλασεν. (2d hand) Ἀνέγνω[ν].
(1st hand)   [γ̅ .... ὁ στρ]ατηγὸς τὰ συνηνεγ[.......]
        [.....]ι ἐν Ὄμβοις διὰ βοη[θοῦ. (2nd hand) Ἀνέγνων].
(1st hand)   [δ̅ ὁ στρατηγὸς πρὸς] τῷ λογιστηρίῳ τη[ ]
        [..............(2d hand) Ἀ]νέγνων.
(1st hand) 15   [ε̅ ὁ στρατηγὸς............]ωδη . [ ]
        [..............]εστώτων . [ ]
        [.....]θεν. (2d hand) Ἀνέγνων.
(3d hand)   [Αὐρήλιος ...].. τὰς ὑπ(ηρέτης) προθὶς δημισα κατεχώρι]σα

Column 2

(1st hand)   [Ὑπομνημ]ατισμοὶ Α[ὐ]ρ[ηλίου Λεοντᾶ στρατηγοῦ]
        [Ὀμβίτ]ου   Ἐλεφαν[τίνης]
        [(Ἔτους) ι]β Αὐτοκράτορος Κα[ίσαρος Μάρκου]

5
[Αὐρη]λίου Σεουήρου Ἀλεξάνδρ[ου Εὐσεβοῦς]
[Εὐτυ]χοῦς Σεβαστοῦ.
[Θὼθ ᾱ ὁ] στρατηγὸς ὑπὸ νύκτα [........]
[ἐ]ν τῷ γυμνασίῳ ἅμα Αὐρη[λίῳ.......]
[ἔ]στεψεν εἰς γυμνασιάρχ[ην Αὐρήλιον]
[Π]ελαιᾶν Ἀρπαήσιος Ἱέρα[κος (?) καὶ ἔθυ]-

10
[σ]εν ἔν τε τῷ Καισαρείῳ κα[ὶ ἐν τῷ γυ]-
μνασίῳ, ἔνθα σπονδά[ς τε καὶ]
[δε]ήσεις ποιησάμενος ἀπ[εδήμησεν]
[εἰ]ς τὸν ἕτερον νομὸν Ὀμβ[ίτην, ἔνθα τῶν]
[συ]νηθῶν ἱερουργιῶν Δι[......]

15
[γε]νομένων καὶ τῇ ἀγο[μένη κωμα]
[σ]ίᾳ τοῦ αὐτοῦ παρέτυχεν. (2d hand) Ἀ[νέγνων].

(4th hand)
[Αὐρ]ήλιος Διονυσόδωρος ὑπ(ηρέτης) προθεὶ[ς δημοσίᾳ κατε-
χώρισα]
[(Ἔτους) ι]β Θὼθ β.

Column 3

(1st hand)
[Ὑπομνηματισμοὶ Αὐρηλίου Λεον]τᾶ στρατηγοῦ Ὀμβί[του
Ἐλεφαντίηνς]
[(Ἔτους) ιβ Αὐτοκράτορος Καίσαρος Μάρκου] Αὐρηλίου
Σεουήρου
Ἀ[λεξάνδρου Εὐσεβοῦς Εὐτυχοῦς Σεβαστοῦ]
[Φαῶφι ᾱ ὁ στρατηγὸς ....]ως τῇ ἐκτράξει τῆς μη[νιαίας
18 chars.]ευσεν καὶ ἐν ἄλλαις κώμ[αις
[........] (2nd hand) [Ἀνέγνων.

(1st hand) 5
[β ὁ στρατηγος ....]α πράξας περὶ ἑσπέραν τοῖ[ς
διαφέρουσιν ἐσχόλασεν. (2d hand) Ἀνέγνων].

(1st hand)
[δ ἱερᾶς οὔσης ὑπὲρ γενεθλίω]ν Αὐτοκράτορος Μάρκου Αὐρ[ηλίου
Σεουήρου Ἀλεξάνδρου Εὐσ]εβοῦς Σεβαστοῦ ὁ [στρατηγὸς]
[ca. 20 chars. τριβού]νῳ τῆς ἐν Σοήνη σπείρης κα[ὶ τοῖς
ἑκατοντάρχαις καὶ τῷ βεν]ιφικαρίῳ καὶ τοῖς ἐνάρχοις [........]

10
[ca. 16 chars. ἐν τοῖς πριν]κιπίοις καὶ ἐν τῷ Καισαρείῳ [ca. 24
chars.]νεσι πᾶσι, ἔνθα τῶν συνη[θῶν ἱερουργιῶν (?)
[γενομένων ὁ στρατηγὸς ἔστεψεν (?)] τὸν κύριον ἡμῶν Αὐτο-
[κράτορα Καίσαρα Μάρκον Αὐ]ρήλιον Σε[ο]υῆρ[ον] Ἀλέξα[δρον
Εὐσεβῆ]
[Εὐτυχῆ Σεβαστὸν καὶ Ἰουλίαν Μ]αμαίαν τὴν κυρίαν ἡμῶν[ν
Σεβαστὴν μητέρα Σεβαστοῦ] καὶ τῶν ἱερῶν στρατοπέδ[ων ...
[ca. 25 chars.]τημηθέντων τε τῶν λαμ[προτάτων ἐπάρχων τοῦ
ἱε]ρωτάτου πραιτωρίου καὶ το[ῦ λαμπροτάτου]
[ἡγεμόνος Μηουίου Ὀνωρατιανο]ῦ καὶ τειμηθέντων τῶν
κ[ρατίστων Μαξιμίνου καὶ υἱο]ῦ Μαξίμου πρὸς ταῖς ἐπισκέ[ψεσιν

15
[ca. 25 chars.]λου παρέτυχεν τῇ ἀγομένη [κωμασίᾳ .... καὶ ἐν τῷ

Καισ]αρείῳ εὐωχήθη τῶν ἐνά[ρχων]
[ca. 25 chars. (2d hand) Ἀν]έγνων.

(1st hand)   [ε̄ ca. 16 chars. προσ[ελθόν[το]ς Φιλάμμωνος [ca. 22 chars.]ινιτῶν
πόλεως καὶ τῶ[ν . . . .]
[ca. 24 chars. Αὐ]ρηλίου Σερήνου ἱπ᾿πέω[ς ca. 22 chars.]ς παρόντος
Φλαουίου Λο[γγίνου νομικοῦ(?)]
[ca. 25 chars.] Ἀγαθὸς Δαίμων ῥήτωρ [ca. 22 chars.]ια εἶπεν· Δίκην
πρὸς ἡμᾶ[ς . . . .

20   [ca. 25 chars.] Αἱ γὰρ θεῖναι διατάξεις τῶν π[ροτέρων
αὐτοκρατόρων κελε]ύουσι τὴν νομὴν κυρίαν εἶνα[ι . . . .
[ca. 20 chars. τὸν μ]ὲν εἰκοσαετῆ [χρόνο]ν ὥρισαν [τοῖς ἀποῦσιν,
παροῦσιν δὲ τὸν δε]καετῆ καὶ οὗτος οὐ λόγος ῥη[
[ca. 25 chars.]αι προσκυνη[.]ι[.]. Εἰ οὖν ε . [ca. 22 chars.].
γεν[ο]μένη, δι᾿ ἧς δεδήλ[ωται
[ca. 25 chars. τ]ὰς ἀσφαλίας τοῦ ἀμφιζβη[τουμένου ca. 15 chars.]
τος ἴσως οὐ βούλεται προ[. . . . .
[ca. 25 chars.] τὰ ἀντίγραφα ἔχομεν καὶ λ[ca. 20 chars. εἰκ]οσαετῆ
χρόνον ἐν τῇ νομῇ ἐχ[. . . . .

25   [ca. 25 chars.] ὅσ᾿ ἔτη διαγέγονεν ἀναγκαίως [ca. 22 chars.]ιν αὐτὸν
μὴ ἐπέρχεσθαι ἡμῖ[ν . . . . .
[ca. 25 chars.]ας παρὼν πυθέσθαι περὶ τούτο[υ ca. 19 chars.
πρᾶγ]μα χρῄζει τοῦ μείζονος καὶ ἀξιο[ῦμεν . . .
[ca. 25 chars.] . υς. Αὐρήλιος Λεοντᾶς ὁ στρατηγὸ[ς . . . .
. . . . . μ]ὲν τὴν δίκην εἰπεῖν πρὸς ὑμ[ᾶς
[ca. 25 chars.] αὐτῷ τὸ πρᾶγμα ἀκέραιον ὡς ἦλ[εν ca. 17 chars.
πρ]οτέρῳ γεινομένης. Φιλάμμ[ων . . . . . .
[ca. 25 chars.]ργων περὶ τῆς νομῆς. Ὁ στρατηγ[ὸς ca. 20 chars.].
ἀναθέμενο[ς] τὸ πρᾶγμα ἀκ[έραιον . .

30   [ca. 15 chars. τῷ ἐπιστρατ]ήγῳ. (2d hand) Ἀνέγνων.
(1st hand)   [ξ ὁ στρατηγὸς δημοσίοις πράγμ]ασι σχολάσας τὴν τῶν ὠνίων
ἀ[γορὰν ἐπεσκέψατο. (2d hand) Ἀνέγνων]

(1st hand)   [ζ ὁ στρατηγὸς πρὸς τῷ . . . .]ῳ διάκρισιν πρακτόρων
ποιησ[άμενος ca. 16 chars.]ουῳ καὶ ἐπὶ παροῦσι τοῖς ἐξάρχοι[ς . . .
. .
[ca. 25 chars.]ης ἐντε[ι]λάμενος πρόνοιαν π[οιεῖσθαι ca. 14 chars.]
ἀπεδήμησεν εἰς τὸν ἕτερ[ον νομὸν
[Ὀμβίτην. (2d hand) Ἀνέγνων.]

(1st hand) 35   [date ὁ στρατηγὸς . . . .] . ἐπεδήμησεν. (2d hand) Ἀνέγνω[ν].
(1st hand)   [date ὁ στρατηγὸς ca 12 chars. δ]ημοσίοις πράγμασι [ἐσχόλασεν.
(2d hand) Ἀνέγνων.]

(1st hand)   [date ὁ στρατηγὸς ca 12 chars.] δημοσίοις πράγμασι σχ[ολάσας
πρὸς τῷ . . . .]ιῳ ἐποίησεν προκήρ[υξιν . . . . . .
[ca. 25 chars.]ει ὑποστέλλει ἔτι τε κα[ὶ ca. 20 chars.]ς τὰ ὑπὸ
Πετεφαῦτος ο[. . . . . .
[ca. 25 chars. μ]εταδοθέντα ὑπὸ τῶ[ν τῆς πόλεως γραμματέων εἰς
πρ]ακτορίαν πρὸς δευτ[. . . . . .

40   [ca. 26 chars.]κα ἴσων ἴσας ενετ[ca 22 chars. κα]ταχωριζομένοις
        ὑπ[......

(5th hand) [Αὐρήλιος .... ὑπ(ηρέτης) προθεὶ]ς δημοσίᾳ κατεχώ[ρισα
        date].

Column 4

(1st hand) [Ὑπομ]νημα[τ]ισμοὶ Α[ὑρηλίου Λεοντᾶ στρατηγοῦ Ὀμβίτου]
        [Ἐλεφαντίνης]
        [Ἔτου]ς ιβ Αὐτοκράτορος Καίσ[αρος Μάρκου Αὐρηλίου
        Σεουήρου]
        [Ἀλε]ξάνδρου Εὐσεβοῦς Εὐτυχ[οῦς Σεβαστοῦ]
5   [date ὁ] στρατηγὸς περὶ ἑσπέρα[ν ἐπεδήμησεν. (2d hand) Ἀνέγνων].
(1st hand) [date ὁ] στρατηγὸς πρὸς τῷ λογιστ[ηρίῳ τοῖς διαφέρουσι σχο]-
        [λ]άσας τὴν τῶν ὠνίων ἀγορ[ὰν ἐπεσκέψατο. (2d hand) Ἀνέγνων.]
(1st hand) [date] ὁ στρατηγὸς πρὸς τῷ λογιστη[ρίῳ τοῖς διαφέ]ρουσι
        ἐσχόλασεν. (2d hand) Ἀνέγνων.]
(1st hand) [date] ὁ στρατηγὸς πρὸς τῷ λογιστ[ηρίῳ τοῖς]
        διαφέρουσι ἐσχόλασεν. (2d hand) Ἀνέγ[νων].
(1st hand) [date] ὁ στρατηγὸς πρὸς τῷ λογιστη[ρίῳ .....
        ποιησάμενος περὶ δείλην ο[....
        παρέτυχεν κωμασίᾳ ἐξ ἔθ[ους ἀγομε]-
        νῃ Ἴσιδος θεᾶς μεγίστης. (2d hand) Ἀ[νέγνων].
(1st hand) [date] ὁ στρατηγὸς πρὸς τῷ Καισα[ρείῳ τοῖς]
        διαφέρουσι σχολάσας ἐγέν[ετο πρὸς τῷ]
        [λο]γιστηρίῳ δημοσίοις π[ράγμασι .... (2d hand) Ἀνέγνων.]
(1st hand) [date ὁ] στρατηγὸς πρὸς τῷ [........ τῇ ......]
20   [. .]ήσει ἐσχόλασεν. (2d hand) Ἀνέγνων.
(1st hand) [date ὁ στ]ρατηγ[ὸς] πρὸς τῷ [..... (2d hand) Ἀνέγνων].
(1st hand) [date] ὁ στρα[τηγὸς πρὸς τῷ λογιστηρίῳ διάκρισιν πρα]-
        κτόρων ποιησάμεν[ος ἀπεδήμησεν εἰς τὸν]
        ἕτερον νομὸν Ὀμβίτην. (2d hand) Ἀ[νέγνων].
(4th hand) 25 Αὐρήλιος Διονυσόδωρος ὑπ(ηρέτης) προθ[εὶς δημοσίᾳ
        κατεχώρισα date].

Column 5

(1st hand) Ὑπομνηματισ[μοὶ Αὐρηλίου Λεοντᾶ]

Appendices

Elements of Form in Greek Commentarii

Sigla to Column "Elements of Form"

1 Extract phrase: (a) ἀντίγραφον
               (b) ἀντίγραφον ὑπομνηματισμοῦ
               (c) ἐξ ὑπομνηματισμῶν
               (d) ὑπομνηματισμοί
               (e) ἐκ τῶν ῥηθέντων
               (f) ἄλλου or ἄλλου ὁμοίως
               (g) other

2 Presiding magistrate(s): n = name t = title

3 Date formula

4 Location: (a) ἐν location;
             (b) πρὸ βήματος ἐπὶ (τοῦ) βήματος πρὸς τῷ βήματι
             (c) ἐν τῇ αὐλῇ

5 Presence phrase: e.g., παρόντων ἐν συμβουλίῳ
                      παρερχομένου προσελθών ἐντυχόντων followed by
                      name(s) and/or description (=δ) or title

6 Participants formula: n = name δ = description t = title
      (a) A πρὸς B; (b) ἐπὶ τῶν κατὰ ... κατὰ/πρὸς ...
      (c) κληθείσης καὶ ὑπακουσάσης/κληθέντος καὶ (μὴ) ὑπακούσαντος
      (d) A διὰ/ὑπὲρ X ῥήτορος (e) παρόντος A πρὸς B

7 Delegation phrase: e.g., ἐξ ἀναπομπῆς

8 "Ellipsis" phrase: e.g., μεθ' ἕτερα μετ' ἄλλα/ὀλίγον

9 Summarizing *oratio obliqua* and/or narrative abstract

10　Reading phrase:　e.g., ἀναγνόντος ἀναγνωσθέντων
　　　　　　　　　　ἀναγνωσθέντος μετὰ τὴν ἀνάγνωσιν followed
　　　　　　　　　　(usually) by quotation

11　Oratio recta of magistrate(s)

12　Oratio recta of participants

13　Narrative ἐκέλευσεν-formula or κρίσις given in oratio obliqua

14　Κρίσις: name and/or title of magistrate + oratio recta introduced by:
　　　(a) no verb (direct introduction); (b) εἶπεν/εἶπ
　　　(c) ἀπεφήνατο　(d) ἀπεφήνατο οὕτως/κατὰ λέξιν
　　　(e) ὑπηγόρευσεν ἀπόφασιν, ἣ καὶ ἀνεγνώσθη κατὰ λέξιν
　　　οὕτως ἔχουσα　(f) dative of addressee

15　Concluding matters:　(a) ἐξῆλθεν ὁ δεῖνα ὑπηρέτης
　　　　　　　　　　　(b) ἀνέγνων　(c) ὑπογραφή/ἔγραψα
　　　　　　　　　　　(d) ἐξεδόμην/ἐξέδωκα τὰ ὑπομνήματα
　　　　　　　　　　　(e) σεσημείωμαι　(f) (magistrate's name)
　　　　　　　　　　　ἐκέλευσεν/εἶπεν ὑπομνηματισθῆναι
　　　　　　　　　　　(g) summary of penalties exacted or summary of action
　　　　　　　　　　　taken at the magistrate's order, introduced, e.g.,
　　　　　　　　　　　ἔστιν δὲ τὰ ὀφειλόμενα

Sigla to "Magistrates" column

ἀντ	ἀνταρχιερεύς	ἱερ	ἱερεύς
ἀρχδ	ἀρχιδικαστής	καθ	καθολικός
ἀρχι	ἀρχιερεύς	καῖσ	καῖσαρ
αὐτο	αὐτοκράτωρ	κριτ	κριτής
βουλ	βουλή	λογο	λογοθέτης
γυμν	γυμνασιάρχος	πρεσ	πρεσβύτεροι
διέπ	διέπων	προ	προέδρος
δικα	δικαιοδότος	πρύτ	πρύτανις
ἔπαρ	ἔπαρχος	συμβ	συμβούλιον
ἐπισ	ἐπιστρατηγός	στρα	στρατηγός
ἐπίτ	ἐπίτροπος	σύνδ	σύνδικος
ἡγεμ	ἡγεμόνος	ὑπο	ὑπομνηματογράφος
ἴδιο	ἴδιος λόγος	χιλί	χιλίαρχος

Additional sigla and abbreviations to "Elements of Form" column

Verbs introducing oratio recta

A	ἀπεκρείθη	G	εἶπεν
B	ἀπεκρείνατο	H	εἶπ(εν)
C	ἀπεκρίνατο	I	εἶποσιν
D	ἀπεκρ(ίνατο)	J	εἰπόντος
E	ἀποκρίνεται	K	εἴποντων
F	εἶπαν	L	ἐπιφώνησαν

M ἐπιφωνησάντων	T direct (no introductory verb)
N ἐπύθετο	U dative of addressee
O ἔφασαν	V λέγων
P ἔφη	W λέγει
Q ἐφώνησαν	X φησιν
R ἐφώνησεν	Y dixit
S λέγοντος	Z respondit

Miscellaneous sigla and abbreviations

≡	fragmentary
±	very fragmentary or missing
?	when following an element = my conjecture
( )	elements contained within an element
[? ?]	conjectured sequence
*	form of element unlike form found in *commentarii*

Defence and Explanation of Appendices 1 – 3. Five large three-ring notebooks full of photocopied *commentarii* resulted from months of dragging papyrological publications from various libraries at Harvard, principally Widener Library, to photocopy machines. When it became apparent that the notes to these photocopies were themselves filling notebooks, it became necessary to devise a way to analyze the patterns of relevant data in an overview fashion. What resulted are Appendices 1 – 3. My gratitude goes to any reader who should actually succeed in understanding the sigla; my apologies to those who do not.

To my knowledge, the list of papyri given below is complete for the period 49 – 350 CE, although more *commentarii* have no doubt been published since my last trek to Widener Library in late 1983.

Explanation of the "Elements of Form Present" column: A few examples in less cryptic language may be helpful to the tenacious reader who has gotten this far. "6na" in long hand translates to "participants formula in which the participant's name is given in the "A πρὸς B" form." "11ntE, 12nE" translates to "*oratio recta* of the magistrate introduced by his name, title, and εἶπεν *oratio recta* of a participant introduced by name and εἶπεν." Elements of form are indicated in the order in which they appear.

Acts of Martyrs and Commentarii

Dated *Commentarii*	Magistrates	Elements of Form Present
P. Oxy. 37 (49 CE)[1]	στρα	1c, 2nt, 3, 4b, 6na, 12ntT, 12nT, 12nT, 14ta
P. Yale Inv. 1528 (63 CE)[2]	ἥγεμ	1a, 6nδa, 11ntA, 9, 11G, 12tI, 9, 14ntb
P. Fouad 21 (63 CE)		1b, 3, 4b, 5nt, 14, 15c
P. Oslo 180 (after 69?)	ἐπισ	1b, 2nt, 6nb, 11t?, ≠
P. Flor. 61 (85 CE)[3]		1ac, 3, 6na, ≡, 12n[?t?]T, 11nT, 12ntT, 12ntT, 12nT, ≡, 12nT, 11nT, 12nT, 11nT, 12nT, 12nT, 12nT, 11nT, 12nT, 12nT, 14f, 9
P. Stras. 226 (90–91 CE)	ἔπαρ	1/2n (in gen.), 3, 6na, ≡, 10? (edict from 69 CE)
SB 5761 (91–96 CE)	ἔπαρ	1b, 6na, 9, ≠, 14a; (2d hand) 3; (1st hand) 15
P. Hamb. 29 (after 94)		(*comm.* from 89 CE) 1b, 3, 6δ, 11n (ἐκέλευσε τὸν κήρυκα κηρῦξαι), 12ntT, 14na (ὑπομνηματισθήτωι) ‖
		(*comm.* from 94 CE) 1/2n, 3, 6nδc, 11nT, ≠ [?12nT?], 11nT, ≠
P. Stras. 227 (99/100 CE)	στρα	1/2n, 3, ≠, 11tT?, 12nT, 12nT, 12nT, 12nT, 14na
SB 9050 (after 114)[4]		(*comm.* from 100 CE) 1b, 3, 12nJ, 12nT, 12T, 11nE, 14 ‖
		(*comm.* from 114 CE) 3, 4a (Naucratis), 5nδ/12nJ, 11nT, 12S, 11nT, 12nJ, 9, 14na ‖

---

[1] *P. Oxy.* 37 = M.*Chr.* 79
[2] *P. Yale* Inv. 1528 = *SB* 8247. B. C. Welles, "The immunitas of the roman legionaires in Egypt," *JRS* 28 (1938) 41f.
[3] *P. Flor.* 61 = M.*Chr.* 80.
[4] *SB* 9050 cols. III–IV = *P. Amh.* 65 cols. I–II. Hubert Metzger, "Zur Stellung der liturgischen Beamten Ägyptens in frührömischer Zeit," *Museum Helveticum* 2 (1945) 54ff. Notice the odd mixture of participles (εἰπόντος and λέγοντος) and direct introductions to *oratio recta* in these *commentarii*, which is due, no doubt, to an idiosyncrasy of the copyist.

		(*comm.* from 105 CE) 1/2n, 3, 4a (Memphis), 10, 9, 14nf
P. Rein. 44 (104 CE)[5]	κριτ	1b, 3, 2nt, 6nδa, 15g, 15c
P. Amh. 64 (107 CE)		3, 10, 9, 14na, 11nT, 14na
PSI 450.2 (107/112 CE)	ἔπαρ	1c, 2n, 3, ≡, 9, ≢
P. Fam.Teb. 15 (up to 115)	στρα	1b, 2nt, 3, 6nδ/nta, 12nT, 11nT, 14nt, 15a
P. Oxy. 706 (ca. 115)[6]		≢, 10, 14d, 14fb
SB 9252 (118 CE)	στρα	1b, 2nt, 3, 4c, 9 (6), 12nT, 11tT, 10, 12nT, 12nT, 14nta, 15b
P. Fam.Teb. 19 (118 CE)	στρα	1b, 2nt, 3, 4c, 6d, 9 (of rhetors), 11tT, 10, 12nT, 12nT, 14ta, 15b
PSI 281 (after 118)	ἔπαρ	(*comm.* from 103 – 7) ≢?, 3, ≢, 4, 14n[?a?] ‖
	ἔπαρ	(*comm.* from 107 – 12) 2n, 3, 9?, 11n, 12nt, 14n ‖
	ἐπισ	(*comm.* from 118) 2nt, 3, 9 (1st party), 9 (2d party), 14n, 15g
SB 8757 (120 CE)	ἴδιο	1b, 2nt, 3, 5, 9, 13, ≢
P. Teb. 286 (121 – 38)[7]	αρχδ	1g, 3, 6na, 8, 10 (rescript of Hadrian and κρίσις), 14nta
P. Teb. 488 (121/122 CE)	χιλί	1b, 3, [?6nδ?], ≢, 11nT, 12nT, 14nta, ≢
Arch.Pap. 2, 125a (123 CE)	στρα	1c, 2nt, 3, 6nta, 9, ≢
P. Teb. 297 (ca. 123)	ἴδιο	≢, 12 (rhetor's speech), ≢
CPR 1.18 (124 CE)[8]	ἔπαρ	1c, 2nt, 7, 3, 6e, 9, 11nT, 10, 8, 13, 15na, 3

[5] *P. Rein.* 44 = M.*Chr.* 82.
[6] *P. Oxy.* 706 = M.*Chr.* 81.
[7] *P. Teb.* 286 = M.*Chr.* 83.
[8] *CPR* 1.18 = Bruns[7] 189 = M.*Chr.* 84.

P. Amh. 66 +	στρα	‡, 9, ‡ ‖
Arch.Pap. 2, 125b (124 CE)		1f, 3, 6b, 9, 11ntT, 5, 9, 13
P. Fam.Teb. 24 (up to 124)	στρα	1c, 2nt, 3, 5nt, 9 (1st party), 9 (2d party), 11nT, 10, 11nT, 10 (14nta, 15a ‖ 1/2n, 3, 14nta, 15b), 11nT, 12nT, 11nT, 12tT, 14nta, 9, 14na, 15b, 3, 15g
P. Mil.Vogl. 25 (126/127)	στρα	1b, 2nt, 3, 6nδ, 12ntT, 12ntT, 12nT, 11tU, 12nT, 12nT, 12nT, 12nT, 12nT, 11tT, 11tU, 12nT, 12nT, 12nT, 12nT, 11tU, 12nT, 14ntf ‖
(127 CE)	ἀρχδ	1b, 2n, 3, 4b, 5?, ‡, 6nδa, 9, 11tT, 9, 14nta, 15a, 3
P. Teb. 489 (127 CE)	ἡγεμ	3, 4 (ἐν τῇ οἰκήσις), 7, 2nt, 6nδa, 5, 12tT, ‡
P. Mil.Vogl. 27 (128/129)	στρα	1b, 2nt, 3, 4a (Tebtunis), 9, 11tU, 12nT, 14nta, ‡
P. Oxy. 1420 (ca. 129)	στρα	‡, 11nt (σκεψάμενος εἶπεν), 9, 13, 15b
P. Oxy. 472 (ca. 130)		‡, 12 (speech of rhetor), ‡
P. Teb. 562 (133/135?)		≡
P. Oxy. 2111 (ca. 135)		‡, 12nG, 9, 11nG, 12ntG, 11nG, 12ntG, ‡
BGU 19 (135 CE)[9]	στρα	1a, 7, 2nt, 3, 6nb, 11ntUG, 10, 8, 10, 9, 12ntT, ‡
BGU 136 (135 CE)[10]	ἀρχδ	1b, 1c, 2nt, 3, 4a (Memphis), 6na, 9, 14nta, 15b
SB 7601 (135 CE)[11]	στρα	1c, 3, 4a (Antinoöpolis), 4b, 9, 15 ‖ 1fc, 2nt, 3, 4b, 6nδa, 9 (1st party), 9 (2d party), 9 (1st party), 14ntf, 15b
P. Oxy. 707v (ca. 136)		‡, 6nδa, 12ntG, ‡

---

[9] *BGU* 19 = M.*Chr.* 85 = Bruns[7] 190.
[10] *BGU* 136 = M.*Chr.* 86.
[11] *SB* 7601 = *P. Lond.* Inv. 1890 + 1892; *Aegyptus* 13 (1933) 516.

P. Oslo 17 (136 CE)[12]	στρα	1c, 2nt, 3, 5nδ, 11tT, 12J, 11tT, 12K, 11tT, 12K, 11tT, 9, 11tT, 14tf
SPP 22.184 (140?)[13]		1g (2, 3, 4a), 6nδd, 12
P. Fay. 106 (ca. 140)[14]	ἔπαρ	⚷, 1, 2nt, 3, 14nb, 15g
P. Lond. 196 (ca. 141)[15]		9, 10 (11nF, 12nT, 11nT, 14nb, 15g)
BGU 587 (141 CE)		3, ⚌, 5n, 12nG, ⚌, 11n?G, ⚷
BGU 969 (142?)	γυμν	1a, 1c, 2nt, 3, 6nδb, 12ntH, 12ntB, ⚷, 12nH, ⚷
M.*Chr.* 372 (after 142)	στρα	(*comm.* dated 117) 3, 9 (6nd), 14ntb ‖
	ἱερ	(*comm.* dated 134) 7+1g (ἐξ ἀναπομπῆς X), 3, 6nδa, 9, 10, 9, 14nta ‖
		(*comm.* dated 115) 3, 9 (6n), 14nb ‖
		(*comm.* dated 115) 3, 9 (6nd), 14nb ‖
		(*comm.* dated 142) 3, 5nδ, 9, 11n, 12n, 14nb ‖
		(*comm.* dated 136) 1g (ἰδίου λόγου X), 3, 9 (6nδd), 11n, 9, 14na
P. Wisc. 23 (143 CE)[16]	ἔπαρ	3, 5nt, 8, 14b
P. Fouad 23 (144 CE)		1b, 3, 5nδ + 12G, ⚷
P. Fouad 24 (ca. 144)	ἀρχδ	⚷, 11ntG, ⚷, 14ta?
P. Phil. 3 (144?)	στρα	1b, 3, ⚷ [?5, 9, 12n, 11t?], 14ta
SB 7516 (ca. 140–50)		⚷, 9, ⚷, 15g

[12] *P. Oslo* 17: in this *commentarius, orationes rectae* of the magistrate are introduced directly by a long curved stroke, the abbreviation for στρ(ατηγός). *Orationes rectae* of participants are introduced, without the speaker's name, by εἰπόντος or εἰπόντων.

[13] *SPP* 22.184. *Aegyptus* 13 (1933) 337–38.

[14] *P. Fay.* 106 = W. *Chr.* 395.

[15] *P. Lond.* 196 = M.*Chr.* 87.

[16] *P. Wisc.* 23 = *SB* 9315.

P. Oxy. 1102 (ca. 146)	ἱερ	1ag (ἀποφάσεων), 3, ±, 5n, 14nte, 9, 14ta, 9, 14ta, 15a, 15b
SB 7558 (148 CE)	ἐπισ	(subjoined to a petition) 1a, 3, 5nδ, 9, 11nG, 12nδG, 11nG, 12nG, 11nG, 12nδG, 11nG, 12C, 11nG, 12nG, 11nG, 12nG, 11nG, 12nG, 14nb
W. *Chr.* 77 (149 CE)	ἀρχι	±, 10, 14nta
P. Ryl. 678 (ca. 150)	ἔπαρ	3, ±, 6c?, 8, 11nG, 12nG, 11nG, 12nG, ±
P. Goodsp. 29 (ca. 150)	συμβ	±, (10), 14tb, 12nG, ±
P. Harr. 67 (ca. 150?)	ἤγεμ	(quoted in a petition?) 1c, 2nt, 3, 6nδa, 8, ±, 14nb ‖ 3, ±, 12, 10 (ὁμ[οίως] ἑρμηνεία Ῥωμα[ι]κῶν κατὰ τὸ δυνατόν), ±
P. Oxford 1 (150/151)	στρα	(quoted in a petition) 14
P. Ryl. 75 (after 150)	ἔπαρ	(*comm.* from 150) 1c, 2, 3, 5nδ, 8, 12nt, 14nb
		(*comm.* from 150) 1g (ἄλλου τοῦ αὐτοῦ), 3, 5nδ, 8, 12nt, 14nb
		(*comm.* from 134) 2n, 3, 5nδ, 8, 9, 12n, ±
BGU 329 (before 152)		unavailable to study
P. Oxy. 899r 20–32 (154)[17]		3, ±, 12nt, 11n, 10, 9, 14nb
SB 8261 (154–58)	ἤγεμ	1c, 2nt, 3, 4, 8, 5nδ, 9, ±
P. Ross.Georg. 2.24 (156–59)		στρα1c, 2nt, 6d?, 9, ±
BGU 2216 (156 CE)	ἀρχι	±, 5nδ, 9, 10, 9, 14ntfb
P. Oxy. 653 (160–62)[18]	ἔπαρ	1c, 2n, 3, 9, 5nδ, 9, 11nG, 12nG, 11nG, 12nG, 11nG, 9, 11nG, 9, 11nG, 9, 14nb
SB 9016 (160 CE)	ἀντ	1b, (2nt), 3, 4, 8, 10 (1b, 2n, 3, 4, 12n, 14na ‖ 1b, 2nt, 3, 9, 13, 10, 8, 9, ±)

[17] *P. Oxy.* 899r = M.*Chr.* 361.
[18] *P. Oxy.* 653 = M.*Chr.* 90.

BGU 613 (160/61?)[19]	στρα	[?quoted in a petition?] 14ntb, 15a
P. Teb. 287 (61–69)[20]	ἐπισ	⩲, 3, 5, 12nt, 14nb, 15b
PSI 1100 (161 CE)	ἐπισ	1c, 2nt, 8, 9, 11n, 12nt, 14nb, 3
P. Oslo 80 (after 161)		⩲, 9, 10? (short *comm.* from 150/51 and 143/44), ⩲
P. Fay. 139r (ca. 161?)		⩲
P. Teb. 291 (162 CE)[21]	ἀρχι	⩲, ≡ [?3, 5, 9, 10?], 9, 14nb
P. Oslo 18 (162 CE)		⩲, 12nt, 11n, 14nb, 15g, 3
BGU 1085 (after 170/71)		⩲, 12n, ⩲ ‖ 3, 5nδ, 8, ⩲ ‖ 3, 5nδ, 9, ⩲
SB 9329 (171 CE)	ἀρχι	5nt, 12nt, 14nt, 3
BGU 347 (171 CE)[22]	ἀρχι	1c, 2nt, 3, 4, 5nδ, 9, 13, 15b
IG 14.830 (174 CE)	προ	1g (ἀπὸ ἄκτων βουλῆς), 3, 2nt, 10, 9, 12n, 9, ⩲
P. Stras. 179 (176–80)	ἡγεμ	1g (προγραφὴ ἐκ δευτέρου τόμου ὑπομνημάτων), 2nt, 3, 4, 5nt, 12nt, ⩲
PSI 1326 (181/83)	ἐπισ	⩲, 11nt, 12n, 8, 11n, 9, 13, ⩲
BGU 361 (184 CE)[23]	στρα	⩲, 12?, 9, 14tb, 15b
P. Oxy. 237 (186 CE)	ἡγεμ	(*comm.* from 128 CE) 1c, 2nt, 3, 4, 5nδ, 9, 14na, 15b, 15e ‖
	ἐπισ	(*comm.* from 133 CE) 1c, 2nt, 3, 4, 6nδa, 9 (1st party), 9 (2d party), 10, 9, 10, 9, 14na, 13, 15g, 15f ‖
	δικα	(*comm.* from 87 CE) 1c, 2nt, 3, 6nδa, 1e, 12n, 11n, ⩲

[19] *BGU* 613 = M.*Chr.* 89.
[20] *P. Teb.* 287 = W. *Chr.* 251.
[21] *P. Teb.* 291 = W. *Chr.* 137.
[22] *BGU* 347 = W. *Chr.* 76.

SB 5693 (186 CE)	ἡγεμ	≡

P. Oxy. 2340 (192 CE)		3, 9 (ἐντυχόντος), 12nt, 10, 9, 12nt, 14nb

P. Ryl. 77 (192 CE)	στρα	1b, ╪, 4, 5nt/nδ, 12 (exclamation of crowd), 12n, 11n, 9, 11n, 10, 14ntb, 15f

BGU 15 (194 CE)[24]	ἐπισ	1c, 2nt, 3, 8, 6nδc, 12ntG, 9, 11ntG, 12ntG, 14nb

P. Mich. 6.365 (194 CE)	ἐπισ	1c, 2nt, 3, 5n, 12nt, 11n, 14nb

P. Oslo 81 (after 197)	στρα	1b, 2nt, 3, 6nδa, 9, 10, 9, 12, 14ta

P. Oxy. 3340 (201/2?)	βουλ	╪, 3, 10?, 12t, ╪

P. Stras. 22 (207 CE)	ἡγεμ	2nt, 3, 6nc, 8, 11n, 12nt, 14nb

P. Oxy. 2341 (208 CE)	ἔπαρ	3, 1c, 2n, 4, 8, 12nt, 11n, 14nfb

P. Oxy. 1408 (210–14)		╪, 11n, 12n, 14nfb

P. Oxy. 2279 (213–15)	ἔπαρ	╪, 11n, 12n, ╪

SB 9213 (215 CE)[25]	αὐτο	╪, 11n, 12n, 10?, 11n, 12n, 10, 14nb, ╪

P. Oxy. 2955 (218 CE)	ἡγεμ	1c, 2nt, 3, 12nt, 8, 12nt, 11n, 9, 11n, 12nt, ╪

P. Stras. 275 (after 225)		(quoted in a petition) 11n, 12nt, ╪

P. Amh. 67 (ca. 232)	ἔπαρ	╪, 12?, 10, 9, 11nt, ╪

P. Paris 69 (232 CE)[26]	στρα	[col. i] (1st hand) 1d, 2nt, 4, 3 + Παχὼν ᾱ ... ἔωθεν, 9, (2d hand) 15b; (1st hand) β̄ 9, (2d hand) 15b; (1st hand) γ̄, 9, (2d hand) 15b; (1st hand) δ̄, 9, (2d hand) 15b; (1st hand) ε̄, 9, (2d hand) 15b; (3d hand) 15 (ὁ δεῖνα ὑπηρέτης προθὶς δημισα κατεχώρισα + date); [col. ii] (1st hand) 1d, 2nt, 4, 3 + Θὼθ ᾱ ... ὑπὸ νύκτα ... ἐν τῷ γυμνασίῳ, 9, (2d hand) 15b; (4th hand) 15 (ὁ δεῖνα ὑπηρέτης προθεὶς δημοσίᾳ κατεχώρισα + date); [col. iii] (1st

[24] *BGU* 15 = W. *Chr.* 393.
[25] *SB* 9213 is sometimes called the *Acta Heracliti.*
[26] *P. Paris* 69 = W. *Chr.* 41.

hand) 1d, 2nt, 4, 3 + Φαῶφι α̅ ... τῇ ἐκπράξει
τῆς μηνιαίας ... ἐν ἄλλαις κώμαις, 9, (2d
hand) 15b; (1st hand) β̅, 9, (2d hand) 15b; (1st
hand) γ̅, 9, (2d hand) 15b; (1st hand) δ̅, 9, (2d
hand) 15b; (1st hand) ≡ [?ε̅?], 6nδ, ≡, 12nδG, ≡,
(2d hand) 15b; (1st hand) ς̅, 9, (2d hand) 15b;
(1st hand) ζ̅, 9, (2d hand) 15b; etc.

SB 5676 (232?)	ἔπαρ	(quoted) 1b, 6nδf, 6c, ⊨, 11nt, 12nt
BGU 705 (234?)		3, 6nδf, 6c, 12nt, ≡
SPP 20.60 (243–49)		⊨, 11ntH?, ⊨, 10, ⊨, 9, ⊭
M.Chr. 93 (ca. 250)		3, 4, 6nδf, 6c, 12nt,
SB 7696 (ca. 250)	ἔπαρ	⊨, 11nt, 12nt, 10, 9, 12nt, 11nt, 10, 9, 11nt, 12nt, 10, 9, (pattern continues), ⊭
Arch.Pap. 4, 115 (258 CE)	πρυτ	3, 11t, 10, 9, 14t, 10, 9, 2 (οἱ ἄρχοντες καὶ ἡ βουλή)
P. Oxy. 1502 (ca. 260)	διέπ	⊨, 12nt, 11nt (or 14ntbf), ⊭
P. Oxy. 1413 (270–75)	πρυτ	⊨, 11t, 12t/nt/nδ, 14tb, 11t, 12t/nt/nδ, 14tb (pattern continues)
P. Oxy. 1414 (270–75)	πρυτ	⊨, 11t, 12t/nt/nδ, 10, 9, 11t, 14tb, 10, 9, 11t, 12t (pattern continues)
P. Oxy. 2612 (285–90)		⊨, 11nt, 12nt, ⊭
P. Oxy. 2417 (286 CE)	πρυτ	≡, 3, γενομένου ὑπομνηματογράφου, 11t, 12t, ⊭
P. Oxy. 1503 (288–289)	ἔπαρ	3, 9, 12ntH, ≡, 11ntH, ≡, 11tH, ⊭
P. Oxy. 1204 (299 CE)	καθ	3, 4, 6nc, 12n, 8, 11t, 10, 12n, 14ntb, 15d
P. Oxy. 3187 (300 CE)		1c, 2nt, 3, 9, 12ntH, 12ntH?, 8, 11tH, ⊭ ‖ 1c, 2 ⊭
P. Ryl. 701 (305 CE)	βουλ	⊨, [?11?], 2t, 3
P. Oxy. 2562 (after 330)	λογο	⊨, 10?, 9, 14tb (5n), 12δ, 15g
SB 8246 (340 CE)²⁷	συνδ	≡, 10, 9, 12ntH, 11tHU, 12nH, 10, 9, 11tHU,

	12nH, 11tHU, 12nH (pattern continues at some length), $\pm$
P. Oxy. 1103 (360 CE)[28]	3, 4, 14ntb
P. Ross.Georg. 5.29 (360?)[29]	$\pm$, 9, $\pm$

Commentarii Only Generally Dated
Second Century CE

Commentarii	Magistrate	Elements of Form
P. Oxy. 2281	στρα	$\pm$, 9, 14ta
P. Giss. 84		$\pm$, 12?, 13
P. Oxy. 3023	καῖσ	$\pm$, 11t, 12n, $\pm$
P. Teb. 569		1c, 2nt, 3, 4, $\equiv$, $\pm$
BGU 592	γυμν	$\pm$, 12nt, 14nte, 15a, 15c, 15b
W. *Chr.* 27	πρυτ	$\pm$, 12nt, 10, 12nt, 11nt, 10, 12nt, $\pm$
P. Oxy. 3015 (109 CE)		3, 6nδa, 1e, 9, 14n (ἔφη) ‖ 3, 1b, 8, 9, 14n (ἔφη)
BGU 2070		$\pm$, 9, 11nt, 12n, 13, $\equiv$, 11n, 12n, 14nb, $\equiv$, 15g
P. Oxy. 2339[30]		

---

[27] *SB* 8246. C. J. Kraemer, Jr., and N. Lewis, "A Referee's Hearing on Ownership," *TAPA* 68 (1937) 357f.

[28] *P. Oxy.* 1103 = W. *Chr.* 465.

[29] Other dated *Commentarii* that are either too fragmentary or were not analyzed in this study are: *SEG* 18.646 (89–91?); *BGU* 163 (108 CE); *BGU* 5 (138?); *P. Mil.Vogl.* 98 (138–39); *Berl.P.* 6982 (147 CE); *BGU* 168 (after 169); *BGU* 82 (185 CE); *HespSupp.* 6 nos. 31–32 (ca. 230); *P. Doura* 126 (235 CE); *P. Doura* 127 (235?); *P. Oxy.* 62r (242?); *P. Erl.* no. 18 (248 CE); *P. Stras.* 5 (262 CE); *P. Giss.* 34 (265/66); *P. Mert.* 26 (274); *P. thead.* 15 (280/81); *P. Oxy.* 2332r (ca. 284); *P. Oxy.* 2187.24–32 (302?); *P. Thead.* 16 (after 307); and *P. Herm.* 18 (323?).

[30] *P. Oxy.* 2339. The editors of this text, E. Lobel and C. H. Roberts, thought this account to be possibly authentic; see my quotation of their remarks in Chapter 3, n. 23. Coles (*Reports of Proceedings*, 61) lists this papyrus thus: *Acta Alexandrinorum?* I have included it among the pagan acts; see Chapter 3.

SB 11170[31]	στρα	‡, 9, 10, 9, 11t, 12, ‡

Late Second Century

P. Stras. 234	στρα	‡, 11n, ‡
BGU 388	ἴδιο	‡, 11n, 12n, 9, 11n, 12n, 14neb, 15a ‖
	στρα	1g (ὁμοίως τοῦ αὐτοῦ), 3, 5nδ, 12n, 14nb
P. Oxy. 2112		‡, 9, ‡, 15g?

Late Second / Early Third Century

P. Oxy. 40	ἤγεμ	1b, 2n, 3, 5n, 12n, 11n, [?‡?]

Second / Third Century

P. Harr. 129	πρυτ	‡, 12n?, 11n, ‡
P. Giss. 99		‡, 12, ‡
BGU 893		‡, 12nt, 11n?, ‡

Early Third Century

P. Oxford 5	ἐπισ	‡, 9, ‡
BGU 925	πρυτ	‡, 10, 9, 12t, 11t, 10, 9, 12t, 14tb
P. Oxy. 1305		‡
P. Oxy. 1415	πρυτ	‡, 11t, 10, 9, 11t, 12t, 10, 9, 12, 11t, 14tb, 12t, 14tb, 12t
P. Oxy. 1504	ἔπαρ	‡, 11nt, ‡
P. Oxy. 2280		‡, 11t, 12, 14tb, 15 (προσαντέβαλον τὸν δηλούμενον ὑπομνηματισμόν)

[31] Other generally dated *Commentarii* of the Second Century CE that are either too fragmentary or were not analyzed in this study are:
P. Aberd. 17; *P. Ryl.* 296; *IG* II 1092; *P. Erl.* no. 16; *SB* 9488; *P. Ant.* 98; *P. Ryl.* 680; *P. Fay.* 322; *PSI* 1159; *P. Erl.* no. 17; and *P. Athen.* 58; *P. Ryl.* 271; *P. Ryl.* 272; *P. Oxy.* 578; *BGU* 868; *PSI* 1411; *P. Fouad* 25; *P. Phil.* 2; *P. Teb.* 574; *P. Fay.* 203; *BGU* 1019.

P. Oxy. 2407	⊞, 11nt, 12, 9, 12, 11nt, 12nt, ⊞

SB 8945	≡ [? 3, 2nt ?], ⊞

Third Century

P. Ryl. 679	⊞

BGU 389	⊞, 11, 12, ⊞

BGU 390	⊞, 9, 12n, ⊞

PSI 293	⊞, 12nt, 10, 9, 12nt, 10,

PSI 294	⊞, 12, ⊞

P. Oxy. 3186	1c, ⊞, 4a (Antinoopolis), ⊞, 9, ⊞

P. Ross.Georg. 5.21	⊞, 12, ⊞

P. Ross.Georg. 2.40	⊞, 12n, 11nt, ⊞

P. Oxy. 3117[32]	ἐπίτ	3, 4a (Oxyrhynchus), 4b, 12ntH (6nδc), 9, 12ntH, 11ntH, 12nN, 12nH, 12nH, 12nH, ⊞

---

[32] Other generally dated *Commentarii* of the Late Second and Third Century CE that are either too fragmentary or were not analyzed in this study are:
P. Gen. Inv. 76; *SB* 7368; *P. Bon.* 16; *Syll.I.G.* 2.607; *P. Stras.* 276; *P. Ant.* 87; *P. Lond.* 1283v; *P. Stras.* 22; *BGU* 7.1567; *C.P. Herm.* 7; *C.P. Herm.* 22; *C.P. Herm.* 23; *C.P. Herm.* 24; *C.P. Herm.* 25; *C.P. Herm.* 26; *Syll.I.G.* 3.1109; *P. Hess.* 16; *Berl.P.* 1944; and *P. Lond.* 1112.

Appendix 2

Elements of Form in Latin Commentarii

Sigla to Column "Elements of Form"

1 Extract phrase: (a) *ex commentario*
              (b) *ex codice*
              (c) *descriptam et recognitum/descriptam et propositam*
              (d) *infra scriptum est/in verba infra scripta*
              (e) *sententia* (+ gen. of magistrate)/*sententiam quam tulit* (magistrate)
              (f) other

2 Presiding magistrate(s): n = name t = title

3 Date formula

4 Location: e.g., *commentarium cottidianum* (of city)

5 Presence phrase: (a) *cum concilio collocutus (dixit) (CCC[D])*
               (b) *in consilio/curia fuerunt*
               (c) *utrisque praesentibus*
               (d) other

6 Participants formula: n = name δ = description t = title
              inter A . . . *et (inter)* B

7 Delegation phrase

8 "Ellipsis" phrase: (a) *causa ex utraque*
               (b) *inde pagina* (+ quotation)
               (c) *et infra/et alio capite*

9 Summarizing *oratio obliqua* and/or narrative abstract

10 Reading phrase: e.g., *recitavit*

11 *Oratio recta* of magistrate(s)

12 *Oratio recta* of participants

13 Narrative *sententia*

14 *Sententia:* name and/or title of magistrate + *oratio recta* introduced by *dixit*

15 Concluding matters

Additional sigla to "Elements of Form Present" column

Verbs introducing *oratio recta*

  A *adjecit*
  B *dixit*
  C *d(ixit)*
  D *inquit*
  E *pronuntiavit*
  F *respondit*

Miscellaneous sigla:

≡ fragmentary
≢ very fragmentary or missing
‖ used to separate distinct extracts
? when following an element = my conjecture
( ) elements contained within an element

Dated *Commentarii*	Magistrates	Elements of Form Present
P. Mich. 3.159 (41–68)	centurion	9, 6nδa, 2nt, 9, 8, 10, 13
Bruns[7] 71a (69 CE)	proconsul	3, 1cad, 2nt, 10, 11nt, 9, 11, 9, 14, 5b (*in consilio fuerunt . . .*)
CIL 11.1.3614 (113/14)	consul	1ca, 2nt; 1d, 2nt, 4, 8b (9, 13, 5b); 8b; 8b; 3, 2nt
Digesta 28.4.3 (166 CE)	consuls	1e, 2nt, 11nt, 12nt, 9, 14nta
Aes Italicense (176/77)[33]		(lengthy *sententia prima* of a senator)
Bruns[7] 186 (193 CE)	consul	2nt, 3, 1e, 6ntδa, 5a, 10 (14), ≢
*Cod.*Just. 9.51.1	Augustus	9, 14nta
P. Doura 125 (235 CE)[34]		
Bruns[7] 188 (244 CE)	prefect	1f (*interlocutiones*), 5nd (gen. of the p.p.v.v.), 11n, 12, 8c, 11n, 8c, 11n, 8c, 5a, 11n, 8c, 14na, 3, 15 (names of consuls for the year)
Just. 9.47.12 (Diocletian and Maximian)		

[33] *Aes Italicense* = Bruns[7] 63 = *Hesperia* 24 (1955) 330–34.
[34] *P. Doura* 125 = *CPL* 328.

Appendix 3

Elements of Form in Bilingual Commentarii

(For Sigla, see Appendices 1 and 2)

Dated *Commentarii*	Elements of Form Present
P. Oxy. 3016 (148)	(Greek) 1 (ὑπομνημ. ἡγεμόνος), 3, 10, 9, (Latin) 12(?), ≢
SB 11043 (152)	≢, (Greek) 4, 6nδ, 12nδ, 11n, (Latin) 12, ≢
P. Ross-Georg 5.18 (213)	(Greek) 2nt, 3, 12 (Iunicius d[ixit] + Greek *or. recta*) 12 (Ἡρακλειδης ῥήτωρ εἶπεν), ≢, 8, 12 (Iunicius d[ixit] + Greek *or. recta*), ≢
SEG 17.759 (216)	(Latin) 3, 9 (2nt), 6, 9, 12 (Aristaenetus dixit + Greek *or. recta*), 12 (Lollianus d[ixit] + Greek *or. recta*), ≢, 11 (Antoninus Aug. d[ixit] + Greek *or. recta*, 15n (d[ixit])
P. Ryl. 653 (321?)	(Latin) 3, 4, (Greek) ≡, (Latin) 11nt, (Greek) 12n, (Latin) 15nt (d[ixit]) (second hand then gives Greek translation of the Latin)
M.*Chr.* 96 (350)	≢ (?, 2nt), 3, 6n, 12 (Gennadius d[ixit] + Greek *or. recta*), 11nt (Fl. Gennadius v.p. iuridic. Alex. ei d[ixit] + Greek *or. recta*), (pattern continues at length), 15nt (d[ixit])[35]

[35] Other Bilingual *Commentarii* that are either too fragmentary or were not analyzed in this study are: *P. Doura* 128 (245?) *OGIS* 2.515 (209/10?); *P. Thead.* 13 (322/23); Theod. 11.39.5 (362); *P. Lips.* 33 (368); *SEG* 13.625 (3d century); and *P. Ryl.* 702 (early 4th).